ED

1996

# Improving
# Higher Education

SRHE and Open University Press Imprint
General Editor: Heather Eggins

Michael Allen: *The Goals of Universities*
Sir Christopher Ball and Heather Eggins: *Higher Education into the 1990s*
Ronald Barnett: *Improving Higher Education*
Ronald Barnett: *Learning to Effect*
Ronald Barnett: *The Idea of Higher Education*
Tony Becher: *Academic Tribes and Territories*
Robert Berdahl *et al.*: *Quality and Access in Higher Education*
Hazel Bines and David Watson: *Developing Professional Education*
William Birch: *The Challenge to Higher Education*
David Boud *et al.*: *Teaching in Laboratories*
John Earwaker: *Helping and Supporting Students*
Heather Eggins: *Restructuring Higher Education*
Colin Evans: *Language People*
Gavin J. Fairbairn and Christopher Winch: *Reading, Writing and Reasoning: A Guide for Students*
Oliver Fulton: *Access and Institutional Change*
Derek Gardiner: *The Anatomy of Supervision*
Gunnar Handal and Per Lauvås: *Promoting Reflective Teaching*
Vivien Hodgson *et al.*: *Beyond Distance Teaching, Towards Open Learning*
Jill Johnes and Jim Taylor: *Performance Indicators in Higher Education*
Margaret Kinnell: *The Learning Experiences of Overseas Students*
Peter Linklater: *Education and the World of Work*
Ian McNay: *Visions of Post-compulsory Education*
Graeme Moodie: *Standards and Criteria in Higher Education*
John Pratt and Suzanne Silverman: *Responding to Constraint*
Kjell Raaheim *et al.*: *Helping Students to Learn*
John Radford and David Rose: *A Liberal Science*
Marjorie Reeves: *The Crisis in Higher Education*
John T. E. Richardson *et al.*: *Student Learning*
Derek Robbins: *The Rise of Independent Study*
Tom Schuller: *The Future of Higher Education*
Geoffrey Squires: *First Degree*
Ted Tapper and Brian Salter: *Oxford, Cambridge and the Changing Idea of the University*
Gordon Taylor *et al.*: *Literacy by Degrees*
Kim Thomas: *Gender and Subject in Higher Education*
Malcolm Tight: *Academic Freedom and Responsibility*
Malcolm Tight: *Higher Education: A Part-time Perspective*
David Warner and Charles Leonard: *The Income Generation Handbook*
Susan Warner Weil and Ian McGill: *Making Sense of Experiential Learning*
David Watson: *Managing the Modular Course*
Thomas G. Whiston and Roger L. Geiger: *Research and Higher Education*
Gareth Williams: *Changing Patterns of Finance in Higher Education*
Alan Woodley *et al.*: *Choosing to Learn*
Peter W. G. Wright: *Industry and Higher Education*
John Wyatt: *Commitment to Higher Education*

# Improving Higher Education

## Total Quality Care

## Ronald Barnett

The Society for Research into Higher Education
& Open University Press

Published by SRHE and
Open University Press
Celtic Court
22 Ballmoor
Buckingham
MK18 1XW

and
1900 Frost Road, Suite 101
Bristol, PA 19007, USA

First published 1992

A catalogue record of this book is available
from the British Library

*Library of Congress Cataloging-in-Publication Data*

Barnett, Ronald, 1947–
    Improving higher education : total quality care / Ronald Barnett.
        p.       cm.
    Includes bibliographical references (p.    ) and index.
    ISBN 0–335–09985–8 — ISBN 0–335–09984–X (pbk.)
    1. Education, Higher—Aims and objectives.   2. Education,
Higher—Evaluation.   I. Title.
LB2324.B37   1992
378'.01—dc20                                        91–43035
                                                          CIP

Typeset by Graphicraft Typesetters Limited, Hong Kong
Printed in Great Britain by St Edmundsbury Press Limited
Bury St Edmunds, Suffolk

For Upma

# Contents

# Acknowledgements

I am most grateful to a number of publishers and others who have given me permission to draw freely and loosely on earlier papers of mine. Some of those writings have informed single chapters; others have been reflected in more than one chapter. They are: Does higher education have any aims? (1988) *Journal of Philosophy of Education*, 22 (2), 239–50 (Carfax Publishing Company); Higher education: towards a definition of excellence (1988) *Reflections on Higher Education*, 1 July, 34–37 (Higher Education Foundation); Institutions of higher education: purposes and performance indicators (1988) *Oxford Review of Education*, 14 (1), 97–112 (Carfax Publishing Company); Entry and exit performance indicators for higher education: some policy and research issues (1988) *Assessment and Evaluation in Higher Education*, 13 (1), 16–30; *Towards an Educational Audit*, CNAA Discussion Paper No. 3 (Council for National Academic Awards); *Changing Patterns of Course Review*, CNAA Project Report, June 1990 (CNAA); Towards the learning academy (1990) *Reflections on Higher Education*, 2 (1), 6–10 (Higher Education Foundation); Communication, competence and community (1991) *Scottish Communication Association Journal*, 1, Spring, 7–17 (Scottish Communication Association); Delivering quality in student learning (1991) in D. Muller and P. Funnell (eds) *Delivering Quality in Vocational Education*, Kogan Page; Quality control and the development of teaching and learning (1989) in M. McVicar (ed.) *Performance Indicators and Quality Control*, proceedings of a conference held at the Institute of Education, University of London (published by Portsmouth Polytechnic). Also, the appendix, containing the outline of a grid, is reproduced from a contribution to the work of the Quality Assurance Working Party, Institute of Education, University of London.

I am indebted to a number of friends who have read and commented on the whole manuscript in draft: Graham Badley, Lewis Elton, Gareth Williams, Peter Wright, and Mantz Yorke. Robin Middlehurst offered advice on Chapter 4. Upma Barnett has given the manuscript a professional editorial scrutiny. Naturally, I accept entire responsibility for any omissions and errors that remain.

# Introduction

## The quality gap

Across the western world, higher education is in something like the following situation (Fig. I.1).

Governments generally have begun to have a renewed interest in seeing an expansion of their higher education system. This motivation gives rise to debates over 'participation rates' and 'access'. Higher education, however, being *both* capital and labour intensive, is a relatively high-cost service and so problems over its funding also appear on the public agenda. One means of funding the expansion is through a diminishing unit cost: the state is hopeful that, in future, each student can be educated at a proportionately smaller cost than in the past. This motivation in turn gives rise to assessments of higher education in terms of its 'efficiency' and 'effectiveness'.

There is, though, a possible conflict of interest between expansion and diminishing unit costs and that conflict is reflected in the diagram. Being pulled in the directions of both expansion and the squeezing of resources, doubts about the quality of the system's products emerge. Can the ensuing quality gap be bridged or is the gap irreconcilable? Is it possible to have both greater numbers and lower unit costs while maintaining quality? Or, given these conditions, will more lead to worse?

Not surprisingly, therefore, 'quality' has become a key word in the public debate about higher education. In the United Kingdom, quality has been flagged by its funding councils as a criterion of resource allocation, and systems of quality evaluation are a prominent feature of a recent Government White Paper (DES 1991). More generally, across the western world, the quality of higher education is one of the three central issues, alongside those of access (how can we get more students into the system?) and funding (how can we pay for them if we do?). Yet, the extent of public interest in matters of quality in no way should be taken as an indication that people have a clear sense of what quality is or might be.

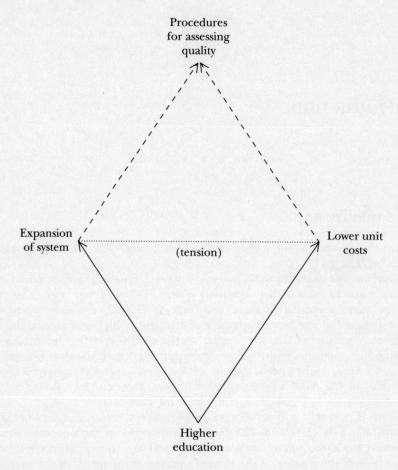

*Figure I.1*   Higher education: the quality gap

## Approaches

How might we get a purchase on quality? In this book, I shall run two perspectives – the philosophical and the sociological – together. The value of the philosophical perspective is precisely that it prompts us to clarify our intentions and suppositions, and to supply reasons for them. The sociological perspective is important because it indicates how we come to be in the position we are in, and charts the options in front of us (McIntyre 1971; Gellner 1974).

Philosophically speaking, the suspicion must be that 'quality' has become simply a hurrah word, a word of approval rather than of dismissal, for all sorts of achievements and characteristics of higher education are called up as indications of its quality. Like 'good', its use is a signal that the user is picking out some element that he or she wishes to endorse. Its expression tells us little about the element in question and much more about the person concerned for its use is likely to reflect the social position of the user. On this initial view, if there could be anything approaching a general theory of quality, it would have to be called the 'emotive theory': the use of the term quality simply betokens an expression of positive inner feeling towards the feature being picked out. If this is not an adequate characterization of quality, then we should be prepared to identify some entities or features of higher education that would command general assent as examples of quality.

This tension between trying to give a general account of quality in higher education and accepting that there are many definitions of quality will run throughout this book.

Philosophically, the crucial question is this: is quality essentially one thing (or set of related things) or is quality justifiably an attribute of different kinds of entity or achievement in higher education? There is a related question: does quality reside in higher education or in the minds of those who use the language of quality? The first question is paramount, however. The answer to that determines whether we can have a real conversation about quality; the second merely indicates what the conversation is about, the contents of our minds or of higher education itself. But if, in answer to the first question, it turns out that we can disagree so fundamentally about what quality in higher education amounts to that there is no overlap between our accounts, then it is difficult to see that the conversation could ever seriously get started. And we have to allow for it turning out that 'quality' is like that.

What of the sociological background? In his book (1983), *The Higher Education System*, Burton Clark introduced a (since well-known) triangle, in which he depicts the forms of influence on the shape and character of the higher education system. He distinguishes between those systems that are primarily influenced by the academic community itself, those in which the state plays the major part, and those that have opened themselves to the market to a significant extent. His claim is that, within the triangular space, each national higher education system can be plotted, depending on the influence of the three forces.

That typification of social forces is helpful in understanding the contemporary situation of higher education in the quality debate, for the three forces (picked out by Clark) can be seen to have given rise to three methodological approaches to quality. What we have here is something like that shown in Fig. I.2.

My hypothesis is that the state will tend to favour performance indicators as a means of assessing quality; that the academic community will tend to favour peer review; and that the market-led system will generate consumer oriented approaches to quality assessment. The systems in Clark's original triangle were in a dynamic condition, moving from one position in the triangular space to another. So too with approaches to quality. The three

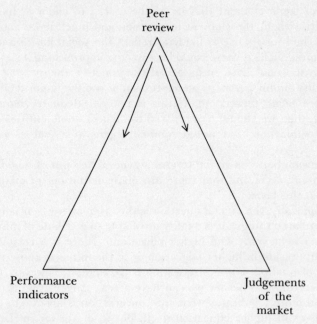

*Figure I.2*  Forms of quality assessment

approaches are pulling against each other: in general, we are seeing a shift away from peer review both to state-led performance indicators and to market-led approaches. All three approaches will, therefore, find their way into the discussions that follow.

However, we can go further than that, for these contrasting methodologies produced by the separate social forces are tantamount to rival definitions of quality (Yorke 1991a). The state, in its determination to promote a more efficient system, will come to regard as of high quality those institutions which, on the performance indicators, show up as being able to propel increasing numbers of students into the labour market at reducing unit costs. The peer review system, favoured by the academic community, will in its operation reflect the values around which the academic class is oriented, namely the values of advancing knowledge and of developing the minds of those who present themselves to the academic community. The market system is anarchic and no predictions can be made about its preferences. That, though, is the point for those who favour the market, for the collective voice of the consumers *is* what counts as quality.

This analysis is clearly over-simple. The academic community may not rest content with peer review and may embrace performance indicators; the state, correspondingly, will be likely to support quasi-peer reviews, in the form of inspection, accreditation or audit whether at the institutional or the programme level. At the same time, there will be accreditation exercises carried out by the relevant professional bodies. So the analysis is deficient in both its range of social forces and its classification of their approaches to quality.

The point of Figure I.2, however, is less to offer a comprehensive summary of contemporary groupings bearing on quality than to pick out the key social forces and their dominant approaches. For my purposes, it does not matter if the situation is in reality much more complicated than that. Indeed, that observation only helps to strengthen my point which is that, in the modern world, there are many social groups (including the parents of would-be applicants and the employers of their offspring as graduates) who are expressing their sentiments about quality, and that the system is responding to these different voices. They are *different* voices, however, and it is far from clear to what extent their contrasting claims can or should be reconciled.

## Perspective

There is less a debate about quality, therefore, than a babel of voices, their different messages reflecting alternative starting points and conceptions of higher education itself. But why, then, has this debate arisen with such noise across the western world? Again, we are in the realm of the background sociology and the salient features include the following:

1. A shift from a system enjoyed by the few to a system in which a large proportion of the population participates and in which an even larger proportion of the population now feels it has claims (so giving rise to talk of 'accountability'). (Contemporary observers are prone to talk of a change from an 'élite' to a 'mass' system, but those terms are both evaluative and descriptive and require extensive qualification in their use if they are to be handled with any precision (Trow 1987).)
2. A shift from a higher education which has been essentially part of the cultural apparatus of society to a higher education which is much more part of the economic apparatus of society, so relegating its finishing-school aspects as it has become a force of production in its own right (Gellner 1964, ch. 8).
3. A shift from higher education being a personal and positional good to being more of a wider social good, having a general societal value.
4. A shift from higher education being valued for its intrinsic properties to its being an instrumental good, especially for economic survival amidst expanding world markets.
5. A shift from a culture characterized by the formation of personal life-world projects to one dominated by the formation of public and strategic policies, so displacing what we might term the educational project of higher education.

Against these shifting currents of the modern age, all of which bear directly on higher education, quality can be seen as a metaphor for the aims of higher education. The debate over quality is none other than the often anguished efforts of the protagonists to find some point of purchase over which they can converse at all. Those contemporary voices include the following: technicist (the imposition of technical instruments); collegial (the collective voice of the academic community); epistemic (the territorial claims of a particular disciplinary community); consumerist (the claims of the participants or would-be participants); employers (the voice of the labour market accepting the products of the system); professional (the voices of the separate professional bodies); and inspectorial (the voices of the state and other external agencies with an authorized right to inspect higher education and pronounce on what they find).

These various voices contributing to the debate are groups of actors attempting to secure their claim either to continue to defend their traditional idea of higher education and their means of valuing it (the academic community), or to impose alternative views of higher education with new means of assessing it. The debate over quality in higher education should be seen for what it is: a power struggle where the use of terms reflects a jockeying for position in the attempt to impose own definitions of higher education.

Seeing quality in this way – as an amalgam of alternative concepts, a concatenation of voices, the different forms of life and interests from which they spring, and the shifting social currents of the age – involves a coupling of philosophical and sociological perspectives. This book can be described, therefore, as an attempt to examine quality in higher education through the perspective of social philosophy.

## Strategy

In trying to shed light on this contest, there are two strategies open to us. One method is to work systematically through the different viewpoints on offer, analysing their components and establishing their relationships with the social and cognitive positions of their holders. What are the different methods of evaluating, and for improving, the quality of higher education under discussion today and can they be brought into some kind of balance? The value of such a strategy is that, seriously pursued, it would identify and illuminate the range of voices there are in the contemporary discussion, it would plot their social location and it would offer an insight into their social and epistemological strength.

However, the strategy adopted here is different and perhaps somewhat more risky. Instead of feeling my way gently through the nuances of the rival vocabularies as my main strategy, I want to develop and exploit a complementary vocabulary. It is a vocabulary which takes seriously the educator's aims towards the individual student. It is not so much a vocabulary in which the claims of the student *per se* are central (for that is the market approach to quality) as it is one in which the key questions are: what are we trying to offer students in higher education? And: how would we know whether what we are offering is of high quality? And even further: how might we improve the quality of those offerings? It is a vocabulary in which our arrangements in higher education *and* their effect on the minds of students are central.

In what follows, I shall try, therefore, to work out a view of quality from within another voice, simply that of the educator. Obviously, if it is to have any plausibility, it has to be developed in a way that is sensitive to the claims of those other voices. If it is to carry any weight so far as quality measures are concerned, then it has to carry weight with a sufficient proportion of the key actors involved. So part of the earlier strategy will also be adopted. We shall engage with the current debates bearing on quality and see to what extent contemporary notions of quality fit with the conceptions being proposed here. Where they can be taken on board without prejudicing the general argument, they will be. Having a clear argument about quality is one thing (assuming there is clarity in the present argument); securing allies for its adoption is another. To pick up our opening observations, views on quality should be tested for their analytical soundness *and* for their political and social attractiveness.

## Argument

In brief, the argument of this book is the following. There are two dominant and rival conceptions of quality in the modern age. One is based on the expression of the tacit conceptions of value and propriety in the academic community. Its reflection in peer review contains the implicit claim that the conversations of the academic community are self-justificatory. This view of quality sees higher education as a 'practice' with its own rules and warrant (McIntyre 1985). On this conception, it is the character and quality of the continuing interactions of its members that is at issue rather than any end-point or definitive outcome.

On the alternative conception, higher education is seen as the issuing of products, with inputs and outputs. Students are units destined for the labour market. On this view, the quality of the system is understood in terms of its 'performance', that performance being captured in performance indicators. An institution's effectiveness is assessed, to a significant degree at least, in terms of its efficiency.

These two conceptions of quality might be termed the communicative and the instrumental versions of quality. The *communicative* version certainly comes close to the view that will sustain the following discussion but it is deficient for, as the earlier characterization implied, it takes the continuing conversation of the academic community as self-sufficient, and it often focuses on the interests of academics as researchers rather than as educators. The communicative view, relying on peer review, bars any outside voices from getting a purchase. Since the conversations have internal meaning, external commentary is *ultra vires*. The academic tribes form and protect their boundaries (Becher 1989). Specialism becomes the refuge of the timid.

In contrast, I shall argue, the *instrumental* approach to quality takes as its point of departure the values and interests of the external world, both as to the purposes of higher education and as to the means by which its quality ought to be assessed and improved. In doing so, internal characteristics of higher education tend to be neglected.

Immediately, questions arise about the relationship between these two orientations to quality: what are their differences and can they be resolved? But even if it is the case that both conceptions of quality have point, *and* that any tensions between them can be eased, neither separately nor in being brought together are they likely to be sufficient to the task of getting to grips with quality in higher education.

Higher education is, whatever else, an educative process. One of the tasks of this book, therefore, is to spell out the nature of an educative process characteristic of higher education. In identifying those features of the appropriate educational process, we will be identifying what ought to be addressed if we are seriously concerned with the quality of higher education, whether in its assessment or in its improvement.

Accordingly, alongside the communicative and the instrumental approaches to quality, we can term the approach being argued for here as *educational*. There is an obvious irony here, for the implication of this classification is that the dominant approaches to quality are not driven principally by educational considerations. That sense of irony is justified. In the western world, the key interest groups – the state, the academic community (with its discipline-based research interests) and the market – are not overwhelmed by an educational sensitivity. The market is educationally neutral in the sense that while some of its collective views might have positive educational consequences, it is not founded on an educational orientation. Its by-products might well be judged equally to have deleterious educational consequences. (We can put to one side for now the difficult questions of who confers educational worth, and what weight should be accorded to the views of the market in that assessment.) The other two dominant approaches to quality – those of the state and of the academic community – have definite interests other than the quality of the development of students' minds as such. Efficient outcomes constitute a key consideration for the one, and (we may judge) the survival of the different parts of the academic class is a central consideration for the other. So the major social forces at work in the 'quality' debate are unlikely to develop a vocabulary which reflects educational concerns for that is not their main motivation.

What I will try to do in this book, therefore, is to offer a vocabulary and an approach to quality to stand alongside the other definitions of the age. It is an approach that takes its bearings from a sense of the educational mission of higher education and places the solitary student in the centre stage, and which has as its central concern the question: what is it to educate in higher education? And, against that understanding, it asks: what is it to speak of, to assess, and to try to improve the quality of higher education?

There is another consideration behind the strategy adopted here. I have already indicated how the various social forces and interests – by no means consistently – are acting in the unfolding debates to produce a new vocabulary for higher education. In this book, I engage with those debates by examining those vocabularies.

The book, therefore, is not a textbook on quality. It does not pretend to offer a complete inventory of all current matters which might be relevant to 'quality' (for example, it has little to say about external examiners, in any case a somewhat parochial British concern; nor does it examine the use of staff appraisal). Equally, although I offer definite proposals for developing institutional quality at the institutional and course levels, this book does not pretend to provide a comprehensive catalogue of quality assurance systems. Nor will those seeking a recipe book for the successful introduction of a quality assurance system in an institution find it in this book. None of these matters is unimportant but I judge none of them to be central to the main debates of the day concerning the improvement of quality in higher education.

This book is a mainly conceptual inquiry, examining some of the key ideas of contemporary debate. It is not, however, a purely conceptual inquiry. On the foundation of the conceptual insights generated from these explorations, I offer some principles for action and practical suggestions in four areas: the assessment of institutional performance; ways in which institutions can improve the quality of their course programmes; course review; and improving the character of the student experience. In short, this book is an exploration of the logic of quality in higher education.

## Plan

The plan of the book is this. The first section (Chapters 1–4) is devoted to getting our conceptual bearings about both higher education and quality. Unless we attempt to reach a position of some clarity about the nature and substance of these concepts and their relationships, any more procedural discussions (about criteria, methods, and forms of improvement of quality) are bound to be unsatisfactory.

The second section (Chapters 5–8) engages with contemporary debates concerned with assessing the quality of higher education, both at institutional and at course levels. It examines the notions of performance indicators, fitness for purpose, value added, peer review, total quality management and academic audit. On the basis of those explorations, a methodology for assessing institutional performance is sketched out, and specific ways in which institutions can improve the quality of their educational provision are suggested.

The third section (Chapters 9–12) engages with current debates concerned with improving the quality of the educational process in higher education. Among the issues with which it grapples are 'the student experience', skills in the curriculum, transferable skills, competence, critical thinking and the idea of 'the reflective practitioner'. Again, on the logic of the considerations yielded by those explorations, some principles are offered to serve as guidelines for the continuing improvement of the quality of higher education.

# Comment

It may be thought that the book is trying to go down two disparate routes. There is a public debate, in which the government, its funding bodies, national accreditation agencies and institutional managers are primarily engaged, about the means by which we assess the quality of our institutional performance. If funding councils are going to take into account judgements about institutional quality, then large stakes are involved. The form of those methods of assessing quality is going to have major implications and it is obviously a matter of public interest how those evaluations are going to be conducted.

The other debate about improving the quality of the curriculum – the teaching, the educational processes and the student experience – is a separate affair; or so it might be thought. This is a debate in which those nearer the teaching situation are involved, such as the subject associations, the professional bodies, the staff developers in institutions, and the national agencies more interested in changing the character of the curriculum than in assessing it for the purposes of resource allocation.

There is one obvious rejoinder to this apparent separation of issues and interests. The funding agencies are becoming directly interested in the quality of individual courses as well as in institutions as a whole. Also, in the UK at least, the evaluations of national assessors of individual courses either have been (Council for National Academic Awards), are (Her Majesty's Inspectorate) or may be (the proposed quality assessment units) linked to the funding process. So several of the key agencies are interested both in assessing institutional performance and in modifying the character of the higher education curriculum.

There is a less transparent feature at work which is just as significant. As I will try to show, definitions of quality at the institutional level and systems being developed for evaluating institutional performance can have their impact on what we take quality to be at the course level. If we conceive of quality as the production of large numbers of graduates at low cost, that is likely to colour our methodologies for evaluating institutional performance but may also have an impact on what we take to be an acceptable and even desirable student learning experience. So the concerns and proposals of the first set of debates spill over into the second. Neither set of debates can seriously be conducted without an eye on the other (although, strangely, both sets of debates are only occasionally brought together in a single discussion (Astin 1985, Berdahl *et al*. 1991)).

# Bearings

In carving up my discussions in this way, I try to show that the maintenance and improvement of quality are the shared responsibility of every person in an academic institution. Quality is neither a matter just for institutional managers to address nor one just for lecturers to confront. Everyone has a part to play, although the parts will vary. That much will command wide support. What I attempt, however, is to demonstrate the *educational* responsibilities of all involved.

In offering a definite viewpoint rather than simply charting and analysing those on offer at present, the book has been written in the belief that quality does matter. While the debate over quality can be seen, sociologically, as an exchange of disparate voices defending their interests, that kind of dispassionate neutral record cannot do justice to the importance of the topic. Higher education is big business and it is seen as having intrinsic worth. But on either count – whether as a large-scale public investment or as a valued social institution – its quality matters. Accordingly, our discussions over quality should not be conducted solely as a technical matter, as if the object of our considerations was some valueless process or artefact.

We should retain always the sense that at the heart of higher education is the student, struggling to make sense of his or her experiences, undergoing a difficult period of adjustment and maturation (at whatever age), and trying to express himself or herself in meaningful ways. If we are serious about quality in higher education – its identification, its conditions, its assessment and its improvement – the character and the complexity of the educative tasks should remain central. That, at least, is the underlying claim of this book.

This book has been written with a number of different readerships in mind. Teachers, institutional managers and staff developers are likely to form the principal groups that may find value in these discussions and suggestions, for the ideas speak immediately, I believe, to their professional concerns. I hope, too, that those connected with higher education funding bodies, with national bodies concerned with assessing higher education, or with professional bodies or other national agencies involved in the development of the curriculum, as well as academic administrators, may all find things of interest here, for the book engages with many of their debates.

Principally, however, the book is addressed to anyone who cares about the quality of higher education and who is interested in its improvement.

# Part 1

The Idea of Quality

# 1

# The Quality of Higher Education

## Getting beneath quality

We cannot form secure ideas about the quality of higher education unless we first have a reasonably clear conception of what might be included under the umbrella concept of 'higher education'. This is such an obvious and rudimentary point that it has an air of banality about it. And yet the modern debate about quality takes place in just such a conceptual void. It is a common assumption that we can make progress in developing our systems of quality assurance and quality appraisal without any such conceptual reflections holding us up. There are, though, two things wrong with that belief.

Firstly, there are a number of contrasting conceptions of higher education. 'Higher education' is a contested concept, 'contested' in the sense that, as a matter of fact, some conceptions of higher education are promoted to the exclusion of others. There are, as I shall show in a moment, not merely different but rival conceptions. That being so, it is somewhat disingenuous to believe that we can simply paper over the cracks of our disagreements about the purposes of higher education, and press on obliviously to work through our ideas and practices concerned with quality.

The second reason follows on. We cannot escape having some kind of conception of the nature of higher education. Whether as students, teachers, researchers, institutional managers, employers, or officers of national funding and auditing bodies, we are bound to take a view of the character of higher education, whether or not we articulate it and whether or not we are conscious of it. Consequently, even if we do not explicitly attempt to give an account – if only to ourselves – of what we take higher education to be, the views we hold will still be reflected in the ideas on quality that we form.[1] In that case, the models and approaches that we develop for assessing and improving quality will take on the form of an ideology.[2] They will be offered as if they are neutral attempts to get to grips with 'quality' but in reality they will contain hidden interests, bound up with our assumptions about the fundamental purposes of higher education.

From these preliminary observations, it follows that sorting out our ideas and methods for assessing, maintaining and improving quality cannot be just a technical matter.[3] Specifying such ideas and methods requires more than clear thinking or systems development or the identification of political possibilities (as institutions and funding bodies weave around each other). For, ultimately, what we mean by, and intend by, 'quality' in the context of higher education is bound up with our values and fundamental aims *in* higher education. We cannot adopt a definite approach towards quality in this sphere of human interaction without taking up a normative position, connected with what we take higher education ultimately to be. In turn, what we take higher education to be will have implications for how we conceive of quality, how we attain it, how we evaluate our success in achieving it, and how we improve it. So if we want to offer a particular view on quality we should be prepared to declare where we stand on the key purposes of higher education.

As expressed here, these remarks are just assertions and will need to be justified, which I shall begin to do in this chapter; but they also constitute a fundamental principle behind the argument of this book.

The principle is that there is a logical connection between concepts of higher education and different approaches to quality, and we can see this link in various forms. For example, if we conceive of higher education as a process of fulfilling particular slots in the labour market with individuals who are going to be 'productive', then one way of assessing quality might be to examine the destinations of the students.[4] The question is not just whether they are employed; but are they employed in the kinds of position envisaged by the course designers? Do law graduates, for instance, actually end up in the legal profession? Further, can we derive measures of the productivity of the different kinds of graduate entering the labour market? Here, we might want to look at the economic rates of return of graduates over, say, a ten-year period: allowing for the opportunity costs and the costs of their education, does it appear that their education has generated extra economic added-value to society?[5] Under this conception, students take on value as, and are described in the vocabulary of, 'products' of the system.

That is one way of assessing the quality of higher education. But if we start from a different value position, a different form of assessing the quality of the enterprise may result. If we believe, for example, that the quality of higher education is more demonstrated in the nature of the intellectual development that takes place in students' minds, in the depth and breadth of understanding that students achieve, in their ability to be self-critical, and in their capacity to apply that understanding and self-critical capacity to all they experience and do, then 'quality' of higher education takes on a quite different character. Under this conception of higher education, a proper appraisal of quality will not rest content with economic indicators of output, but will turn to exploring the educational processes within our institutions. For there is a logical connection between the development of worthwhile states of mind and the experiences and educational processes to which students are exposed in their courses (Hirst and Peters 1970). A conception of higher education of this kind will prompt an examination of the types of intellectual challenge presented to students; and that in turn will begin to produce an illumination of the internal life of our institutions.

## The idea of higher education

In the modern world, there are not just these two but many different conceptions of higher education. That is how it should be, many will say. The pluralism of views regarding the purposes of higher education is the inevitable and proper reflection of a democratic society, in which no single ideology is driven forward by the state but in which institutions of higher education are increasingly encouraged to carve out their own niche and mission for themselves in the totality of higher education provision as it takes on the form of a quasi-market.[6] I agree with that response, but two qualifications can be made.

Firstly, the ready acceptance of disparate views on the nature of the enterprise called 'higher education' all too easily fails to ask whether there are any criteria that institutions need to satisfy in order to justify the title 'institution of *higher* education'. Are there no boundaries to the use of the term? Surely the title – if it is to be more than an administrative convenience – has to carry some kind of educational import? 'Higher' education is not merely 'additional' education; not simply more of what has gone before. The title signifies a particular kind and, indeed, level of intellectual attainment. In the philosopher's language, 'higher education' is as much an achievement concept as it is a task concept (Peters 1967). Processes of higher education have – as with all educational processes – an enduring character, and require effort from all involved. But they also imply attaining some kind of standard, in order to justify the appellation 'higher' education.[7]

Plato talked of the acquisition of knowledge as 'the ascent to see things in the upper world' (1971: 231). In the nineteenth century, Cardinal Newman – in articulating his view of the purposes of the university – said that 'if we would improve the intellect, first of all we must ascend; we cannot gain real knowledge on a level . . . in every case, to commend it is to mount above it' (1976: 125). Today, in justifying the idea of 'higher' education, we are faced with the challenge of giving a modern expression to this imagery of levels of knowledge without the attendant metaphysical baggage;[8] but that difficulty must not dislodge us from the task. Otherwise, the general conception of higher education is liable to be reduced in scope and is likely to fragment, with a consequent diminution of the core of the idea of higher education.

The second reservation, over the too easy assumption of a plurality of views about higher education, is a corollary of the first. The disinclination to see if any unitary description can be given to 'higher education' results in the different views that are on offer turning out to be partial descriptions, reflecting certain kinds of interest. Consequently, when a particular approach to quality assessment is being offered, it makes sense not only to enquire into the conception of higher education that it springs from, but also to ask: what set of interests is being defended? Precisely what form of partiality is being promoted? Unless such questions *are* asked, definitions of what counts as higher education will be determined by the big battalions wielding power and influence both outside and inside the academy.[9]

Of course, it follows that the same questions can be addressed to the case set out in this book, since a particular approach to quality assessment is argued for here. But I hope, at least, that the background values, the underlying conception of higher education and the ensuing proposals about quality are explicit and coherent, rather than hidden and offered in a misguided sense of value-neutrality.

Let us then turn to identify some of the key conceptions of higher education which can be found beneath debates on quality.

## Concepts of higher education

Four dominant concepts of higher education underlie contemporary approaches to, and definitions of, quality.

*(1)    Higher education as the production of qualified manpower*    This is a view we have already encountered, in which higher education is seen as a process in which students count as 'products', as outputs having a utility value on the labour market. On this conception, quality tends to be identified as a function of the ability of students to succeed in the world of work, as measured by their employment rates and, more especially, their career earnings (or 'rates of economic return').

*(2)    Higher education as a training for a research career*    Here, the definition of higher education is framed by those members of the academic community who are themselves active in research. Quality, on this conception, is measured less in terms of the achievement of students than in the research profiles of the *staff*. There is an assumption that the related input and output measures – the number of Fellows of the Royal Society, the amount of research income and the publications output – are themselves indicative of educational quality.[10]

The assumption itself overlies an image of worthwhile qualities being passed on to students by osmosis through their being in the midst of that kind of 'quality' environment. Along with this viewpoint goes a tendency to think that the osmosis – the transmission of the high academic culture – is best achieved by small groups of students in the company of the recognized researcher. Consequently, low student : staff ratios tend to be another favoured performance indicator. In so far as students' accomplishments come into play, it is in their formal qualifications *on entry* (as evident, in the UK, in A-level point scores); the assumption here is that it is those entrants with 'high' entry qualifications who have demonstrated their ability to survive in the academic culture and to acquire the accoutrements of academic discourse and interaction.

*(3)    Higher education as the efficient management of teaching provision*    Through

the 1970s and 1980s, UK institutions of higher education have seen the student : staff ratio moving steadily upwards. Their unit costs have, correspondingly, witnessed a continuing reduction. Part of the accompanying story is that numbers of students in the system as a whole have grown remarkably (having doubled to nearly one million) in that period. Couple that with the reflection that, even if the social class composition has not changed, the student body has changed so that it contains both relatively and absolutely a larger number of mature students, more younger students who are admitted on the basis of entry qualifications other than A levels, and increased numbers of entrants from non-traditional backgrounds of all kinds. Together, all these factors place increased demands on institutions to husband their teaching resources so as to achieve an ever-higher level of efficiency.

On this conception, institutions are understood to be performing well if their throughput is high, given the resources at their disposal. Their total efficiency is what is in question here: not only how many students they can accommodate, but also with what velocity their students are successfully propelled into the wider world. As the dictionary indicates, 'efficiency' is 'the ratio of the energy output of a machine, device, etc to the energy supplied to it'.[11] Accordingly, here, indicators of performance are sought which can capture this sense of efficiency. Non-completion rates and proportions of students obtaining 'good degrees' are drawn on. So too unit costs, especially as reflected through student : staff ratios themselves, as well as other financial data, come into play as key means of assessing the performance of institutions. If these indicators are giving the appropriate message, then an institution that does well by them will account itself as one of high quality.

*(4)  Higher education as a matter of extending life chances*     This final contemporary conception is none other than that of the potential consumers of higher education.[12] The metaphor of consumption is deliberate, for on this conception higher education is valued for its ability to offer opportunities to participate in the dominant institutions and to enjoy the benefits of modern society.

As a result, higher education here becomes the outcome of unfettered student demand, whatever it turns out to be. And that may be just as instrumental, if not more so, than the first and third perspectives. The attempt to switch round our institutions so that they are fully open to and compliant with student demand is seen most obviously in more 'flexible' admissions policies and practices as moves are made towards open access. But the orientation to student demand is also evidenced in its effects on the curriculum, both through the continuing introduction of new fields of study into higher education and through the incorporation of more flexible course structures, with the onward march of modular, open-textured, credit-based course provision.

The key indicator of institutional achievement here lies in the percentage growth of student numbers and in the range of entrants. In particular, do they reveal a widening of the intake to include students from socio-economic backgrounds normally under-represented in higher education? (One UK polytechnic has set as targets specified proportions of its intake from students of ethnic origins.)

As with the previous concept, there is a leaning towards high student : staff ratios, since it is understood that the associated move towards a mass higher education system will only be accomplished by a system resourced at a lower level of unit costs than that enjoyed by a smaller, more exclusive system. In any case, the institutional achievement is thought to be all the higher for meeting wider student demand on a relatively low resource base.

That is a sketch of four dominant conceptions of higher education (admittedly in outline only), and it indicates the way in which different ideas as to the purposes of higher education lead in turn to different kinds of definitions *and* measures of quality. Three qualifications have to be made to this analysis, however.

The first qualification is that the four viewpoints just identified are not mutually exclusive. In the UK, the universities are predominantly associated with conception two, but also to a lesser extent with one and three; the polytechnics are very much associated with one, three and four. So while, as I began by saying, some conceptions of higher education are pressed forward to the exclusion of others, that exclusivity does not lie between these four conceptions. Indeed, while there are differences across these four conceptions of higher education, they also have much in common.

In all four conceptions, higher education is a total system, in which students enter as inputs, are processed, and emerge as outputs. It is a view of higher education in which the educational experience of students is neglected, unless it turns out that there is something amiss with the output (when employers complain, for example, that their graduate employees are either insufficiently specialized, or – increasingly today – are insufficiently 'flexible', a code word for more general knowledge and skills). So the dominant approaches to quality are characterized by a consensus of a systems approach in which higher education becomes a black box: it does not matter what goes on in the black box as long as the quantity of desired inputs and outputs is achieved.

## Alternative concepts

The second qualification is that the analysis presented so far is some way short of being a comprehensive survey of the possible conceptions of higher education. Let us, then (for the moment anyway), leave these conceptions of higher education which are essentially systems-based and turn to views of higher education which take seriously the educational processes to which students are exposed, or which are intimately concerned with the students' development. Such conceptions include higher education seen as:

1. The development of the individual student's autonomy, with students acquiring intellectual integrity and the capacity to be their own person.

2. Higher education as the formation of *general* intellectual abilities and perspectives ('the general powers of the mind', as Robbins called it a generation ago (1963)), the student attaining a breadth of vision and grasp beyond the confines of a single discipline.

3. The enhancement of the individual student's personal character. Here, higher education becomes, in effect, the acquisition of cultural capital, not only as at Oxbridge from the mid-nineteenth century onwards,[13] but more generally through the acquisition of a distinctive socio-linguistic form of interaction, characterized by a facility with a communication style in which language is distanced from the speaker in a non-personalized mode of discourse.[14]

4. The developing competence to participate in a critical commentary on the host society (so sustaining an oppositional function for higher education (Scott 1984)).

Although, on any serious analysis, these must be considered to be significant conceptions of higher education, they are not in any obvious way reflected in the contemporary debate over quality assurance in higher education (whereas the previous four are). This empirical fact has two sides to it. Firstly, this second group of purposes contains ideas about higher education that do not lend themselves to institutional practices easily captured by system-wide and systematic evaluation procedures such as numerical performance indicators. In contrast to the first group of four, the immediate concern of this group is with the educational processes that students undergo, not with inputs and outputs and their relationships.

Secondly, the first group of conceptions reflects the thinking about higher education that characterizes the national policy makers, funders and institutional managers, and other national interest groups. Whether springing from an interest in enhancing the economic power of UK Inc., in advancing the life chances of those under-represented in higher education, in ensuring the continuity of the research community, or in reducing the unit costs of an institution, the interests driving the national debate and development work in quality assessment are essentially *external* to the process of higher education and are informed by a systems approach.

The second group of conceptions, on the other hand, are essentially *internal* to the process of higher education and are informed by a concern with the experience of the individual student. But their not fitting the standard model of performance assessment does not affect the validity of such conceptions of higher education. On the contrary, it is testimony to the conceptual impoverishment and feebleness of the dominant models of quality assessment.

Our conceptions of higher education should not have to fit our models of quality assurance. On the contrary, if they are to be adequate to revealing the character of the extraordinarily complex human interactive process that we term 'higher education', our models of quality assurance should, rather, fit our concepts of higher education. Unfortunately, though, it is at present a case of the performance indicators' tail wagging the quality dog. A single-minded use of numerical performance indicators as an approach to quality serves to marginalize conceptions of higher education that are actually focused on the character of the educational process. Paradoxically, then, in higher education, performance indicators act to rule out of court concepts that are concerned with the essence of higher education itself.

## Concepts and ideologies

The third qualification about the analysis of the concepts of higher education provided so far is even more fundamental. It is that, as presented, they are hardly real concepts at all.

Purely to chart the territory, I have set down various conceptions in a simplified and abbreviated form. In that form, the first four conceptions emerge more as social functions of higher education than genuine concepts. To say that higher education is a preparation for the labour market, for instance, is an external description of the way in which higher education works in society. It is the view of the analyst or the systems planner. It becomes a concept of higher education when it is a view of the enterprise to which someone is committed. An idea or view is properly called a concept when there is some element of intentionality attached to it, when it is not just indicative of what is happening from the outside but also a proposal of what should happen as advocated by an actor within the total arena. And that might be an employer, but it might also be a lecturer or it might be a student (Peters 1964).

Since a concept has these elements of intentionality and of implicit recommendation, it contains other elements as well. Being held by individuals, and being articulated by them, a concept of education has a justificatory component too. That is, in being held with commitment, in being proffered and advocated, a genuine concept – as opposed to a piece of ideology – opens itself to the responses: what do you mean by that? How do you justify it? What are your grounds for believing that to be the case? In turn, its adherents should not only be prepared to respond to such probing, but also have a set of arguments to substantiate the point of view being argued for.

It is at this point that the analysis becomes debate and the discourse takes an interesting turn. For everything hangs on the arguments adduced to back up a particular point of view. Obviously, the defence will vary, depending on the kind of conception being held. Academics interested in seeing students go on into the research community might wish to argue for 'knowledge for its own sake', which in turn raises questions about the nature of knowledge. Is it assumed, for instance, that the value of knowledge lies in its having an objective character? If so, the underlying assumption – that objective knowledge is attainable – is itself debatable.[15]

Alternatively, if the viewpoint being held is that higher education is a matter of responding to student demand, one defence might be that higher education should in principle be open to all who wish to take advantage of it (perhaps along the lines of the Open University). When pressed further, the advocate might argue for universal access on the grounds of improving life chances. Generalized, this defence would turn on an argument in favour of a form of democratic education (Gutmann 1987).

Arguments for other conceptions of higher education might resort, for example, to utilitarianism (that expenditure on higher education is justified by the general social good that results), or perhaps to an argument for the development of the mind (which in turn raises questions about what we take the mind to be). The point is, though, that it is only when *some* kind of articulated justification is to hand that we can sensibly say we are being offered a *concept* of higher education.

The reason that this seemingly pedantic point matters in the context of issues of quality is that, as we have seen, there are different approaches to the matter of quality. In turn, those approaches to quality derive from different views about what higher education is or should be. So, when faced with an analysis of quality – however elaborately wrapped up in technical jargon about institutional systems, international comparisons and lists of performance indicators – a key issue is: what is the underlying conception of higher education which informs this particular approach to quality? Is it a conception based on a thought-through set of substantiating arguments? Or, instead, is the approach to quality based on a relatively shallow conception of higher education? In other words, are we being faced with a rational approach to quality (prepared to enter into debate) or are we, rather, faced with a piece of ideology (an unconsidered reflection of social interests?)[16]

There is also a distinction, which I hinted at earlier, between the two sets of viewpoints I have sketched out. The first four conceptions of higher education have an external perspective about them, whereas the latter four are essentially concerned with the internal character of the educative process. In turn, the philosophical rationale backing the two sets is also likely to reflect that difference.

Within the first set of conceptions, the point is obvious enough in relation to the labour market and access conceptions, which clearly derive from a point of view external to the educational process. But the research orientation is external too, in the sense of deriving from the interests of the academic community rather than from a concern with the student's development as such. Even the conception which looks to the success rates and retention rates of students is a conception which is taking a hold in virtue of an underlying managerial interest in the efficiency of the system, rather than its intrinsic quality.[17] In contrast, the four conceptions in the second group are conceptually connected with the internal purpose and nature of the educational process, with the intended character of the student's development, and with the accompanying student experience that will help to foster that development.

A general pattern, therefore, seems to be emerging. The dominant approaches to quality assessment are associated with inputs and outputs in higher education, derive from an external vantage point and, in turn, are

*Table 1.1*   Forms of approaches to quality

|  | Dominant approaches | Neglected approaches |
|---|---|---|
| *Focus of methodology* | Inputs/outputs | Processes |
| *Viewpoint* | Outsider | Insider |
| *Justification* | Extrinsic | Intrinsic |

based on external justifications of higher education. On the other hand, conceptions of higher education which are under-represented in current approaches to quality derive from a concern with the internal processes of higher education, are to be found among those who are committed to their teaching activities or who sympathize with that viewpoint (such as staff developers) and, in turn, are supported by justifications which appeal to the intrinsic value of those educational processes. This analysis takes the form shown in Table 1.1.

Two fundamental questions arise from this analysis. Firstly, what approaches to quality would derive from conceptual viewpoints oriented around the character and value of the educational process *per se*? And secondly, is it possible for such approaches to quality to have a hearing amidst the systems-planning approaches that dominate in the contemporary scene? This book is an attempt to provide positive answers to both questions.

## Whatever happened to liberal education?

From its explicit and clear formulation in the mid-nineteenth century in the hands of Newman, one important justification of higher education has been argued in terms of 'liberal education'. Admittedly, 'liberal education' is a slippery term, susceptible to many interpretations itself.[18] Perhaps, as it was for Newman, the key idea is that of 'knowledge as its own end'[19] or, in the language of the first three-quarters of the twentieth century, knowledge for its own sake. But a new century is upon us and with it the emergence of a new language of higher education, that of competence, skills, enterprise, capability and outcomes. Consequently, the phrase 'knowledge for its own sake' is itself being passed by, and is taking on the sense of the language of a former age.

However, the idea of knowledge for its own sake has *always* had its opponents; it has always been controversial. Newman felt compelled to argue its case so passionately and at such length precisely because of the countervailing pressures from nineteenth-century professional and industrial society of which he was conscious. And that debate has continued ever since. The 1960s saw the formation of a group of green-field universities, owing something of an allegiance to the idea of knowledge for its own sake.[20] At the same time, the 1960s saw the reinforcement of another, more service-oriented, tradition in higher education (Burgess 1982). Colleges of advanced technology were permitted to enter the universities' club and, in the polytechnics, a new sector of higher education was created to form a more 'socially responsive' kind of provision. But that service tradition, for the last 150 years, has been fought for in conscious determination against the liberal tradition. Indeed, as testimony to the pull of the liberal tradition, Robinson (1968), in producing an eloquent apologia for the polytechnics, felt bound to offer a rebuttal precisely of 'knowledge for its own sake'.

I draw two observations from these reflections. Firstly, any view of higher education which wishes to be taken seriously should show how it relates to the traditional accounts of higher education. If it is to be read as more than a piece of rhetoric, then the onus is on its proposers to explain the weaknesses of conventional viewpoints. In other words, the debate should be joined. And that requires, at least in part, giving some analysis of the relationship of the new viewpoint with that of the liberal viewpoint. If there are deficits in the liberal perspective, they should be argued through and not just assumed to be self-evident.

Secondly, there is a corresponding onus on those who still wish to hold on to a liberal viewpoint. It will not do simply to defend it in the language and assumptions of the mid-twentieth century, as Peter Scott has recently observed (1990). It is not just that the stance is no longer credible to the wider audience, for whom liberal higher education is associated with unjustified claims on the public purse, narrowness of delivery, élitism of access and academicism of outcome.

It is also that the stance is no longer tenable on intellectual grounds. Academic debates over the past thirty years have questioned the grounds of knowledge in general and have pointed to the way in which higher education has become incorporated into the modern state.[21] Consequently, two axioms on which the liberal idea rested – the objectivity of knowledge and the autonomy of institutions of higher education – have been undermined.[22] The onus is therefore on those who maintain a liberal perspective to show how that perspective can withstand the *intellectual* assaults of the modern age.

## The essence of higher education

I began by saying that higher education is a contested concept, and went on to argue that our different conceptions of higher education in turn give rise to varying approaches to quality – its definition, assessment and improvement. The question remains open though: is it possible to identify a conception of higher education which has some general validity? Is there an irreducible core to the idea of higher education, which – in our attitudes to quality – we should not overlook? I want to suggest there is.

We can begin by asking: what is 'higher' about higher education? Conventionally, three answers are given. Firstly, higher education is simply the highest part of the education system, in terms of student progression, the acquisition of educational qualifications, its status and its influence over the rest of the educational system. This may be true and may be reflected – so far as quality is concerned – in a presumption of high quality on the part of the academic community being inherent in higher education. But it is largely an administrative point, and is irrelevant here.

Secondly, higher education is thought to advance students to the 'frontiers of knowledge' through their being taught by those who are working in that difficult territory. However, knowledge is expanding so fast, particularly in the sciences, that academics are themselves acknowledging that it is impossible to take undergraduates to the boundaries of current thought. In any case, the term 'frontiers of knowledge' is misleading. Knowledge does not have a clearly marked boundary, with harmonious security on one side and the void of an unknown region on the other. Rather, it is a bloody battlefield being fought on many fronts, with the boundary line often lost in the quagmire.[23] So we should abandon this imagery of sharply defined boundaries as a definition of higher education.

Thirdly, higher education is said to impart the deepest understanding in the minds of the students, rather than the relatively superficial grasp that might be acceptable elsewhere in the system. In higher education, nothing can be taken on trust and the students have to think for themselves so as to be able to stand on their own feet, intellectually speaking. There is certainly something in this idea, supported by international research, as we shall see in the final section of the book. But as a response to the question 'What is higher about higher education?', it comes a little oddly. For the metaphor it offers is one of reaching some kind of depth, whereas the metaphor implicit in the question is one of gaining height.

So another tack is needed. Here, let us return to the two quotations from Plato and Newman. Both saw the acquisition of true understanding as one of ascending above conventional understanding. But while they both saw genuine understanding as the taking on of a new perspective, over and above that of common sense, they also employed the metaphor of ascending, not in the sense of rising above the clouds and becoming cut off from the earlier viewpoint, but of being able to look down on that earlier viewpoint, to impart a perspective on the viewpoint itself, and to see its limitations and partialities.

We do not have to share the metaphysical baggage which informed both Plato's and Newman's accounts to see that there is something of value in this imagery of ascending levels of understanding. In more modern, and less tendentious terminology, it can be expressed in three ways.

Firstly, we can say that the clusterings of knowledge constituted by different disciplines have been built up over time, so that their internal concepts are not simply interdependent but that some concepts stand on other concepts and are, in that sense, logically superior to others, having greater explanatory power. Such 'higher order' concepts and perspectives are what a genuine higher education is about, rather than the acquisition of low level facts and information.

Secondly, from within 'postmodernism', in which the search for ultimate foundations of knowledge has been abandoned (Rorty 1980), *and* from modern learning theory (both in higher education and in professional settings[24]) comes a single powerful unifying idea. In everyday language, it is that of critical reflection or, in more technical jargon, reflexivity. If there is no end point in the search for knowledge and sound practice, if even the criteria by which we think and act are impossible ultimately to establish, then one way out of the cul-de-sac lies in rigorously evaluating and, if necessary, reconstituting our own thoughts and actions. We claim to be rational, and our claims to know are always open to criticism, so – even if no secure redoubt is available – we have to be prepared to entertain criticism of our own claims to know. There is no end point in thought and action, only conversation (in which even the language and concepts of the participants may be different). And true conversation means taking seriously the critical viewpoints of others, perhaps even entering a different world held open by those others (Rorty 1989). That means being prepared to be self-aware and self-evaluative. We all have to become 'reflective practitioners' (as I shall argue in a later chapter).

Thirdly, modern learning theory offers a separate line of support for the metaphor of hierarchy of levels of knowledge and understanding. In taking on a reflexive attitude, we are in effect taking a view of our knowledge from a higher level. To employ another piece of contemporary jargon, it is to embark on 'metacognition' (Baird 1988). In order to gain a vantage point from which to attack a form of thinking or action, we have to climb to a higher level of thought. So the idea emerges of a hierarchy of levels of thought. Once we accept that a statement about a class of entities can only be made at another level, in turn that new statement can be evaluated from another – and higher – level. In theory, therefore, an unending hierarchy of levels of understanding arises. We do not have to enter into those higher levels; the key point is simply that we should be prepared to recognize that our claims to knowledge are always susceptible to further and ever-higher forms of evaluation.

## Higher learning in action

This analysis of higher learning has application both to the individual student and to the institution of higher education.

The first point is clear enough: students on courses of higher education should be encouraged to enter into a continuing conversation (Oakeshott 1989), be prepared to take on the point of view of others and become comfortable in conducting that critical dialogue with themselves. To do that seriously will require the acquisition of high-level concepts *and* a breadth of frameworks so that that critical evaluation can be conducted from a variety of perspectives. In turn, developing the intellectual strength to offer a point of view but modifying it in the light of counter-evidence or argument calls for a range of higher order intellectual abilities. As well as knowing that something is the case and understanding certain concepts, students have to acquire the ability to analyse an argument, to examine evidence, to integrate material from contrasting sources and perspectives, and to draw different kinds of inferences (empirical, evaluative, logical). It is, therefore, through a combination of higher order thinking and higher order cognitive abilities that students acquire the intellectual autonomy that is associated with a genuine higher education.

The second application of the idea of critical reflection, namely to institutions of higher education, is perhaps less obvious but equally important if our approaches to quality are to be soundly implemented. I start here with the observation that institutions can reflect on themselves and can critically evaluate their own policies and activities. But if that is accepted, all that we have said about critical reflection in the mind of the individual student holds for institutions of higher education, however large they may be. In other words, they can become learning institutions in the double sense: not only do they provide for student learning, but they also become adept at learning about themselves.

The ideas of conversation, of higher order discourse and of continuing exploration should, for example, typify to some degree the internal transactions of academic life. To say that, admittedly, may sound like a regression to a 'pre-Jarratt' age in which, against a managerial perspective, universities were characterized by never-ending debate in committees with little direction or outcome (CVCP 1985). But nothing that has been said so far justifies talk for the sake of it; nor does it give support for any disinclination to take decisions. What is at issue is whether the decisions taken find a resonance in the conversation of the institution's academic community. I shall develop these ideas in later chapters.

## Conclusions

Talk of quality in higher education is not fully honest. Those who use the language of 'quality' do not always make explicit the conception of higher education from which their approach to quality springs. This is readily understandable, for often they have not made their ideas about the purposes of higher education explicit to themselves. Consequently, proposals for quality assurance and quality improvement tend to become the party lines of the different groups.

As we have seen, the contrasting approaches to quality partly derive quite honestly from legitimately held but alternative concepts of higher education. Higher education is a complex public good in modern society, giving rise to different definitions of its purposes. The question, then, is: can we uncover any set of principles basic to quality that is grounded in the essential character of higher education; or, in these postmodern and pragmatic times, are we reduced merely to shrugging our shoulders and saying 'anything goes' (Feyerabend 1978: 28)?

I have suggested, and in this book will try to take further, the belief that we should not give up the struggle peremptorily. There may be some guiding ideas that we should hang on to. Contained within the idea of higher education are the notions of critical dialogue, of self-reflection, of conversation, and of continuing redefinition. They do justice to the idea of higher education because it is through such processes of the mind that a *higher* level of understanding – and ultimately, of action – is achieved. I have suggested that these ideas are helpful in understanding the processes of educational development that we hope to see in the individual student; and also in understanding the processes by which every institution of higher education should conduct its affairs, learn about itself and improve the quality of its work. It is in the presence of such higher order processes that we can legitimately talk of institutions of *higher* education.

# 2

# Aiming Higher

## Aiming for quality

A central observation of the last chapter was that there are many, and even rival, conceptions of higher education. One way of reflecting this situation, so far as quality is concerned, is to say that purposes in higher education vary. Then what counts as quality must vary too. Our sense of quality – it might be said – should reflect 'fitness for purpose' (Ball 1985).

This approach to quality at once throws the onus back on the providers to consider their purposes in offering higher education. What are they trying to do? What are, or should be, their aims? Prima facie, such questions are benign enough. For this approach to quality is denying that there are absolute conceptions of quality that can be laid down for all courses and all institutions. On this account, quality is a more relativistic concept. It is up to the providers to spell out what it is they are about as they intend it.

In making these moves, it looks as if spelling out specific aims can be of real help to us in assessing quality. Tell us your aims, and the standards and possibly even the methods for assessing the quality of delivery will follow.

But the matter is not that simple, for talk of aims raises conceptual questions which are more important than they may seem. Who takes aim in higher education, and who achieves the aims that are set out? Does anyone really take aim, in any real sense? These philosophical questions may appear remote from the issue at hand – the nature of quality and its improvement – but they are vitally important. If we are going to ensure that our arrangements and practices in higher education are of high quality, and if we want also to go on improving their quality, then we have to have a sense not only of the direction we are going in, but also of who is involved in the journey. Whose efforts are central in the achievement and promotion of quality?

In this chapter, I will argue that it is the students who do the achieving, not the teaching staff, or the senior personnel, or the institutions. Those other actors and the institutional environment may help the student to achieve; and when we describe educational processes as being of high quality, it is the staff (including the support staff) who rightly deserve credit. But in so far as we can identify aims in higher education, it is the student who attains them. For aims of higher education are essentially a filling out of the particular characteristics and aspects of intellectual and personal growth which educators intend their students to acquire.[1] Seeing students as central to the achievement of higher education is not an empirical point about what happens in practice, but a conceptual point about what we take higher education to be. Neither institutions nor teaching staff are necessary for higher education to take place. The students, though, *are*; and it is they who should be central to our thinking about achieving quality in higher education.

In what follows, I shall try to justify this viewpoint and go on to draw out its implications for our policies and practices within higher education.

## Aims in higher education

Talk of aims in higher education takes place on two levels. On the one hand, there is talk of aims by those responsible for designing courses of higher education, especially within the UK polytechnics and colleges sector. Here, particularly in the context of course approval and review, the usage is essentially operational: course teams justify to their peers the general aims of a course and demonstrate their ability to deliver those aims. (Specific objectives or outcomes of a course are often, especially in polytechnics, identified at the same time.) The specified aims provide a means of direction for those in positions of responsibility to guide and, later, to evaluate the achievement of those purposes.

This sense of 'aims' is course-specific and, while not being confined to the higher education part of the education system, is particularly associated with it. For in higher education, as distinct from the other sectors of the educational system, we find discrete courses which are entirely designed, planned, delivered and assessed by largely autonomous institutions.

At present, institutions of higher education in the UK have real *institutional* freedom in this sphere (and hence the value of getting them to specify their separate educational missions). Despite national initiatives which are beginning to affect the higher education curriculum, such as the Enterprise Initiative and the establishment of the National Council for Vocational Qualifications with its competency-based approach to curriculum design, higher education institutions retain a high degree of institutional autonomy.[2]

That freedom goes even deeper, to the internal life of departments and course teams where perhaps the strongest impact on aims is that of the disciplinary home of a course of study. As Tony Becher has recently shown, the academic community is a collection of many 'tribes', organized around discrete disciplines (Becher 1989). Consequently, course aims reflect, at least in part, the culture of the core discipline(s). What counts as a proper appropriation of knowledge, what intellectual skills are most desired, or where the balance is to lie between theory and practices differs across subjects. Compare, for example, the kinds of competencies and development that graduates in computing, in archaeology, in philosophy and in nursing are expected to demonstrate.

It is in these circumstances of local direction that we find course teams being asked to give an account of themselves, as compared with the more central direction that characterizes other parts of the educational system. Admittedly, the UK universities have been relatively free from such account-ability procedures but, with the advent of the Academic Audit Unit (1991a, b), the staff of universities are beginning to experience some form of peer evaluation over their teaching activities, as universities introduce their own internal evaluation procedures to meet the Unit's desiderata.

There is also a sense of 'aims' employed by philosophers of education and others who talk in an overarching way of 'the aims of education'.[3] If these aims are ever given any cash value, they offer a view as to the general ends that an educational process should serve, in order that what is on offer can really be thought to count as education. These aims are supposed to hold across all the educational processes within higher education; this usage of 'aims' is a quasi-conceptual perspective.

However, identifying such general aims across all of higher education is fraught with difficulty, for different sets of overarching aims are on offer. As we saw in the last chapter, not only are there competing conceptions *within* the academic community (between those who are research-oriented, those who give priority to the general intellectual development of students, and those who have an eye to the demands of professional bodies and working life), but there are also general conceptions held by influential interest groups *outside* higher education.

This debate over the general ends of higher education – which might be said to be a matter of competing ideologies (Collier 1982) – is important: are we just faced with these competing ideologies or can we detect some indisput-able conceptual core to the idea of higher education? That was the topic of the last chapter, where I began to sketch out a conceptual analysis of higher education which has, I argued, some internal logic; a view of higher edu-cation which latches on to the sense of higher order levels of reflection and understanding and which, I suggested, is contained within the idea of higher education. But, irrespective of my argument for an essential core to the idea of higher education, there are nevertheless these competing general con-ceptions of higher education, which translate themselves into different sets of general aims.

So aims are to be found at both course-specific and system-wide levels of higher education. And at both levels, aims contain an implicit 'ought' element (Moore 1974). Either, as system-wide aims, they are in effect a set of recommendations to the wider world as to the character that higher educa-tion ought to have; or, as course-specific aims, they are in effect a reminder to the course team itself that this is the kind of course they have in mind and they ought, therefore, to work towards the conditions that favour the realization of the aims in question. On both counts, the specification of aims is an attempt to spell out the kinds of attribute that are desired for successful graduates. Aims are not, therefore, so much descriptive as they are value-statements, reflecting the values of their holders.

## The problem with aims

Aims cannot be ducked. Even if the course does not have stated aims, and even if the teaching staff responsible for it have never sat back and worked through their teaching 'philosophy', some set of aims will still come through. Whether we realize it or not, whether we wish to recognize it or not, as educators we must have aims. All educators, if they are serious about the task, must operate with the intention of achieving some kind of outcome (White 1982).

But, as we have noticed, specifying aims has more positive features. At the course-specific level, apart from aims being helpful for self-guidance to a course team, they can act – increasingly in a market-oriented system – as a signal to prospective student recruits. Also, because courses of higher education have quite different ends built into them, it is partly through the articulation of those ends that we can begin to make judgements about the level of the quality of a particular course. The identification of the course aims provides a mark against which course evaluation can take place.

At the system-wide level, particularly if argued through cogently, aims serve not just as a piece of rhetoric but also as a means of persuasion or influence about the direction of higher education as such. They help to develop a rational debate within society about the ends and character of higher education overall.

Yet, despite all these uses and despite their inescapability, the language of 'aims' *and* of 'fitness for purpose' is profoundly misleading. Both terms put the emphasis on the educator's intentions. I use 'educator' in the broad sense to include national bodies concerned with higher education and institutional managers, as well as those at the sharp end, course leaders and teaching staff. Extending my sense of 'educator' in this way is justified because the two terms (aims and fitness for purpose) are applicable to conceptions of systems, institutions and courses, conceptions held by those in positions of power to drive forward the delivery of higher education at its various operational levels.

The problem with placing the focus on the educator's intentions is that that approach to conceptualizing higher education smuggles in a sense of a course (or even an institution or a system) being designed and imposed on students. The purposes and the aims talked about are those of the course designer, or the teachers, or – at the higher levels – the institutional managers or the system planners. Unwittingly, talk of aims (and fitness for purpose) assumes pre-set conceptions of higher education which are presented as a *fait accompli* to the students. Even the educational processes they experience, under this conception of higher education, are things that are done to the students. After all, we do not, in the usage of the terms, hear much talk of students' aims, or students' purposes. It is the course aims (as envisaged by the course team), or the mission of the institution (as set by its academic staff), or the purposes for which the sector is intended (as envisaged by the members and officers of the relevant national body) which carry the day. Of students' aims or purposes we have heard very little; although admittedly that state of affairs is beginning to change as student recruitment takes on more of a market character.

The point is that, in teaching, educators cannot achieve their aims by themselves. The outcome is realized through another person, the pupil or student. Given this indirectness, educators have to have some notion of what they are hoping to see in their students. That is what is meant by having an aim or a set of aims. But things are more complicated still in the educational processes which characterize higher education.

## The self-achieving student

In the last chapter, I argued that – despite the legitimate contest over its ends – the concept of higher education contains at its core the idea of critical reflection by the individual student. Through this critical reflection are attained *higher* order levels of understanding and *higher* order states of mind. These notions, I am suggesting, are not particular sets of aims, but are part of the essential logic of the concept of higher education.

Evidence for this can be uncovered through an analysis of conventional discourse; and not just that of academics. There is a widespread, though tacit, consensus that part of what is meant by 'higher education' is the attainment of a certain degree of intellectual autonomy on the part of individuals (Baird 1988). We understand it to be amongst the capacities of successful graduates that, in their own subject field at least, they can recognize sense from nonsense, have a personal understanding of key concepts and of the framework and style of thinking and activity associated with a domain of intellectual inquiry or professional action, and are able to form a well-supported argument within it. These capacities may require the mastery of some kind of informational content, but they are not in themselves a matter of learning *that* so-and-so, or learning *how* to do so-and-so. They are capacities at a higher level, which enable the student to 'form a view' of his or her learning (in Newman's terminology). And, as constitutive of the central purposes of higher education, they are capacities that are developed across all subjects and all forms of programme.

This is not, admittedly, how students always see things. For different reasons, they may come into higher education with a dependency orientation, suffering from an overestimate of what can be done for them. Characteristically likely, perhaps, to show this syndrome are 'mature' students, who either have been out of the academic environment for many years or were never in it. In these consumer-oriented times, many quite rightly want their money's worth out of their attendance, especially if they are attending

part time and coming to sessions after a busy day's work. There is, especially
in the technological or business areas, a tendency for them to think that their
'money's worth' is demonstrated in the quantity of information they can
acquire from their lecturers, or in the techniques they can pick up. Weaning
students away from such narrow definitions of intellectual progress, so that
the information and the techniques become vehicles for greater insight,
understanding and autonomy, then becomes one of the key roles of the
teacher.

This gap between student expectation and what can actually be done for
students is not new. Until he went up to Oxford in 1832, Mark Pattison
(later to have perhaps the single greatest influence on reshaping nineteenth-
century Oxford (Sparrow 1967)) had been largely self-taught. In his memoirs,
Pattison recollected how disappointed he had been on the standards at
Oriel at that time: 'Having had next to no teaching at home, I exaggerated
in imagination what a teacher could do for me' (Pattison 1969: 53).

# A commitment to truth

Strange as it may seem, we can gain some philosophical warrant for the
progress available to the autodidact by examining what it is to engage in a
truth-oriented discourse. 'Strange' because what I want to argue is that that
form of engagement is necessarily an interpersonal activity. Truth-telling
contains elements both of personal aloneness and of intersubjectivity. Here,
I draw on the work of the contemporary German social theorist, Jurgen
Habermas.

In his endeavour to locate a secure foundation for rational discourse,
Habermas argues that, in order to enter a truth-oriented discourse, a person
is committed to four validity claims. Simply to make a proposition with any
seriousness, the claimant must be implicitly wedded to the proposition's: (1)
truthfulness; (2) intelligibility to the intended recipient; (3) appropriateness
to the context in which the proposition is made; and he or she (4) must
be sincerely committed to the proposition (Habermas 1979). These ethical
demands are built into the structure of any communication oriented towards
truth.

Several things follow from this analysis of the demands on individuals
engaging in a discourse intended to uncover truth. Whether it is Nobel prize
winners or first-year undergraduates who are making truth claims, the proffering of a proposition as 'true' is necessarily an *action* (indeed, a set of
actions) on the part of the individual concerned (Habermas 1989). Holding
and espousing a truth claim cannot be done passively. A proposition with a
claim to truth carries inbuilt demands on the individual which – as a matter
of logic – cannot be shirked. A truth claim does not simply float freely in a
neutral space, beyond human affairs, but is invested with elements of intentionality and the ownership of anyone who puts it forward.

A truth-oriented discourse, therefore, is a conversation, but it is also a conversation of a particular kind, being heavily structured and requiring all participants to abide by certain rules (of sincerity, comprehensibility, openness to critical comment and appropriateness).

In addition, participants have to be willing to temper their own inputs and allow others opportunities for a hearing. No one should be permitted to unbalance the pattern of contributions except through the force of the argument (a view that Habermas has developed in his consensus theory of truth and his concept of the ideal speech situation).[4] Even the non-speakers, therefore, are active in this conversation; for simply getting to grips with what the speakers are saying is itself a complex and demanding activity. In any case, the difference between speakers and non-speakers is not a sharp one. First-year undergraduates become speakers as soon as they attempt to formulate their thoughts and reflections on what has been encountered, even if only to themselves.

What is the connection between this analysis of discourse focused on getting at the truth and the self-developmental powers of the autodidact? The one is about communication between persons while the other is about individuals. The link is this. The autodidact who makes real progress is one who has internalized the rigour of the critical examination of rational discourse. Indeed, the self-examination can often be especially demanding. The conventions of social life often prevent the underlying validity claims from being questioned. We are not always prepared to ask: 'But do you really mean that?' or 'Are you just saying that?' or even simply 'What do you mean by that?' By ourselves, however, the gloves are off: other than individual imagination and energy, there are no limits to the scrutiny of the self-examination. The self-taught committed individual sets down propositions for herself; and being the author, knows full well whether there is real commitment to and understanding behind the propositions. Wanting genuinely to advance her knowledge, she knows that there is no advantage in self-deception. There is, for the autodidact above all, an inbuilt incentive to be honest, to be persistent in her intellectual endeavours, and never to be satisfied with her present intellectual position.

The general principle to be drawn from these reflections is not that the educator is superfluous to requirements. Rather, it is that, in so far as higher education is an achievement concept, it is the student who does the achieving. The understanding, the forming of intelligible propositions underpinned by personal commitment, the opening of oneself to critical examination, and the determination simply 'to get to the bottom of things' (as Richard Peters once put it) are personal capacities that can only be achieved by individuals for and by themselves. They can be helped to do all these things. But precisely because of the inbuilt ethical demands of truth-oriented conversation, a proposition made by a student has to be owned by the student himself; it cannot be owned by anyone else. Even if the same words or symbols are uttered or written by another student, it is not on those occasions the same proposition. For the two students open themselves to questioning about those strings of words or symbols. They have to be prepared to give their reasons, their *own* reasons, for that particular ordering of words or symbols.

Far from being redundant, the educator can play a significant role in assisting the student in advancing to this position of intellectual autonomy. There is, therefore, an achievement on the part of the educator in being effective in this way. But it is supplementary to the key achievement promised by 'higher education', which is that of the student himself. No one can make the intellectual journey which the student must undergo for him. No one else can take the pressure off the student and acquire the necessary mental toughness for him. The ethical demands of a determination to get to the truth, to offer a point of view and to be flexible in the face of justified critical comment will require and will develop an intellectual maturity which has to be the student's alone. Centrally, it is the student's own accomplishments that count.

## Action at a distance

It might be countered that, especially in higher education, this account undervalues the possible impact of the teacher. For there, whether in the laboratory or lecture hall, we find some teachers having an effect which lasts for the rest of the students' lives. Graduates often look back to the influence that a certain teacher had on them, an influence connected in some way with the personal intellectual qualities of the teacher as a teacher (whatever his or her research and scholarly status might have been). Indeed, the graduates may quite consciously become ardent followers of their former teacher, passing the baton of his or her teachings to a new generation of pupils or students (if they enter the academic profession or become teachers elsewhere in the education system) or into their chosen professional settings.

In so far as this picture of devoted disciples continuing to transmit earlier teachings across generations has validity, it is rather depressing. One of the purposes of higher education is not to produce uncritical followers of charismatic stars, but to enable students to be able to formulate and argue for their own views or – in the professional world – their own actions. To the extent that graduates are able to take on the mantle of their teacher in an open way, willing to probe for weaknesses and prepared to try their own formulations and courses of action, then to that extent the picture of a charismatic pied piper is misleading.

Consequently, the close and often influential interaction between teacher and taught can easily be misread. The immediacy of the day-to-day contact that accompanies this influential relationship is seductive to educators. And, perhaps in the company of particularly striking behaviour or performances by their tutors in the lecture room or laboratory, the students themselves are sometimes seduced in this way. But, if the desired independence of mind is also achieved, what we have here is a case of action-at-a-distance, not a cloistered equivalent of the laying-on-of-hands. In the end, it is the student's own cognitive and practical perseverance that is crucial to attaining intellectual and personal maturity.

No matter whether the number taking the student's course is large or small; or whether the students are attending full time or part time; or whether there is much staff: student contact or little (as with the Open University); or whether teaching methods include significant elements of group work or practical work under supervision: in all cases, in the end, the student's achieving of the promise of higher education has to depend essentially on his or her efforts. There is an ineradicable element of aloneness in the role of student, as indeed there is in being a full member of the academic community.

This aloneness emerges in such phenomena as problems over studying and examinations which many students experience and which not infrequently lead to acute stress and even psychological disturbances. It is also apparent in the language of higher education where, although we use the term 'teacher', we just as often talk of 'lecturer' or 'tutor'. Without getting into the social and linguistic origins of these terms, part of their meaning is that they do not stand for a simple model of transmission between teacher and taught. The terms are indicative of a certain degree of cognitive distance between the two. Learning in higher education is not a matter of imbibing what is encountered for subsequent recall, or of re-performing an activity enacted before the students. The processes of higher education are not like that, for they require in part a personal involvement in, and commitment to, what is taken on board as well-founded belief or action.

All this is testimony to the point that, in higher education, the staff are but one kind of resource on which the students can draw. They are certainly an important resource, but the extent to which they are necessary to the student's success is contingent on local circumstances. The development of distance learning alone suggests that the belief in the importance of a continuing and immediate interaction between teacher and taught can be overplayed (Weidemeyer 1981). It is also indicative that the real value of the teacher (in higher education, as elsewhere) lies in the assistance given to the student in providing a set of meaningful learning experiences which lead on from the student's current stage of knowledge and understanding.

## Silence in the library

Learning can be, and should be much more, accomplished through student interaction. Teaching in groups is becoming much more widely advocated (Bligh 1986; Collier 1990; Jaques 1991). But learning ultimately has to have an inescapable solitary aspect. This is apparent in the library, which after all is a necessary facility in every institution of higher education. Quite often, these days, academic libraries are crowded places, as student intakes rise rapidly, as more use is made of open learning and as staff find themselves under pressure to do more research. Usually, though, all that activity in the library is undertaken silently, as individuals go about their own activities. Objectively speaking, the ritual is a strange affair, for it is not just a silent group activity (like some religious rite) but a collection of personal endeavours.

For many students, the library constitutes their most important resource as book prices outstrip the size of their grants or loans; and at postgraduate level or on part-time undergraduate courses, many are self-payers with families and other financial commitments and cannot indulge in much personal book buying. The significance that students attach to the library frequently emerges in student surveys: the opening hours and the availability of titles in both range and number (that is, duplicate copies) figure repeatedly as matters of concern to the students themselves (Bourner *et al.* 1991). This pressure from the students is entirely proper. With rare exceptions such as mathematics, across the disciplines it is the student's growing familiarity with a specialized literature and his or her personal responses to it that are important. This is so whether the relevant written words are readily available in books or whether – as in the natural sciences, medicine and some other professional areas – the important written words are to be found in the latest journals. The number of titles on the shelves of an institution of higher education and its ability to replace them with up-to-date stock remain important indices of its status and quality as an academic institution, even in an age of handouts to students.

The student's success, however, is not simply a function of the number of words that he or she has read or remembered. Rather, it is the degree to which the student – through that reading – has got on the inside of a literature, has become used to the shape of relevant academic conversations, and has grappled with an unfamiliar language until it becomes his or her own language. Even this is not sufficient, however, for the full promise of higher education to be achieved. For that, we look to the student forming a personal appropriation of what has been encountered, learnt and understood. In the end, the really successful students reach a state of independence from their learning.

# Taking aim

From this discussion, it emerges that talk of aims of higher education is a misleading depiction of the processes of higher education. Someone has to hold an aim or set of aims; and the most obvious candidate is the educator. But, strictly speaking, the teacher's aims, while not exactly beside the point, are not *to* the point. The achievement of the promise of higher education must ultimately be the work of the student, and the significant responsibility for making the educational process effective is borne by the students themselves.

Nevertheless, talk of aims is far from redundant if we are concerned about quality in higher education. As we saw earlier, each educator has to have an aim (or set of aims). We have also seen that aims are contested or, at least, open ended; so it is important that educators know where they stand and what they are trying to bring about. At the same time, holding a particular set of aims, the educator has the task of arranging the conditions of learning so that the student has the most favourable opportunity of achieving those particular aims *and* the general educational ends of personal autonomy implicit – as we saw – in the idea of higher education. The educator, therefore, has to have both the specific aims of the programme of studies in mind and the general purposes of higher education. We can legitimately retain the vocabulary of aims, therefore, with the proviso that we remember that – especially in higher education – the educator cannot achieve either kind of aim directly, for the achievement belongs to the student.

The ballistic metaphor of aiming has a certain aptness in the context of higher education, because once one has taken aim and fired a shot, one is normally powerless to affect the outcome. In other words, the tasks of aiming and shooting are separate from the outcome: while the former affects the latter, the latter is not a simple function of the former. Various factors may intervene to prevent the missile reaching its intended target; and it may reach its target in spite of, rather than as a result of, the accuracy of the initial shot. We can see these occurrences in higher education. Students sometimes emerge with lively critical minds at the end of their course in a way that seems quite mysterious, especially when they have been offered – what might appear to the outside observer – a dull and undemanding programme of study. The explanation is that the students were somehow able to frame for themselves a wide and challenging experience, either through their own efforts or through their extramural encounters (for example, in training placements or study abroad).

Aiming in higher education is more like playing snooker than firing a rifle. In snooker, rather than aiming at the target directly, one aims the cue (white) ball at an intervening object (the coloured ball). The direction of aim is seldom in line with the pocket down which the coloured ball is expected to fall; and even where it is, the immediate focus has to be on the contact with the cue ball, rather than the pocket. At the same time, in addressing the cue ball, the competent player will also have in mind the further consequences of the shot. There will be an immediate set of concerns which interact with a set of larger, though less specific, strategies.

Similarly in higher education: the tutor tries to set the student off on the right path, and hopes to see the student being successful. Once the contact has been made, the outcome is to a considerable degree uncertain. The tutor cannot control the outcome; for it is largely what the student makes of it. It follows that if a student is unsuccessful – if he or she fails the course – the responsibility must lie in the first place with the student. Questions can and should be asked about the character of the student experience, and the support given to the students. But unless the number of students not completing the course was unusual in any way, the first line of inquiry will be oriented around the student, and his or her problems, rather than the teacher(s) concerned. This is in no way to diminish the responsibility that teachers have towards trying to ensure that students *are* successful. It is to make the logical point that, in human affairs, matters cannot be assured; trying to bring something off and actually succeeding are different matters.

There is one sense in which the gap between aim and process is not as sharp as I have implied. Educational aims are not just evident in outcomes. They also have to be evident in the educational transactions that lead to those outcomes. If we want our students to develop the arts of critical thinking and problem solving, for example, then these aims have to be built into our educational processes. Processes and outcomes are logically interwoven. But there is a necessary gap between the curriculum experiences provided by the tutor and what the student makes of them.

Employing the metaphor of aiming in another way, we can say that aiming in higher education is more like trying to hit the end point of a stick in moving water. One cannot successfully aim directly at the target; one has to make allowances for refraction and other intervening factors and hope for the best; and the water may be a little murky. To some extent, the tutor has to aim 'blind'.

## The educational gap and how to bridge it

Usually, in higher education, students embark willingly and legitimately on pre-established courses offered by institutions. The programmes they sign up for normally have a high degree of structure to them. But even then, the student's time is never fully accounted for. A significant part of the student experience is the way in which students use the time which is at their own disposal.

It follows that in a programme of study of high quality, the student is obliged to construct the educational process partly for himself. In effect, the curriculum is the result of a negotiation between the student and the staff responsible. This is obviously the case in instances of open learning or where there is a significant amount of project work, where by definition the work is to some degree under the control of the student. The degree in independent study offered by the Polytechnic of East London is perhaps the most striking example, because the total programme is designed by and negotiated with the student and is delivered through independent study (Robbins 1988). But the point I am making is that all programmes of study in higher education – to be worthy of the title *higher* education – are to some extent under the control of the student. This is because, as we saw earlier, the student has to give something of himself if the personal autonomy implicit in higher education is to be realized; and the timetable has to allow space for students to organize their efforts in their own way. Ultimately, the student has to develop beyond a relatively passive assimilation of a curriculum and become an active partner (even if a junior one) in it.

If this account is plausible, if there is this necessary gap between the efforts of the teacher and the achievements of the students, how do staff in higher education improve their effectiveness? With this indirect relationship between effort and effect, better teaching is not a matter of simply being clearer about aims, or of shaping efforts in a particular direction, or of making more effort or teaching more hours. Rather, improvement comes – as with students' own performance – through critical reflection by the staff concerned on the total process of teaching and learning. As we saw earlier, processes of systematic critical reflection are more advanced in the polytechnic sector of UK higher education (Barnett 1987; Harris 1990) but they are developing with more rigour in the universities too (CVCP 1986–89). We shall look more closely at these procedures later on; in this section, we are concerned with conceptual matters. The point is that the development of systematic processes of course review is entirely appropriate, since staff in higher education cannot aim directly at the target – of an autonomous, self-critical, competent student – but can only *subsequently* appraise the effectiveness of their efforts and make adjustments that seem sensible in the light of the available evidence.

## Conclusions

Although this chapter has consisted of a conceptual exploration of the processes of higher education, certain practical conclusions stand out. There are three areas in which general principles can be drawn out: course design, course delivery and course evaluation.

In designing a course, and in determining the curriculum, we need to remind ourselves that the principal educator is the student; staff and institutions are supportive players in the proceedings. To think in this way amounts, for most teachers in higher education, to nothing short of a paradigm shift in the way in which they think of their roles and their relationships with their students. On one contemporary conception, a course is put on, is offered to the market, and students are invited to purchase it as consumers. The transaction is one of a passive consumption of what is available. On the conception being argued for here, the relationships are inverted: a course makes sense only *if* it makes sense to students. That means that efforts have to be made to identify the students' starting points, and their aspirations, and to design a set of curriculum experiences which build on that platform. It also means providing students with sufficient non-programmed time and intellectual space so that they can make explorations of their own of the terrain being opened to them.

Secondly, on course delivery, the discussion in this chapter suggests that a key principle is that the teaching methods should be such as to promote students' personal insight into concepts and frameworks of the subjects studied. The methods should also enable the students to be self-sufficient. Students' learning should be accompanied wherever possible by an encouragement to form their own judgements or views or suggest possible procedures of their own (for example, within programmes of professional education). Students should become responsible for a definite part, at least, of their own learning. More generally, the learning, even at 'the frontiers of knowledge', should be seen simply as a vehicle through which the students come to be critical and self-critical.

Lastly, in the realm of course evaluation, there should be at least some focus on students' educational experiences and their intellectual progression. The course team has to so recognize the value of course evaluation that it becomes part of the ethos of the course. Continuous feedback should be sought, principally from the students, so that the course is always under review and undergoing modification (however slight). Evaluation and feedback, and even modification, are of little account in themselves, however. They count where they lead to a more effective and a more worthwhile student experience. But we can only know this indirectly through evaluation and feedback; it cannot (I have argued in this chapter) be achieved directly. Nor can it be assumed that where processes are – on the evidence – success-ful, that they will continue to be so. For students are different and will respond differently, both individually and as a cohort. Evaluation cannot usefully, therefore, be held at the end of a course but must be held through-out; and, if necessary, adjustments in approach and delivery must be made continually.

All these points can be interpreted as general principles which can inform attempts to improve the quality of higher education. However, the signs are mixed as to whether these principles are being reflected in the internal life of institutions. For example, the new consumerism and the emergence of a competency-based approach (under the direction of the National Council for Vocational Qualifications) could lead to more tightly structured curricula. On the other hand, moves towards a mass higher education system may bring in a *more* open-ended curriculum approach, as managers look to open learning for efficiency gains and – through the Higher Education for Capa-bility initiative of the Royal Society of Arts – learners generally are encouraged to take responsibility for their own learning.

In relation to course review, again the signs are ambiguous. On the one hand, the Council for National Academic Awards – which has done much to promote an internal culture in institutions of looking systematically at course offerings – is being disbanded. On the other hand, the UK universities are beginning to establish their own quality assurance mechanisms through the prompting of the Academic Audit Unit (now being assimilated into the new Higher Education Quality Council), and new though uncertain arrangements have been foreshadowed in a White Paper.

The operational future of the principles I have just sketched out is unclear, then. That uncertainty in no way diminishes their logical status and their potential for guiding possible improvements in higher education.

So, to return to our opening question 'Does higher education have any aims?', we can answer yes; but its aims are less fixed points we steer towards, than compass bearings we steer by.

# 3

# The Idea of Quality

So far, we have looked at the idea of higher education and the peculiarities of its associated educational processes. It is time to turn to the idea of quality itself. What is 'quality' in the context of higher education? How is the term being used in contemporary discourse and debate about higher education, and with what underlying assumptions? What are the relationships between 'quality', 'standards' and 'excellence'? What is meant by 'quality control' and 'quality assurance', and how do their meanings differ? How helpful are the ideas of total quality management, of academic audit and of quality circles? This is a broad conceptual field and I shall tackle only the first three of those questions in this chapter.

## Quality contested

The assessment methodologies of national bodies, institutional managers, heads of department, researchers and lecturers, quite apart from employers and other external groupings, are almost certainly going to differ, for there is no reason why we should expect their concerns and expectations in higher education to be identical (Yorke 1991a). Given the concerns of:

1. a national funding body to secure a trans-institutional means of comparing quality with its dominant interests in limiting expenditure and in seeing a high proportion of students graduating in the sciences and technologies;
2. an institutional manager to defend the particular mission of his or her institution perhaps in expanding access to identified groups in society or in wanting to support, say, its modular structure of undergraduate programmes;
3. large segments of the academic community, in wanting to demonstrate their productivity through their research record;
4. some lecturers in wanting encouragement and assistance from their peers in teaching a new subject or perhaps wishing to move an existing course radically in the direction of open learning;

it would be very surprising if there were unanimity on ways of assessing the quality of higher education.

These different approaches are testimony to the point that quality is a contested concept (see Chapter 1); so much so, that the different groupings, despite their overlaps and interlinks, constitute distinct sub-cultures within the totality of local, national and international networks that pass under the banner of higher education. The contemporary debate over quality is a vivid exemplar of the postmodern society, in which rival definitions of large issues are defended without any obvious way of either arbitrating between them or erecting a supra-cultural definition.

With that said, it might be thought that the discussion over quality cannot  fruitfully go much further. Different interest groups will have their own ideas as to what constitutes quality and how to measure it; and in any democratic society, the actual arrangements in use will be the outcome of a political, economic and social interplay (if not conflict) between the competing interest groups. That is a defensible instance, but I want to try to steer a path through the debate to reach a definite position.

In the contemporary debate over quality in higher education, certain issues are prominent. For example, how can we assess it? To what extent can we compare the quality of provision across institutions? Who is to do the assessing? What is the evidence that assessors should look at? But while procedural issues of this kind are frequently raised, very little attempt is made to confront the key question head-on, namely: What is quality in higher education?[1]

There is good reason for this reluctance to face explicitly the second-order conceptual question, and to concentrate attention on first-order procedural and technical questions. As we saw in Chapter 1, the different approaches to quality reflect different conceptions of higher education itself. Consequently, it is far easier to raise technical and procedural issues than to raise fundamental issues connected with the aspirations and ultimate values which lie behind different approaches to quality. But we should not allow the debate on quality to be reduced in this way; and those underlying values or principles will be present anyway and will reflect themselves in our attitudes to quality, whether we recognize them or not.

I shall state a view of my own in this chapter but, for now, I want to develop an overview of current conceptions of quality. I begin by offering a classification which, while it has all sorts of offshoots to make it more complex, is fundamentally simple. It rests on a single division, between what I shall term *objectivist* and *relativist* conceptions of quality.

## Objectivist conceptions

The fundamental assumption underlying objectivist conceptions of quality is that it is possible to identify and to quantify certain aspects of higher education, and that the same assessment can be accorded to all courses or all

institutions (depending on one's focus of interest). Using a common methodology across the system, by looking at the same aspects and quantifying them
in the same way, an objective measure of quality results, or so it appears for
those who adopt this approach. It is assumed that precisely because the
elements in question have been identified and have been assessed in the same
way, the figures that result tell a story not only about this institution but also
about this institution in relation to others.

In the jargon, this treatment is applied to 'input' and 'output' features of
institutional life. On the input side, for example, it is sometimes thought that
the most important feature of higher education is the quality of the teaching
staff. Very well, the logic goes, let us look at their qualifications and their
research records. How many fellows of the Royal Society or British Academy,
how many staff with higher doctorates, and how many recognized authorities
does an institution have? As we saw in Chapter 1, this approach assumes that
there is some kind of direct and positive relationship between the staff's
research record and their ability to teach effectively. In doing so, it reflects
the academics' belief in the superiority of research over teaching. So, what is
offered as an objective means of assessing quality hides a particular set of
values and, as such, functions as an ideology, protecting a group's social
interests.

If assessments of staff are problematic, then let us look for another input
indicator which is firmer and more substantial; and what could be more firm
and substantial than the buildings or equipment (including libraries and
computers) that an institution of higher education has at its disposal? Capital
resources *are* important elements in establishing modern systems of higher
education. A higher education of sound quality cannot be offered today without proper resourcing. However, an appraisal of resources of this kind, in-
animate as they are, can tell us very little about their use. A concern with
capital resources is not out of place, but it can lead to an over-concern.[2]
Buildings become admired for their architecture or their age. But the character of the human interactions taking place within them is too easily
overlooked.

A final example of input measures, employed by those favouring an objectivist approach to quality, rests with student entrants. Despite the influx of
non-traditional entrants, the dominant means of evaluating the quality of an
intake still lies (in the UK) in an arithmetical valuation of entrants' examination performance in their school or further education college, scores being
derived by assigning numerical values to their A-level performances (Johnes
and Taylor 1990). This indicator is essentially retrospective; it looks to past
performances of entrants.

It is extraordinary that the concern with A levels as a commentary on the
quality of higher education could have been so longlasting. Doubtless many
assume that there is a positive relationship between A-level performance and
degree results (although the empirical evidence is uneven and often weak
(Johnes and Taylor 1990)), but the claim hardly takes us any further
forward in understanding the quality of higher education. As a matter of

logic, a student's performance at one moment in time cannot be an indicator of the quality of the educational processes that the student will experience *subsequently*. (I shall return to this issue in a later chapter.)

The objectivist conceptions of quality have also favoured an assessment of outputs. Typical indicators here are non-completion rates, degree results, and subsequent patterns of employment or postgraduate education (Johnes and Taylor 1990). Again, all these are quantifiable, and encourage a ranking of institutions by their numerical scores on any of the indicators. A sensitivity to the difficulties of attaching weight to individual indicators has prompted the appearance of 'value-added' in the language of performance indicators. As a term, value-added contains a double claim. Firstly, that input and output measures in themselves do not have the objectivity they appear to exhibit; and secondly, that a measure of the added value can overcome that difficulty. The supposition at work is that by putting input and output indicators into a relationship with each other, a fairer measure of institutional effectiveness can be produced (Johnes and Taylor 1990).

I shall examine the soundness of that supposition later (Chapter 6); my observation here is that value-added represents in itself a qualification on the apparent objectivity of existing indicators. Value-added measures, being relational, cast doubt on the legitimacy of absolute measures of performance. But, in the classification I am developing here, such measures still remain within the objectivist fold. For value-added promises to offer a *more* objective means of identifying and ranking the performance of institutions than those otherwise available. Value-added is objective through and through.

## Relativist conceptions

This approach has both public policy and theoretical backing, though in an unexpected combination.

In the sphere of public policy, we see the following move in the discourse. Faced with the charge from the UK polytechnic sector of higher education that it is not being funded at the same level as the universities in offering courses at the same level and at the same standard, one response from those in national bodies and close to national decision-making – as we have seen – is that 'fitness for purpose' should be the test of performance. In determining the appropriate level of funding and provision (the 'inputs' of performance), consideration should be given to institutions' strategic and relational functions in the system, rather than to any absolute sense of what institutions of higher education are entitled to enjoy.

Alongside this line of thinking, we find a parallel set of reflections from a quite different and more theoretical source. Social theory and several domains within modern philosophy (including philosophy of science, of social science, and of education) have been paying considerable attention to the idea of relativism. Relativism comes in different varieties (Margolis 1986), but its essence lies perhaps more in what it denies than in what it asserts. Its central claim is that there are no absolute criteria to hand by which we can assess either thought or action. Relativism does not imply that no sense can be given to the notion of truth, but it does suggest that there are different ways of slicing up reality and gaining a valid insight into it. In this way, there can be no absolute claims to validity.

It is perhaps strange to see these two relativist perspectives being run together. One comes from the world of public administration and policy making, and springs from an essentially defensive posture on the part of the dominant powers and agencies. The other comes from the world of intellectual reflection, and, for many, is a subversive doctrine. Conservatism and radicalism somehow seem to be marching hand in hand. If so, then either the bureaucratic relativism of national policy making is more radical than it is being portrayed as or the radicalism of philosophical relativism is more conservative than I have implied. I want to suggest that both possibilities are true. We can see both perspectives at work in contemporary views on quality in higher education.

To unravel this conundrum, we can usefully turn again to the idea of 'fitness for purpose'. It has two interpretations. It can be an ideological term, wearing an apparent democratic concern on its sleeve, but all the while acting as a mask for a *hierarchical* view of higher education. Not far from 'fitness for purpose' we may hear talk of 'the gold standard' of higher education. Yes, institutions of higher education should be so resourced that they can fulfil the demands of their function within the total system of higher education, but we should not be surprised if some institutions attract more resources than others. In their public reputation, their historic place in international higher education, the staff attracted to work in them, and the calibre of entrants enrolled on their courses (as evident in their A-level results), some institutions rightly attract greater esteem *and* are considered to be of higher quality than others.

If this is the view of some traditionalists within the academic community, it finds an echo in the central agencies of national policy making and resource allocation. With the demand for higher education exceeding the available national budget, ways have to be found of lowering the unit of resource. If the 'purpose' of one sector can be so defined that it cannot easily justify the support historically given to the other sector, then 'fitness for (that) purpose' becomes a means of legitimizing a differential funding base.

Deployed in this way, 'fitness for purpose' is ultimately an incoherent notion. For it pretends that the quality of institutions of higher education is different only in kind (in their 'purpose'), but it acts to defend a hierarchical relationship. Its relativism is only skin deep; its real core meaning is one of ordering and ranking (Fig. 3.1). All institutions are equal, but some are more equal than others.

'Fitness for purpose' can have an alternative interpretation, that of a *parallel* approach to quality assessment (Fig. 3.2).

Here, institutions are indeed seen as equal but different, and it is against thinking of this kind that they are encouraged to produce and implement

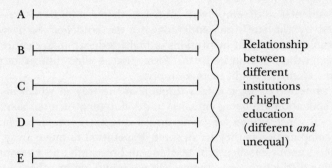

*Figure 3.1* The hierarchical form of 'fitness for purpose'

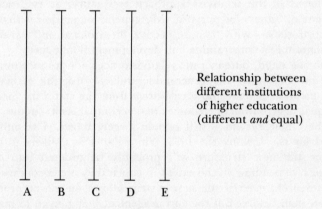

*Figure 3.2* The parallel form of 'fitness for purpose'

their own 'mission statement'. In contrast to the hierarchical conception of 'fitness for purpose', this approach to quality assessment – if it could be successfully implemented – would be tantamount to ruling out of court comparisons across institutions. Each institution would be responsible for determining its own profile of activities and the priorities between them. Comparison would be a non-starter, for we would not be comparing like with like.

That, at least, is the logic; but there is an incoherence here, too. If institutions want to count themselves as institutions of higher education, then presumably there must be points of similarity so that they are recognizable as institutions of higher education. Admittedly, *pace* Wittgenstein's notion of 'family resemblances' (1967), we have to be ready to find that there is no single aspect of their internal life that all institutions of higher education have in common, but there would have to be points of contact between them. Can we not say – at a minimum – that almost all institutions of higher education, whatever else they do, offer programmes of study to students at or near or beyond first-degree level, and have students, programmes of study taken by those students, staff employed to teach them, and forms of assessment arranged by the staff and undergone by the students? So it would seem implausible to hold that institutions of higher education are entirely different from each other. Yet, in its *parallel* form, that is what 'fitness for purpose' in mission statements might seem to imply.

The same forced logic comes through in the way in which institutions of higher education are being enjoined to develop their own mission statements. As a result, institutions are being driven into extraordinary conceptual and policy complexities as they try in some desperation to move away from bland statements about excellence in teaching and research and attempt to fashion something distinctive about themselves not found in any other institution.

We can now try to justify the double claim made earlier, that it appears that there is little difference in practice between the conservative and the radical forms of the relativist approach to quality, as evidenced in their perceptions of 'fitness for purpose'. My general suggestion is that both relativist approaches – with their respective hierarchical and parallel conceptions – contain *both* constraining and developmental influences.

On the one hand, bureaucratic relativism does not produce total inertia in the system. Certainly, the general hierarchical ordering of institutions of higher education is under no great threat from the state; the inequality and the unequal distribution of resources that accompanies it – across sectors and across the whole system – will remain largely intact. The unitary system proposed for the UK by the 1991 White Paper is unlikely to disturb this point, for the new structure will probably be ordered into divisions of institutions, depending on the extent to which they are encouraged to pursue funded research, even if the new system allows for easier promotion and relegation than before. But the encouragement being given to institutions to work out their own 'niche' in the total system and to identify the particular services they have to offer, including the range of programmes and the segments of the student market to which they especially wish to appeal, is bound to have the effect not just of widening access and the participation in higher education, but also of broadening our very conceptions of what can legitimately fall under the honorific title 'higher education'. So the 'fitness for purpose' of public policy making has an inner dynamic.

On the other hand, the philosophical and social relativism that can be glimpsed behind contemporary efforts to clarify quality in higher education is not as radical as it might appear. The justifiable sensitivity towards differences across institutions, including their contrasting histories, traditions and values, certainly helps to maintain a variety of provision at a time when the dominant forces of modern society are a stimulus towards narrowing uniformity. But that sensitivity contains a charitable dimension which all too easily can allow institutions separately and the system as a whole to comfort themselves that their traditional values, perspectives and definitions of purpose have an inner justification requiring no external justification.

So both conservative and radical conceptions of 'fitness for purpose' have elements of inertia *and* openness to change.

# Developmental conceptions

I have been arguing that our contemporary conceptions of quality in higher education are dominated by two perspectives, an objectivist approach and a relativist approach. They both have shortcomings. The objectivist approach suffers from an insensitivity to the differences of purpose, tradition and social location across institutions of higher education; while the relativist position (in its extreme form) implies that anything goes, that there are no boundaries to what is to count as higher education, and that cross-institutional judgements are *ultra vires*.

Against these conceptions, I want to draw out a third conception of quality, not (for the moment, anyway) to advocate it as such but to fill out the general schema in a way which does justice to contemporary ideas. I am not claiming that this third approach is hardly to be found. On the contrary, it is well established, especially in polytechnics, and is growing in universities. The problem is that it is more part of the internal culture of institutions, whereas the other two are to be found in national policy making and the pronouncements of politicians and administrators. Consequently, the third approach is largely unmentioned in public debate; it is under threat and liable to be marginalized, with its subsequent neglect leading to its disappearance.

This third perspective is what I shall term the *developmental* approach to quality, and it has a number of aspects.

Firstly, the relativist and objectivist conceptions are external viewpoints, in which either outside agencies find ways of forming an assessment of what an institution is up to, or an institution itself performs the assessment with an eye to its external constituencies. The developmental approach, in contrast, is that of internal members of an institution (staff and students) reviewing what they are about for themselves. This is not to deny that, within those reviews, those people will often want to take into account external interests, such as those of employers or professional bodies. And they may well wish to engage the services of others outside their institution to assist them in that assessment. But those considerations are embraced and the external advisers are brought in as part of an overriding concern of the key actors themselves to improve the quality of their own activities. It is, in this sense, an internalist approach to quality in higher education.

Secondly, both the objectivist and the relativist approaches are built around an assessment of an institution's past performance. Certainly, the relativist conception allows for, even encourages, the formation of institutional goals, and in that sense has a futures aspect to it. But both conceptions are essentially different ways of forming an assessment of how well institutions have been performing. The relativist approach adds the rider that we can only do that with any degree of sophistication by attending to an institution's agreed aspirations for itself.

In contrast, the developmental viewpoint is oriented towards improving the quality of the work of an institution. It may be rejoined that that, too, is one of the purposes of the evaluations conducted under the other two conceptions; but that response should cut little ice. That outcome can, at best, be a by-product of what they are about. In the jargon, those approaches to quality assessment are essentially summative, producing judgements on past performance so as to guide policy or financial decision-making (whether at institutional or national levels). Nor is that function to be disparaged. But improving the character, mode of delivery and sheer effectiveness of programmes of work are not their guiding principles, as they are under the developmental approach. Accordingly, the developmental approach to quality assessment is a kind of formative evaluation.

Thirdly, the objectivist and relativist approaches to quality assessment have evolved principally as methods of assessing the performance of institutions. Admittedly, they can be applied nearer the point of delivery. Indeed, we see just that, especially as objectivist conceptions prompt the use of discrete performance indicators (such as non-completion rates or degree results) to evaluate the performance of individual courses. But both conceptions have their origin in the assessment of whole institutions, whether by institutional managements or as a tool in the national resource allocation procedures.

The developmental conception, in contrast, has its source in the activities associated with the delivery of programmes of study. It has its force where it is used in connection with recognizable units of educational delivery. Typically, these would be individual courses. But they could be substantial elements of individual courses, such as modules within a modular structure; or groupings of cognate courses, taught by staff who recognize an affinity with each other and perhaps forming a department, a professional school or a faculty grouped around linked subjects or associated areas of professional interest.

## Making comparisons

Finally, the developmental approach has its drive in trying to improve the quality of an *individual* course (or module, or subject). Certainly, ideas for improvement or beneficial change, or critical questions, which emerge in such a review may – indeed, should – be prompted with an eye to best practice elsewhere. To that extent, contemporary practice across higher education forms the context for developmentally inspired evaluations. But no explicit cross-institutional judgements need be undertaken as such. On this approach, it is the future development of a particular course which is the main motivation, not trying to place it in some kind of hierarchy or relationship with its rival offerings.

By contrast, cross-institutional evaluations are of the essence in objectivist approaches at least. There, the whole drive is precisely to produce 'objective' measures of performance which make possible neutral and simple comparisons across institutions. (The simplicity is not in doubt; the same cannot be said for their neutrality, the main reason behind the rise of relativist approaches.) The motivation behind the consequent development of numerical indicators is clear enough: with available public expenditure on higher education being insufficient to meet the demands placed on it, some apparently neutral and value-free means is required in comparing the performance of institutions.

Surprisingly, the relativist approach is not totally immune from cross-institutional comparisons either. Its comparative elements are more hidden than in objectivist approaches. And the strength of its presence differs between the hierarchical and parallel varieties of relativism we encountered earlier. The presumption that it is legitimate to compare institutions of higher education is particularly evident in the hierarchical strand of relativism. There, it is acknowledged that institutions differ in their mission, in what they are trying to be, but it is still assumed that there are overriding criteria by which performance can be judged. Different currencies *and* the single gold standard of institutional performance are held to exist alongside each other, producing (I suggested earlier) an incoherent position on the part of those traditionalists who hold it.

In one sense, given that higher education provides cultural as well as economic goods (Bourdieu and Passeron 1979), there is an important element of truth in this. A BA achieved at Oxbridge does count for more in subsequent career advancement than a BA awarded at a local college of higher education. Indeed, a third-class degree from Oxbridge would probably count for more than a first-class degree from a local college of higher education. In all advanced countries, a hierarchy of esteem overrides formal elements of equality between institutions. So 'gold standard' relativism is correct as a sociological observation on the way in which the higher education world *is* appraised in society, but debatable as a normative recommendation guiding rational decision-making.

As we have seen, the parallel form of relativism eschews hierarchical rankings of institutions. It says that things are more complicated than that: modern institutions of higher education can legitimately pursue differing sets of purposes. The first priority is, therefore, to see how far an institution has fulfilled the goals it has set itself. Institutions will then emerge with varied profiles of performance, reflecting in part at least those activities to which individual institutions wish to give specific attention as part of their own mission. Accordingly, cross-institutional comparison on this form of relativism is difficult, if not illegitimate. So cross-institutional comparisons should not be thought to be a motivation behind this approach to quality assessment.

Consequently, we can say that the relativist approach to quality is a hybrid so far as cross-institutional comparison is concerned. And it falls midway between the objectivist approach (for which cross-institutional judgement is crucial) and the developmental approach (in which it is irrelevant). This hybrid character of the relativist approach is also evident in the last point of comparison between the three approaches that I want to bring out.

## Qualities and quantities

The final element of comparison that distinguishes the three approaches is that of the extent to which they favour quantitative or qualitative methods of information gathering. 'Qualitative' is another ambiguous term in the quality debate. That it has come to mean simply non-quantitative is in itself a commentary on the dominance of quantitative approaches; qualitative approaches are understood in terms of what they are not. But it is worth noting that the term – '*qualit*ative' – represents an attempt to identify, and to assess the extent of, qualities inherent in the educative process, which is to say worthwhile features of a process being educational. On purely linguistic grounds, therefore, we might expect *higher* marks to be given to qualitative approaches; but public policy-making is not normally held up by a deference to linguistic niceties.

The objectivist approach is coupled with quantitative techniques, while the developmental approach is coupled with qualitative methods of assessment. Again, the relativist approach occupies a mid-way position between the objectivist and the developmental methodologies. That such broad general-izations can be made is symptomatic of contrasting underlying motivations; it is not just coincidence. We have seen something of those motivations already: the determination to produce an unchallengeable ('objective') basis for cross-institutional comparisons in the one case, and the desire to assist specific groups of teachers in their quest to improve the quality of their own work in the other.

But the quantitative–qualitative distinction has taken on something of a clash of ideologies, each approach representing for the other side just that which is undesirable in quality assessment. For those adopting quantitative techniques, qualitative methods of appraisal are unreliable, unable to inform third parties about the quality of the programme or institution in question. They are fuzzy soft, and lacking a cutting edge for decision-makers (Yorke 1991c). For those favouring qualitative methods, peer judgements, words and dialogue are preferable to numbers, for human interactions and evaluations require more subtle forms of statement than are possible in the language of arithmetic. Numbers, as a way of making statements about the complex of activities we call 'higher education', may have the replicability demanded of reliable instruments of assessment but (for this side) in the end they must lack validity.

Quality of higher education, like the quality of wine, cannot be adequately described in numbers. Admittedly, wine tasters do give marks for taste; but the numbers are supplied alongside the qualitative assessments which employ a language of their own (of the *taste* of blackcurrants or strawberries). The numbers are intended to make comparisons between wines easier but are not meant to supplant the language of felt experience. In Wittgensteinian vocabulary, quality and numbers inhabit different language games and forms of life, and it is illegitimate to believe that qualitative expressions are reduc-ible to quantitative formulations.

The relativist approach tries to hold the middle ground in this debate. On the quantitative–qualitative issue, it is neutral; so it is prepared to accept both methodologies. Indeed, not having a particular position to defend, it is prepared to accept both forms of methodology being applied together in a single evaluation, so that a composite picture is established which assesses different aspects of provision using a variety of methods. The particular contribution of the relativist approach lies in its insistence that each methodology should be appropriate to the goals or elements being evaluated. Since institutions vary in their aspirations or in the priority they accord to their goals, the methodology should begin from an institution's prior definition of what it is about, or what the course in question is attempting to do. The relativist approach eschews any particular methodological stance as a given; in some situations, one may be more fruitful, while other circumstances may point to another assessment method.

By way of summary, Table 3.1 represents the distinctions made in this discussion. Having achieved some conceptual bearings on quality, we are now in a position to turn to two other key concepts, standards and excellence.

## Standards

The concept of standards I take to be independent of the concept of quality. The standard of an enterprise is the measure or criterion (or set of criteria) against which the enterprise is to be judged. It is the performance of the enterprise against the standards in question that determines whether the enterprise is of high quality or not.

So, in higher education, we could find comparable institutions being assessed against the same standards and being found to be of differing quality, their performances varying when judged against the standards in question. Correspondingly, and picking up our depiction of hierarchical (or 'gold standard') relativism, we might uncover an example of a quite different kind of relationship between quality and standards.

Assume the existence of two institutions of higher education, but where one set the standard by which it wished to be judged as 'the gold standard' and where the other institution, having a different kind of societal mission, was happy to be judged according to different and arguably lower criteria. Suppose further that on a certain aspect of their institutional performance – for example, the quality of the teaching – the second institution was judged to perform as well as the first institution. Given the separate standards by which the two institutions were being judged, we might be justified in saying (somewhat colloquially) that the second institution – in terms of teaching quality at least – was of high quality while denying the accolade to the first institution even though its relative quality was similar. Indeed, when measured against the standard by which *it* wished to be judged, we might even wish to say that the first institution – again, in terms of its teaching – was actually of poor quality.

*Table 3.1*  Approaches to quality: an analytical framework

| Approach | Source of approach | Dominant level of assessment | Purpose | Focus of evaluation | Form of performance indicators | Institutional context |
|---|---|---|---|---|---|---|
| Objectivist | External | Institutions | Summative | Inputs and outputs | Quantitative | Comparative |
| *Relativist ('Fitness for Purpose')* | | | | | | |
| Hierarchical ('Gold standard') | External | Institutions | Summative | Inputs and outputs | Quantitative | Comparative |
| Parallel (non-judgemental) | External | Institutions and courses | Mainly summative, but possibly formative as well | Inputs, outputs, and processes (marginally) | Quantitative and qualitative | Non-comparative |
| *Developmental* | Internal | Courses | Formative | Processes | Qualitative | Non-comparative |

In short, we could find institutional performance of low quality against high standards, and of high quality when measured against comparatively low standards. This typification of the relationship between quality and standards, however, begs many questions and illustrates that 'standards' is conceptually of less interest than 'quality'.

The concept of 'standards' only gets a purchase if we can identify varying standards against which different kinds of institution or programme are to be judged. More could mean just different (parallel relativism) or it could mean that we would have to accept varying levels of performance (hierarchical gold standard relativism). In either case, our standards will affect our judgements of quality.

The interesting issues arise in the latter case, where the system shifts towards permitting different levels of performance, that is, where different standards exist within a single system of higher education.

Institutions may be concerned about differential standards being imposed, especially if they feel that they are being disadvantaged. For instance, institutions being resourced at a lower level in relation to others – whether for teaching or for research – are likely to voice their sense of injustice. So far as teaching is concerned, they would be justified if they could show that their level of resourcing did not enable them to offer a genuinely 'higher' education. However, the empirical base does not yet exist for such a claim. In the UK, the unit of resource has been progressively lowered over the past decade, particularly in the polytechnic sector, while the overall level of degree class obtained has continued to rise (Johnes and Taylor 1990).

Of more general significance, however, is the question: Do we accept a move towards differential standards of degree awards? Do we allow that a degree at university x will be awarded for work at a standard that would not have attracted a degree at university y? The belief in a common standard of award has provided the justification for the UK external examiner system and, even if the idea of a common gold standard was a fiction, what is on the cards now is the acceptance of differential standards as an act of public policy. This is not just a theoretical matter. As more entrants are admitted from non-traditional backgrounds lacking formal qualifications, as entrants are admitted on to science and technological courses without the traditional science A levels, and as students are admitted on to postgraduate courses with professional rather than academic backgrounds, this issue arises with real bite at examination time. By what standards should the students be judged?

This is a serious question, but I shall not attempt an answer. Its resolution will be worked out pragmatically and with much anguished soul-searching between teachers and external examiners over the years to come. As the clientele of the system widens in age and background, and as the character of the programmes changes, so we are likely to see the pretence at common standards explicitly relaxed. The conceptual point I want to make is that even if the standards are relaxed, that should have no bearing on the quality of work that students can be encouraged to strive towards and which is held out for them to aspire to. The quality of learning, understanding and skill envisaged of students, and of the teachers' professionalism in helping them advance towards that quality, can and should be maintained irrespective of the standards in operation.

In terms of the progress made by students, the 'value-added' at the individual level, we may in the future wish to award a degree where the award might have been denied in a more uniform system. In that sense, standards might fall. But there is no reason for the desired quality of work to fall. Quality should remain paramount, even if the standards are moving, and even if that movement is downwards.

The distinction between quality and standards can be put in terms of another distinction, that between outcomes and processes. The *outcomes* may not reach the expected high standard, or may just comply with an acceptable low standard, but the *process* should remain of the highest quality.

Is there no bottom line? In the formation of a mass higher education system, could the standards by which some institutions are judged and operate be adjusted continually downwards? I want to suggest that there is an ultimate end-point to the movement of standards, an end-point that has a conceptual basis in the idea of higher education (see Chapter 1). It is at least plausible to argue that in order to warrant the title 'institution of higher education', there are certain activities – connected with learning, understanding and human development – which an institution necessarily should be promoting *and* that those activities should be conducted with regard to certain minimum standards. That is to say, unless the students were reaching higher order intellectual capacities, unless they were able to form and substantiate independent thought and action in a coherent and articulate fashion, we would have to say that we were not in the presence of 'higher education'. For a process of higher education to exist, it cannot be the case that anything goes. Standards are not a completely movable feast.

Even if every institution could be said to be of acceptable quality, questions would still arise as to how we might improve the quality of institutional performance. There might be no concern over the standards by which the institutions are operating (bona fide degrees for bona fide work) but the quality of the services and activities that constitute higher education can always be enhanced.

We can conclude, therefore, that matters of quality can always get a purchase in matters of higher education whereas the same is not true of standards. The concept of 'standards', while it will give rise to important and perplexing issues in the coming years, turns out to be a thinner concept than 'quality'. Whatever the standard in force, the teachers' expectations of their students must remain of the highest quality. Higher education is necessarily a demanding process, both for the qualities and the quality it exacts.

## Excellence

Talk of excellence has faded (in the UK, at least) over the past decade as quality has come more prominently into public debates. This slippage, we may judge, is not unconnected with the background context which we observed in the introduction to this book. Excellence is a term more compatible with a highly selective 'élite' system, whereas the system is taking on 'mass' characteristics so giving rise to issues of quality as a matter of public interest. Issues of quality arise where there are doubts about the capacity of the system to sustain an acceptable level of quality; it is the expression of concern that the *general* level of performance in higher education may be slipping below an acceptable quality. Excellence, on the other hand, is perhaps more an expression of confidence that the very highest standards are being maintained, at least in *some* institutions. Quality, we might say, is an inclusive term; excellence is an exclusive term.

Excellence has classical origins, attaching both to persons and to objects where they fitted fully the ends for which they were destined. (In that sense, it is akin to 'fitness for purpose'.) So far as persons were concerned, it implied a hierarchical society, where one's station in life (as warrior or senator) was given, and where the virtues appropriate to one's role could be specified relatively narrowly. This, then, was a conception of excellence which just some individuals were assumed to be capable of meeting.

In the contemporary and more egalitarian age, excellence suggests not just 'élitism' and narrowness of achievement but also the implicit labelling of some as failures. The egalitarian point of view looks instead to the promotion of the potentiality of all persons, whether or not they are likely to achieve excellence in any abstract sense. At the same time, from the perspective of the business community, excellence may seem to mesh uneasily with the well-rounded team players that the modern form of corporate life now requires. Also, the waste in human capital to which an over-insistence on excellence may seem to lead, and the consequent marginalization of many from the process of economic development, are matters of regret. So contemporary society sees a coincidence of perceptions, social and economic, running counter to a defence of excellence.

Perhaps, though, we should not give up the notion of 'excellence' too readily. If excellence is taken to mean exceeding by some margin the standards expected, then surely the term has a place in our language of higher education? In relation to individual students, it seems to be a particularly worthwhile locution. Excellence of achievement requires that a student submits herself to, and masters, certain kinds of discipline: of conceptual understanding, of handling techniques, of clear and orderly expression, and of professional competence. Self-expression, authenticity and creativity – other aspects of excellence – only have point where founded on the disciplined involvement in the student's chosen subject or professional field. These are surely desirable goals for the educator to have in mind for every student in a cohort even if only a few will actually excel in those ways.

Nor should these aspects of personal development be felt to be purely the ends of the academic community. The open, though severely structured, interplay of the imagination, of critical thinking, and of pure concentrated listening which excellent performance calls for points to features of human interaction which are surely in demand in the wider society, both in corporate life and more generally.

But if excellence as a concept has merit in the context of student performance, by extension it must have application to institutions and to teachers. An excellent institution of higher education would be one that, as an institution, strove for excellence in its central activities, particularly in the way it enhanced the character and quality of student achievements (Badley 1992). Correspondingly, excellent teachers are those who try seriously to bring about excellent achievements in their students (Badley 1989; Elton 1990). At both levels, the description of excellence only makes sense on the basis of extensive and sound evidence being available from the institution or the teacher concerned.

Excellence of performance is not simply to be prized when it occurs serendipitously; in higher education, it should be constitutive of what we take to be the desirable form of performance for every student and, therefore, for every institution. The price of its neglect, even in a system of mass higher education, may be an underestimate of the levels of performance that individual students are capable of producing.

## A 'suggestive' definition

I take it (indeed, I argued in the first two chapters) that the term 'higher education' refers at least to some kind of educative process. That means that, for an educative process to be going on (to warrant the appellation 'higher education') there must be students present. And, even in an open learning situation, or in an institution – like the Open University – oriented around non-formal learning, there will be teaching staff present assisting those students with their learning. The qualifier 'higher' has also to be explicated and, even if the account offered in Chapter 2 is felt to be debatable, there would, I suggest, as a minimum be a general agreement that we should hold on to the idea of those educative processes taking students to a level of intellectual development in which they are able to recognize the contingency of all that they think and do (Perry 1970).

These may seem simple points, but their apparent banality is their strength; they carry us far in developing a general framework for discussing the three key issues before us: the meaning of 'quality' in higher education, its assessment and its improvement. For what those ideas supply is, in the terminology of Lakatos, a 'hard-core' to the idea of quality (Lakatos 1977). Whatever else is going on in higher education (and to which we may wish to pay attention in assessing its quality), the quality of higher education – wherever it is provided, in whatever country and in whatever circumstances – will be evident in the character of the educational development and the educational achievements of the students engaged on the programmes of study in question. If there were no processes to which those notions – of student development and achievement – could be applied, we would not be in the presence of higher education.

Clearly, all sorts of other entirely legitimate activities and expenditures of effort and resources could be going on, in opening access, widening the forms of educational provision, prosecuting research, developing links with industry and the professions, and so forth. Where they are on the agenda of an institution, it will be entirely justifiable to assess the quality of those activities. But the education of the students, to the level and with the character implied by the description '*higher* education', must remain central to the business of evaluation.

If this is agreed, we emerge with a 'suggestive' definition (Barrow 1991) of quality. Whatever else it might be, 'quality' in higher education, we can say, is at least:

> a high evaluation accorded to an educative process, where it has been demonstrated that, through the process, the students' educational development has been enhanced: not only have they achieved the particular objectives set for the course but, in doing so, they have also fulfilled the general educational aims of autonomy, of the ability to participate in reasoned discourse, of critical self-evaluation, and of coming to a proper awareness of the ultimate contingency of all thought and action.

This formulation of quality is intended to have applicability across all forms of higher education. It is intended to apply to all kinds of programme (whether undergraduate or postgraduate, full time or part time, modular or unitary). And it is also intended to apply to all kinds of subject, whether pure or applied, single or multidisciplinary and formed around disciplines, broad fields of inquiry or professional settings. (I shall try to bring out its general applicability in Section 3 of the book.)

# Conclusions

There are, as we have seen, radically different ways of approaching quality in higher education. But there is a pattern to the differences we have identified. Indeed, they cluster in more or less distinct groupings as the perceptions and value-preferences of separate sub-cultures within the total higher education enterprise. These include:

1. Teachers and students working together and concerned with the character of students' educational experience.
2. Academics engaged in their research with their eyes on their next paper or book and approbation from their peers.
3. Institutional managers wanting – quite reasonably – to balance the institution's books and to define a special niche for the institution in the higher education market.
4. Employers, industrialists and those engaged in the professions, looking for graduate employees with certain aptitudes and abilities.
5. The national resourcing bodies and national decision makers.

Each of these constitutes a sub-culture of its own, forming more or less a network of those with like interests, and inevitably working out its own definition of quality in higher education and seeking – amidst a shifting pattern of power relationships – to impose its definition on the contemporary debate and policy making.

The question that this reflection raises is obvious and simple: can the different definitions of quality to which these sub-cultures give rise be brought into balance in any way that these groupings would consent to? Though the question appears simple enough, there is an intractability in answering it. For the sub-cultures, as we have seen, orient themselves around different starting points, values and expectations of higher education. Their definitions of quality are self-definitions. Seeing the quality of higher education in the productivity and valuation of its research is part of the way in which a significant segment of the academic community defines itself; similarly with the other groupings. This being so, the prospects of finding a definition of quality which might attract a wide, even if not universal, support across the sub-cultures do not appear to be high. Nevertheless, that is the task of this book.

As a start, I want to offer two propositions which emerge out of this chapter.

I have distinguished three different approaches to quality assessment, which I have termed (1) objectivist; (2) relativist (which I divided into (2a) hierarchical (gold standard) relativism and (2b) parallel (out and out) relativism); and (3) developmental approaches. The key point to draw from that analysis is quite simple. Our assessments of quality in higher education will never be complete unless they embrace developmental approaches. What the balance should be between all of the four approaches and how they might be integrated – if at all – are secondary matters.

The other proposition to emerge from this discussion is this. Whatever else we may be interested in, whether in the success of graduates in securing employment or in widening access or in the value of research, there remains at the heart of higher education the individual student, his or her educational development, and the quality of that development. If there is a unifying idea, this is it. Quality in higher education, and its improvement, cannot be understood without attention to it.

I will now state the general position which I hold and will try to substantiate as I proceed. We are likely to make most progress in ways that do justice to the educational promise of higher education by weighting our approaches to quality assessment towards a combination of approaches 2b (parallel relativism) and 3 (developmental approaches), subject to two important qualifications.

The first qualification is that objectivist (1) and hierarchical (2a) approaches will have a part to play, but in supporting roles. The second qualification is that the relativist approach being supported here has real limits. Higher education is a demanding process, calling for the development and expression of worthwhile human qualities. Certainly, there is room for debate over what those qualities might be (hence relativism), but there is a lower limit on the standards appropriate to a genuine process of 'higher education'.

'*Higher* education' implies an educational process of a certain quality. This logic of higher education has implications for managing quality, and for its assessment and its improvement.

# 4

# Can Quality be Managed?

## Introduction

Managing institutions of higher education is becoming more onerous and complex. As news breaks with increasing frequency of institutions facing financial difficulty, and as the new UK funding councils make clear that 'quality' is one of the criteria by which bids from institutions for funding are being judged, the management of institutions becomes critical for their survival. In addition, institutions are being enjoined:

1. To find ways of using their resources to better effect and to generate more resources.
2. To be seen to be more 'accountable' to the wider society, through implanting effective means of assuring academic standards.
3. To develop improved systems of strategic planning and institutional management.
4. To engage more fully with the host society, whether at the level of access for students or links with other educational establishments, or through offering courses, consultancies and applied research attracting remuneration.

Together, these pressures combine to ensure that the arts of management are both more demanding and more central in maintaining institutional effectiveness. The senior member of an academic institution has, so the argument runs, to be a manager; indeed, to be the 'chief executive' of the corporation (CVCP 1985). And, in the UK, we see that some principals of colleges of higher education are changing their title to 'director'.

In the wake of these developments arises the following question for our present discussion: can 'quality' be managed? Quality is a key concept for the modern institution; it is but a short step to assume that the maintenance and improvement of quality must be a responsibility of an institution's senior managers. I want to examine this assumption in this chapter.

My argument is that institutional managers have a crucial role to play in relation to quality but that there are important limits to the application of the idea of management in this sphere of institutional matters. I want to argue for a concept of management *for* quality, rather than the management *of* quality.

This chapter has, the reader should note, limited objectives. It offers a conceptual exploration primarily of the way in which senior management can be said to bear on academic activities. It does so by examining, from a conceptual point of view, some issues that impinge on the role of senior managers in discharging their responsibilities for academic matters. Issues, no doubt important, concerning the concept of management as such and its diverse range of interpretations are not taken up. Nor does the chapter seek to offer a detailed analysis of the managerial responsibilities towards academic quality at the different levels within institutions, for example, those of heads of department, course leaders, or lecturers.

Three matters prompt this particular discussion. In UK higher education, senior institutional managers are increasingly being given explicit responsibility for academic quality. Most institutions now have a named postholder with such responsibilities. Usually, these responsibilities have been given to existing postholders, typically to a pro-vice-chancellor or deputy director; on other occasions, new posts – for example, of 'Director of Academic Quality' – have been established. So the issue of how to construe quality management at this senior level has practical bite.

Secondly, moves to install quality assurance systems in higher education are often, whether tacitly or consciously, looking to practice in business life, particularly in manufacturing processes. Comment on this connection is commonplace, *both* by proponents and by those who are sceptical of these attempted linkages (Day and Edwards 1990; Harris 1990). The question here, though, is what are the presuppositions behind the metaphor of 'assuring quality' in these different contexts? Is there anything distinctive about educational transactions which might make illegitimate the adoption of commercial conceptions of quality, and which institutional managers should, therefore, bear in mind?

Lastly, by examining this issue of managing quality, key features of the nature of academic quality will become apparent and so, too, how it might be improved.

## Is academic management distinctive?

The message implicit in many recent reports on the management of academic institutions is that it is largely a technical matter: directing and monitoring the performance of institutions through financial indicators and measures of efficiency.[1] Underlying this conception of academic management is an assumption that there is nothing special about it as a species of management. The problems facing academic managers of meeting demands which outstrip the readily available budget, and of setting objectives and priorities and managing resources efficiently to meet them, are common across all management settings in the public sector (such as the health service) as well as in industry and in commerce. The underlying presumption, that academic management is simply a subspecies of management in general, *is* a presumption, though; and it deserves to be critically examined.

Any serious conception of the work of academic management has to begin with some conception of the character of the life of the academy (the institution of higher education). What are the purposes of those engaged within it, and what are the connections between those purposes? In answering these questions, we are bound sooner or later to stumble across the term 'the academic community'. That phrase will seem *passé* to some, redolent of an almost bygone age of collegiality and of a recognition amongst academics of sharing in a common enterprise. In contemporary academic life, disciplinary sub-cultures proliferate and it is through them that academics secure not just their social identities and status, but also their actual livings (as contracts and funding come to depend on research output or students successfully taught). In this climate, everyone inevitably fights his or her own corner: competition, individualism and departmental separateness (if not antagonism) become the determinants of an institution's internal life (Schuller 1990a).

Yet there is something valuable about the idea of the academic community, which institutional managers may overlook or neglect but which stubbornly remains. Despite the disciplinary divisions of academics and their activities, there lies beneath those contrasting forms of life an unwritten but universal code tying every member of the academic community together. That higher level commonality is founded, in the terminology of the American theorist, Alvin Gouldner, on a 'culture of critical discourse' (1979). The term 'discourse' is important because it reminds us that the academic community is characterized both by the use of language and by persons seriously engaged in its use. And that, in turn, raises the issue of whether or in what sense the 'culture of critical discourse' can be managed.

The academic community, we might say, is engaged essentially in a conversation (Oakeshott 1989). It is, though, a particular kind of conversation. As the qualifying term 'critical' reminds us, it is a highly structured and self-critical conversation, oriented towards securing truth. To borrow once more from Habermas's analysis of the structure of communication aimed at closing on truth, its practitioners adhere to certain norms: they are truth-seeking; are sincere in their utterances; offer understandable propositions; and adopt appropriate forms of communication. The participants in the discourse may not be conscious of these embedded commitments but, nevertheless, these inner validity claims are always present in truth-oriented discourse in the sense that anyone proffering a statement could justifiably be challenged in any of these four domains (truthfulness, sincerity, comprehensibility, appropriateness).

Certainly, individual forms of knowledge and inquiry in the academic world contain their own presuppositions and cognitive values, a field that Becher has done much to chart (Becher 1989). Nevertheless, my claim here is that all disciplines, in order to warrant entry to the academic world, have to abide by these four norms. They override the individual subject claims and perspectives, for they are simply conditions of a rational discourse.

Drawing out the features of academic discourse just a little further, we can say that it is elaborate (in the sense of being built on abstract concepts, and a network of interconnected theories and evaluation criteria); bounded within particular language communities, but all the time on the move, with an internal dynamic; structured; and critical. In being 'critical', it is first and foremost critical about its own achievements and projects, with academics' debate being focused on academics' own 'findings', ideas, perspectives and practices. Whatever its preoccupations on the surface level with affairs of the world, or even of the universe – whatever its apparent concern to improve the state of the nation, or the quality of life – the conversation is, at a deep level, interested in itself.

The conversation will be about something in the world. (Even philosophy is 'about' important concepts, and they are in a sense entities in the world.) But if the participants in an academic discourse want to be taken seriously, they are bound to want to advance the conversation itself. The hidden structure of the discourse is to reflect on salient offerings, to evaluate them (according to any new evidence, or their internal reasoning, or presupposed values) and to offer a further contribution. That further contribution may be just an observation on, or a reformulation or an empirically sounder version or a complete transformation of, what has gone before. The point is that the conversation has not just been sustained; it has been carried forward in some way.

This analysis has already gone sufficiently far to indicate that the application of the concept of 'management' to academic discourse is problematic. It is not so much the empirical fact that the academic community is a collection of loosely coupled groupings (Clark 1983), with their inner identities and loyalties, that is the issue; though that is not insignificant. The key point is conceptual in character. Given this account of academic discourse, concepts of academic freedom, professional autonomy and professional freedom begin to come into view and, insofar as 'management' may imply some degree of control, its use in this sphere must run into difficulties. I do not, however, wish to develop the point now but want, instead, to take another tack.

To these reflections about the character of the relationships between members of the academic community we have to add the analysis of the educational processes which are constitutive of 'higher education' (drawn out in the first two chapters). Briefly, we saw that what is being asked of students is not any simple process of assimilating what is being put before them, but (in Oakeshott's phrasing) an active 'engagement' in a conversation which has been going on perhaps for generations. Real demands are placed on students in higher education not only to 'give something of themselves' (as R. S. Peters once put it), to form a view of their learning and to rise above it in the sense of not being bound by it, but also, through their own responses and evaluations and through imparting their own stamp on that experience, to become independent of it.

That is why the use of the term 'the transmission of knowledge' cannot offer an adequate conception of higher education. 'Transmission' carries the connotation of a message being carried from A to B such that there is, if not an actual identity, at least a one-to-one correspondence between its points. That kind of vocabulary can hardly do justice to the personal involvement that has to be expected of all students in higher education, and the manipulation of the ideas that are encountered. Higher education always carries within itself room for the unexpected; and even if the emerging ideas are apparently 'the same' as those encountered, so long as they are imbued with personal understanding, involvement and meaning, we can say that we are in the presence of higher education.

## Academic management and conversation

What bearing does all this have on academic management? Can there be connections between these theoretical and abstract observations on the life of the academic community and the day-to-day tasks of managing, leading and administering a large institution of higher education, with perhaps a budget of tens of millions of pounds per year, a thousand staff of various kinds, and several thousand students?

I want to try to show that there is such a relationship. If the account just sketched out of the internal life of an academic institution is to any degree accurate, it is to that degree incumbent on those with responsibility for managing such institutions to take account of that internal life so that, at least, the academic community is not unnecessarily thwarted or hindered in conducting its conversations (whether in the field of teaching or scholarship or research).

In fact, what our analysis has revealed is that the concept of management has certain peculiarities when applied to the academic institution. Those engaged in the various academic enterprises maintain their own interactions, with their own debates, vocabularies, presuppositions, values and forms of interaction. That is to say, they have their own conversations. Even within disciplines, the segments tend to be relatively tightly bounded, with little passing trade between them. As a result, institutions of higher education have an internal dynamic; literally, a life of their own that goes on, whether managed or not.

To this, it might be responded that the senior management in every kind of organization is faced with the interactions of its personnel, and one of the tasks of management is to ensure that those interactions are as effective as possible, so as to maximize the chances of fulfilling the organization's aims. But this kind of rejoinder is misleading. The conversations of members of the academic community with each other, of teachers with their students or of students with each other have point, irrespective of the motivations of an institution's senior management, and an internal value; so much so that it is largely on them that the quality of the institution rests. It may be an exaggeration to say that it is those conversations that are entirely constitutive of the institution's *raison d'être*. But, still, those conversations may follow their own course, without being 'managed' in any sense by the institution's senior management; and the institution may in turn derive status, and perhaps even income, from the character and quality of those conversations.

Logically, an institution of higher education is no such institution at all unless those conversations are going on fruitfully within it; that is, unless they are going on with an unpredictability and perhaps even excitement of their own. This is not to argue that management is an inappropriate concept in the context of higher education. But we need to sort out the character of the relationships between institutional management and the academic community, and to have a sense of what the senior level of management can achieve and what is beyond its legitimate scope.

The first conclusion from the analysis so far is that there is a responsibility on institutional managers to be sensitive to the special character of the institutions in which they work. I do not say 'the institutions for which they are responsible' precisely because, as we have seen, managers in academic institutions can have only limited responsibilities towards the internal conversations which go on in those institutions. Those conversations cannot be 'managed', *even* by the participants themselves. For 'management' implies at least an attempt to bring off predictable outcomes; and academic conversations are *necessarily* unpredictable. Academic managers, therefore, cannot be held entirely responsible for all that goes on; the members of the institution – both teachers and students – have to bear a degree of responsibility too. But the managers' responsibilities are no less real and onerous, for all that.

At a minimum, senior managers have so to take account of the internal life of the institution that the academic community is not impeded in conducting its conversations. For example, the academic manager who understands and is sensitive to the character of the interactions and dialogue of the institution's academic members (including the students) will understand the threat to the free flow of information inherent in any policy that has the effect of diminishing academic freedom. Such an academic manager will:

1. Shrink from adopting policies that lead to freezing journal holdings in the library.
2. Pause before cutting the number of committee meetings or reducing the membership of committees.
3. Be alert to the possible educational loss in promoting programmes of study for undergraduates built around distance learning (for the empirical evidence is that undergraduates value some element of direct contact with staff (Bourner *et al*. 1991)).
4. Hesitate before advocating thorough-going credit-based programmes of study (sensitive to the reduction in inter-departmental or inter-faculty cooperation that might result as staff work at their own discrete modules, or the possible loss in the coherence of students' programmes of study).

These are largely negative proposals; they suggest actions that the academic manager ought not to take or should weigh carefully before implementing. But the role of the academic manager can be construed in a much more positive way.

If an academic manager is to be fully alert to the academic character of the institution, there are general obligations that mark out the kinds of activity that the manager ought to undertake. Obviously, academic management as a positive practice will seek to reflect both general educational aims and values and an institution's self-declared mission in the development of institutional structures, planning processes and admissions policies. But if the essence of the academic community lies in its communication, albeit a variety of forms of communication, then the highest level of academic management must lie in the active support and advancement of that communication. The difference between these negative and positive concepts of academic management is the difference between systems maintenance and systems development.

## Leading rather than managing

There are many spheres of practical action vital to the institution's wellbeing, in which institutional managers can quite legitimately 'manage' in straightforward senses of the term: those of control and bringing off specific intended outcomes (such as in finance, estate management, and personnel functions). But even in those domains, the manager has to accept a level of accountability to the academic members of the institution; for it is in their interests that the institution is 'managed'. It makes no sense to think of areas of activity for management, and areas of activity for academics, with the two separate from each other. Those pools of apparently non-academic activity, such as control of the institution's finances, ultimately leave their imprint on academic activities. But more than that, the character of an academic institution resides in its academic activities; and the quality of the institution is determined by the demonstrable quality of those academic activities. Managerial activities gain their legitimacy, therefore, to the extent that they advance the academic activities of the institution in ways which secure the support of the academic community.

For example, academic managers are fully entitled to launch a debate about the 'mission' of an institution, to develop a five-year plan working through specific academic priorities, or to propose that all an institution's courses be linked through a credit accumulation scheme (notwithstanding the qualification just made about credit-based courses). And the key papers may be entirely drafted by senior managers, perhaps even with the assistance of relatively junior members of the secretariat in the registrar's department. But those papers carry no authority in their own right. They take on authority through gaining the assent of the academic members of the institution. Leadership, political persuasion, the proffering of economic rewards and other arts may all be in the armoury of the management in trying to bring off its plans. Even so, it remains the case that, in an academic institution, the support of the academics is vital.

It may be said that all this is commonplace in corporate life. The successful organizations in the private sector are well aware of the need to involve their employees in fulfilling the organization's mission. Through its employees' dress or uniform, their language and style of interaction with their customers and even their facial expression, the character of the company – its culture and self-understanding – is exemplified. The employees are not mere cyphers; their identification with the company, its aims and mission, and where it sees itself in the market is a necessary requirement for corporate success.

In both higher education institutions and in the private sector, therefore, the management has to pay close attention to the employees, to secure their active understanding of and commitment to the organization. So it looks, after all, that perhaps there is no significant difference in the demands placed on the management in the two spheres.

But there is; and that difference needs to be declared. The conversations and self-understandings of the members of an academic institution – in their teaching and scholarly activities – have a legitimacy, have their own purpose and movement, irrespective of the claims that the institution's management may make on them. Those conversations are, in themselves, constitutive *of* the institution in a way that the conversations of employees in private sector organizations are not. For those conversations that arise in teaching and scholarly situations have their own *internal* point. The conversations of employees in a private sector institution have point only in so far as they contribute to the organization's wider goals of expansion and profit-making. *Their* justification is an external one. In short, the academic institution gains its credibility from the quality of the internal conversations of its members, whereas the internal conversations of a private sector corporation carry no weight in themselves.

However, even if this analysis of the relationship between the academic management and the central activities of an institution's academics is granted, it does not follow that the management role is heavily circumscribed. The academic manager, as the earlier examples show, is fully justified in leading from the front; for instance, in taking initiatives in attempting to change attitudes, to introduce educational developments, or to bring about a shift in an institution's mission. But the assent of the academic community will always be necessary. Whether that assent is to be sought formally through established decision-making structures (using the Senate or senior planning body) or is to be secured through other routes (perhaps by directly drawing in the whole academic body in an institution-wide debate) will be a matter of judgement; and is not a matter for this discussion.

The concept of management, in some of its senses at least, turns out, then, to be problematic when applied to an academic institution. The main activities of the institution – its teaching, scholarship and research – are not 'managed' by the senior personnel in the senses of being directed or controlled by them. The concept of management is still helpful, however, in other senses of the term. For example, the concepts of leader, motivator, change agent, developer, budget administrator, systems designer, staff developer and institutional flag-waver may all have more application so far as the senior managerial roles of the institution are concerned.

## Quality and management

Post Jarratt (CVCP 1985), some will say that this analysis, in preserving an area of independence for the faculty, is a relic of a former age. The view here, it might be thought, constitutes an apologia for the collegial model of consensual debate and decision-making which is inefficient and unproductive; and is inappropriate to an age in which rapid and massive change in policy, character and mission is called for from every academic institution. If the modern academic institution is to prosper, then a strategic plan has to be formulated, carried through and implemented; and that is the job of the senior managers. Managers have to manage.

I have indicated that, in the long term (or even the shorter term), this description cannot offer a satisfactory account of successful management in an academic institution. The idea of management *is* of value in the modern academy but it has to be properly conceptualized. The groups of academics, and their teaching and research activities, found in academic institutions have an internal momentum carrying within it their own legitimacy. We can see this in practical terms in the way in which quality is 'maintained'.

I put quotation marks around 'maintained' because, again, the idea of maintaining quality, while it might have easily understood meanings outside the academic world, is problematic within that world. To have real substance in the academic institution, 'quality' has to have application to the conversations of the academics, in both their teaching and research roles; and it *should* have application.

Academics' research and teaching activities should be activities of quality. Maintaining that quality is important, too. Academics who have published papers recognized as important by their peers, or have put much energy into teaching so that the students have become enthused by what might be otherwise an esoteric subject, may find that, with all the pressures on their time, there is a temptation to rest on their laurels – or at least on the personal capital that has been accumulated. So the maintenance of quality is an idea that does have application in the academic world; it cannot be taken on trust. Effort, commitment and care require continual renewal.

But the notion of maintaining academic quality is misleading, if it is taken to imply that institutional managers can *directly* affect quality. What institutional managers can do is to provide the right kind of conditions, incentives and assistance in order for academics to maintain the quality of their work. Through establishing and improving guidelines, rewards and support systems, and through the internal resourcing systems, they can have a positive effect on the quality of the work of the academics.

Only very rarely will they be in a position to 'manage' that quality in the sense of have a direct impact on proceedings. I argued earlier that the effect of teaching on the learner is a case of action-at-a-distance, so that there is a *necessary* gap between teaching and learning achievements. But if that is so, there must be a necessary gap between the activities of the institutional manager, including heads of department, and the quality of the learning experience of the students.

The gap to which I am drawing attention is, therefore, a conceptual gap. There is also a trivial empirical sense in which there is a gap; in complex organizations like institutions of higher education, senior managers are geographically removed from the teaching and research activities for which they have responsibility. Occasionally, in endorsing research applications on behalf of the organization, or in chairing course review panels, they may be in touch in a literal sense with those activities. However, even then, their involvement is at one remove from the performance of those activities themselves.

This empirical point does, though, alert us to a more important conceptual point. Even involvement by senior managers in key activities does not indicate managerial control.

Assume another example. It might be resolved, at the institutional level, that a staff development programme should be offered to the academic staff, designed to encourage them to reflect on their teaching methods, their admissions procedures (how adept are staff at assessing applicants' experiential learning?), the character and quality of their assessment procedures or the effectiveness of applications for research grants. There is no reason that, in principle, the interested academic manager should not initiate such programmes, and perhaps participate in or even direct them.

Managers can, therefore, be directly involved in efforts to improve quality. But the teaching and research activities in question are not themselves being 'managed', for the activities remain under the control of the academics.

It might be countered that this indirect relationship of management to the ultimate point of delivery has its parallel in the private sector, where senior managers do not themselves conduct all the company's affairs, but try to manage it by imparting the necessary understanding to their employees who are meeting the public on a day-to-day basis. But the analogy is not watertight. The academic has a degree of *authorized* control over the end-point delivery that is denied to the employee in a firm. This is not a matter of chance or a purely empirical matter.

There is, then, a second and more important limitation on the place of management in the sphere of academic quality, connected with the concept of authority. Academics have to have a degree of ownership in all they do. Whether in their teaching or in their research, in their engagement with students or with their peers, they have to be committed to what they are saying and doing. This point derives from the conditions of a truth-oriented discourse that we saw earlier. In what they say and do, academics have to be prepared to be examined on the veracity and comprehensibility of their propositions, their sincerity in proffering those propositions, and the appropriateness of those propositions to the context in which they are made. In short, their propositions have to be *theirs*.

There is here a first-person authorship in academic activities denied to the employees in a private enterprise. In a conceptual sense, individual academics are the authors of what they do, not so much in terms of initiation (though that normally is the case) but more importantly through their authorization of what they do and say. Someone else (a head of department, or another colleague or a staff developer) may make a suggestion that is taken up, but the individual has to be committed to what he or she then says and does. This commitment is not the commitment of the airline employees in their interactions with the airline's customers. The commitment in the academic sphere is a necessary commitment, for the academics lay themselves open to further questioning about *their* reasons for their words and actions.

In commercial life, in contrast, the commitment is merely contingent. The company owns the activities of its employees in a way that is inapplicable to the relationship between an institution of higher education and its staff. The identification between an employee and a firm has no immediate parallel in the academic sphere. A company in a commercial setting has a substance, in the way in which it exerts a pull on its employees, which is necessarily denied to an institution of higher education.

Given these analyses of control, authorship and ownership in academic settings, the use of a phrase like 'senior management' in relation to an institution's academic activities being managed can be misleading. Academics *have* to have a personal investment in what they say and do as academics.

On occasions, others who also carry authority – such as external examiners and professional bodies – are charged with legitimizing the academics' activities; and, in that sense, conferring authority on those activities. But that further authority in turn derives from a recognized level of authority in those other bodies. Were the academics' activities to be managed by someone else, the personal commitment to and involvement in the communication would be put at risk; and with it, the essence of the quality of the academic community. For in such a situation, individuals whose sayings and doings are in question would no longer be required to give their own reasons for their truth claims and actions. They could simply say that the authority lies elsewhere. So there has, in every academic action, to be some element of independence from external managerial control.

## Managing the quality of courses

For a generation, the polytechnics and colleges of UK higher education have developed systematic and explicit systems of course review. Formerly under the direction of the Council for National Academic Awards (CNAA) and centralized as a national system, those procedures are now under the ownership and direction of the polytechnics and other major institutions of that sector since gaining 'accredited' status from the CNAA. In parallel, across universities, the Committee of Vice-Chancellors and Principals has – through surveys and its subsequent conclusions – encouraged universities to develop their own quality assurance systems, particularly through the establishment of institutional course monitoring systems. The establishment of the Academic Audit Unit is almost certainly adding to the impetus building up in the universities in this direction. (Corresponding developments are in place around the western world.)

In UK institutions in general, then, we are seeing the formation of systems of course review internal to each institution, and under its control. Each institution, as a result, is also becoming responsible for demonstrating that it is in command of the quality of its courses. The procedures for course review have to be explicit and systematized. Validation requirements, criteria for assessment, timetables and procedures themselves have to be written, understood and implemented across each institution.

All this implies that course review – if it is to come up to these expectations – has to be properly managed. The establishment of course review procedures, appropriate to an institution's stage of development and overall portfolio of work, is a complex process in itself. It is far from being a purely bureaucratic matter, for the whole institution has to be involved, its collective understanding drawn on and developed, and a consensus of support achieved. New skills have to be developed, in chairing review committees; and new attitudes formed, in embracing the spirit of mutual critical dialogue. Pulling all that off is highly complex and demanding. Maintaining course quality and being seen to do so, therefore, calls for effective and high-level managerial skills. Yes, but there is more to be said.

Assessing the quality of a course calls, in part at least, for a *judgement* to be made. The idea of judgement contains the three elements of (1) an assessment by a person or persons authorized to judge, (2) coming to an evaluation of what is being inspected, and (3) that evaluation not being an exact science but calling for skilled discrimination. The complexities of that discrimination are such that the rules, the considerations and the criteria for its operation cannot be written down. Still less can they be fed into a computer and applied in a technocratic fashion, for the adoption and exemplification of values are inescapably involved. In this last of its three component ideas – that of making fine discriminations and assessments against an unwritten background of rules and values – judgement has something of the character of connoisseurship.

The complexities, and the grounds for debate and even dispute, are such that the judgement of academic activities has often come to depend on the combined judgements of a number of evaluators. Peer review, as it is termed, has been long accepted across the sectors of UK higher education in assessing applications for research funds received by the research councils and the independent trusts. Among polytechnics and colleges, it has also been employed for a generation to assess the quality of courses and, as I remarked upon earlier, that process too is beginning to be introduced into the universities.

Admittedly, the collective views of peers are not always sought in the academic world. Where the fate of individual students is concerned, reliance is often placed on the judgements of individuals, whether individual admissions tutors or external examiners acting by themselves. There is nothing sinister in this; it is simply a case of seeing that the weight of judgement is proportionate to the matter in hand. Admissions tutors make judgements about individual applicants; and they very often act in pairs, or are required to seek the views of a colleague where the admission of a non-standard student is involved. In examining too, especially on large courses, a team of external examiners may be used; and their judgements are more a means of publicly endorsing the views of the course team than standing by themselves as judgements on the students as such.

Technically, judgement about the quality of a course could be made as a paper exercise. A set of documents about the course could be produced, documents that might go well beyond the purely descriptive to include analyses of student throughput and even critical analyses of the course content, philosophy and delivery produced by the course team itself. Those documents could be sent off to the evaluators for their independent judgement, and their responses either collected through correspondence or formed as a collective exercise in a meeting, perhaps some distance from the institution offering the course. Some countries operate systems of course appraisal in this way, with the evaluators and the evaluated at arm's length from each other (Neave 1991).

In practice, though, as soon as judgement is exercised on a collective basis, there is an inbuilt momentum for those exercising their judgement to engage in a dialogue with those being judged. The resolution of differences of response amongst the assessors will suggest the need to avoid coming to a precipitate judgement by engaging with the course team directly. If judgements are going to be soundly based, the assessors will wish – at some point or other – to give the course team an opportunity to reveal more fully the meanings and intentions behind the written words. If the exercise of judgement in assessing the quality of a course cannot be fully captured in written procedures and criteria, still less can be the organization and delivery of a course, with its manifold consequences for the student experience. But a face-to-face dialogue can at least go some way to uncovering some of the nuances, intentions, presuppositions, assumptions and understandings, both as seen by the author of any such document (say, the course leader) and by the individual members of the course team. *Their* differences of viewpoint, about course aims, delivery, recruitment strategy and assessment criteria, may well emerge in such a dialogue, in a way that may surprise even the course team itself.

A dialogue of this kind may have an agenda; and even an agenda agreed between the parties. If it is a real dialogue, it will have real elements of open-endedness about it: both parties will be free to contribute as they see fit.

At any moment, the dialogue is liable to veer off in unforeseen directions. So, both at the level of detail and of general shape, the notion of 'management' in this sphere has limitations, in so far as management contains a sense of controlling for specified outcomes, for here again we are in the realm of unpredictable outcomes.

Even if members of the review team were to sit in on teaching sessions in practice, they would still have to engage in a dialogue to be able to place what they had seen in context, against the intentions of the individual teacher and the position of the class in the overall programme of studies. So the open-endedness of the dialogue cannot be avoided, if an informed appreciation of the quality of the course is to be obtained.

## Where does the buck stop?

Who is responsible for trying to see that activities at the level of individual courses and of the student experience are of the highest quality? To what extent does the idea of management make sense at those levels, especially bearing in mind the essentially unpredictable character of the responses students make to their learning environment?

The problem is nicely captured in the terminology given to the person with responsibility for managing the administration associated with a course of study. In the university sector in the UK, the title 'course tutor' is more often found, while in the polytechnics and colleges sector more use is made of the term 'course leader'. In addition, just beginning to be used across both sectors is the term 'course director'. The term 'course leader' suggests a strong sense of the person concerned having responsibility not just for the administrative arrangements but also to act as the first amongst equals, exercising leadership for improving the quality of the course. In contrast, the term 'course tutor' implies a restricted role, where the person concerned is simply one of the staff associated with the course held responsible for the routine course administration, in dealing with the registry over admissions and examinations and so forth. Behind these terms there is also, in the university sector, a sense of staff members making their individual contributions to a course, with relatively little coordination between them; while, in the polytechnics and colleges sector, there is a greater tacit sense of staff teaching on a course seeing themselves as a team, with the task of the course leader being to develop common understanding and approaches, and team spirit.

The point of this excursion into academic semantics is that these differences across the sectors are indicative of different cultures and different perceptions of the way in which management has a part to play in course organization and delivery. Traditionally, there was – characteristically in the universities – a culture in which academics, even if they taught on the same course, worked largely independently of each other. The idea that their efforts could be coordinated by someone else was outside the self-understandings within that culture. Over time, as accountability has increased – whether to the market, to the Council for National Academic Awards as an external validating body, or to the more intrusive scrutiny of funding bodies – individuals have come to form course 'teams' and the idea of leadership has justifiably come to enjoy widespread currency.

Yet the relationship of 'management' to the activities of individuals, even if they are working together in teaching a course or – in another sphere – in handling a large research project, must always be in tension. To repeat, in academic activities worthy of higher education, there remains an ineradicable element of unpredictability and personal ownership of what is said and done. Interactions with students, writing research reports or journal papers, or the signing of pass lists by external examiners: these cannot be managed in any real sense by third parties. What is said and done has to be the personal expression of the persons directly involved.

The idea of academic freedom is, in part, testimony to this element of personal ownership in academic life. Sincerity, spontaneity and liberty of expression are essential ingredients of that life. In that sense, 'management' – *if* it implies the legitimacy of external influence on thought and action so that personal involvement and responsibility are to any degree diminished – is anathema to the academic life.

The question remains, therefore: if, in the key happenings in the academic world – of teaching and research – the concept of management has limitations, do we say that 'quality' is largely a reflection of the competence of individuals as professionals, of their capacity to perform up-to-standard? Nothing that has been said so far would justify such a simplistic belief (even though just that idea has probably been a dominant approach to quality in higher education, especially across UK universities). There are, as I have indicated, all sorts of ways in which management can have a real and positive part to play in the maintenance and improvement of academic quality; but there is a separate point too.

It follows from the analysis of personal ownership of thought, language, action and interaction offered here that academics – perhaps more than in any other profession – have to be absolutely responsible for their actions, for what they say and the way they say it. This means that the responsibility for assessing those actions and forms of communication and for improving them must fall – in the first place – on the individuals producing them. 'The unexamined life is not worth living', as Socrates put it. But the self-critical mode of life being urged on us here falls directly on those who claim to value the critical form of life characteristic of the academic world.

It might seem that the idea of academic management – even at the point of delivery of academic actions – can be saved after all through the use of the modern concept of 'total quality management'. The logic of that idea is that everyone in an organization shall bear responsibility for the delivery and quality of the final product. To call up the historic notion of academic institutions as bodies of self-critical intellectuals surprisingly seems to mesh nicely with the idea of personal responsibility being taken on by all participants in an organization. The idea of management appears to be strengthened because what is being called for is that every person – including all academic members of staff – shall be responsible for managing themselves and ensuring that their work is of the highest quality and that it is kept always under review and improved wherever and whenever possible. Socrates was a manager before his time.

There are elements of truth about this view:

1. Self-responsibility for the quality of utterances, interactions and manner of self-presentation (in spoken language, in the written word or in non-verbal communication).
2. The promptness of communication (whether in returning essays to students with helpful comments or in returning a manuscript sent by a journal editor for review).
3. The clarity and appropriateness of one's own writings (whether course guides for students, reports for research councils or books for the general market).

However, this can be exaggerated. Yes, there are elements of self-management in these and doubtless many other of the central academic activities. But to repeat, the conversations in which teachers, researchers, examiners and reviewers are engaged must be unconstrained, if those interventions and contributions are to bear the weight of personal ownership and accountability.

Self-management can mean self-control *or* self-censorship (World University Service 1989: 10). The former is desirable and is in keeping with the academic ethic. The latter is an undesirable internalization of third-party requirements, which may be the perceived requirements of the institution's own management; 'undesirable' because undue constraint is then exercised on the conversations in which academics are engaged, and the free discourse of the academic community is thereby surrendered. All too easily, with an eye to the main chance, or to a possible institutional closure, or to gaining approval for a new course or to securing the admission of weak entrants, the discourse of academics can be subtly influenced. Things can be said or done with the possible external consequences in mind, as well as their internal truthfulness. Self-management can, then, be a force for improving the quality of academic work; but it can also be a force for its distortion and even corruption. Correspondingly, the maverick's way of doing things may be managerially disruptive but just may lead to a Nobel prize.

## Conclusions

The conclusions from this chapter can be quickly stated, but are far from straightforward in their implications.

Good management is certainly important for the effective conduct of institutions of higher education, and the quality of their activities is – by definition – also important. Institutional managers can play an important role in identifying elements constituting the institution's quality assurance systems, in making them explicit, in establishing frameworks for maintaining quality, in sharpening the responsibilities towards quality of different postholders, and in raising awareness across the institution that quality matters. Heads of department and course leaders have corresponding responsibilities at their levels. Course leaders, as well as overseeing the redesign of a course, should also have an eye to detail; for example, in getting agreement of a course team that essays will be returned with detailed advice and comment within a week. Nor is all of this to be captured by the idea of leadership, helpful and essential as that concept is. Planning, organization, execution and simply rolling up one's sleeves all come into play.

And yet, for all the value of good management in academic matters, the character of academic activities is in profound and subtle respects resistant to management. Personal ownership of utterances, sincerity, openness to criticism, open-endedness, unpredictability of interactions and the essential individuality of student development: all these are aspects of human engagement characteristic of higher education which fall outside the sphere of management.

This is why, for example, simply delineating the elements of a quality assurance system, and promulgating timetables for action, will not secure in themselves a higher quality of services and activities. For that, the staff have to be engaged, intellectually. They have to take on the idea of quality maintenance for themselves, and become committed to it themselves. And that, in turn, requires both the initiation of an institutional debate about quality and allowing the faculty to own and develop the framework of quality assurance for itself. Management, in the form of tight specification of deadlines, procedures and responsibilities, is likely to be counterproductive.

The idea of management is diffuse and open to many interpretations. It turns out that an idea of management *for* quality is both appropriate and desirable; but that the management *of* quality is to be mistrusted. Academic management is more like that of the leadership and direction exerted by an orchestra's conductor than by an army's general.

The first implication of this analysis, so far as quality is concerned, is that all those centrally engaged on academic activities have to accept responsibility for their quality. The second is that however professional and skilful, however much pursued with an eye to improving quality across the system, can be said to be the quality of an institution's senior management, there has to be a recognition that academics must be free to manage (and to accept responsibility for) their own utterances and actions. The third is that those in senior institutional positions of academic responsibility have the task not of managing quality directly, but of establishing and orchestrating – and, indeed, *managing* – the framework in which those centrally involved in teaching and research are enabled and encouraged to go on improving the effectiveness of their professional efforts. Some hints at how this might be done have already been given, but I will tackle in the next section the implications of this analysis for improving quality in higher education.

# Part 2

Improving the Quality of Institutions

# 5

# Institutional Purposes and Performance Indicators

## Distinguishing purposes

Two key distinctions impress themselves on us in considering the purposes to which institutions of higher education (IHEs) might declare their allegiance.

Firstly, there is the distinction between the purposes that any one IHE might set itself and the purposes that attach to all IHEs, in virtue of which they *are* IHEs and not, say, industrial concerns or even colleges of further education. If any serious meaning can be given to such a high-sounding phrase as 'the purpose – or – the purposes of higher education', it would consist of a set of general conditions that any IHE has to satisfy in order to warrant the title 'institution of higher education'. (Later in this chapter, I shall suggest what those general conditions might be.)

Clearly, the specific purposes that a single institution might set for itself have to be consistent with the general purposes of IHEs. An IHE would not normally be justified in using its funds to run a casino, since that kind of activity would fall outside the *general* purposes of what it means to be an IHE. Still, within that framework, these institutions are entitled to choose their own way of interpreting and implementing the general conditions. IHEs have, at least in theory, a reasonably wide measure of freedom as to the specific purposes they set themselves (Berdahl 1988).

In fact, however, IHEs in the UK have not really taken advantage of the opportunities available to develop an individual character of their own (Burgess 1981). This is evident in the very limited extent to which IHEs in the UK vary over the key purposes for which they stand. The idea of academic institutions setting down in a public document their own 'mission statements' has been relatively slow to catch on. Institutions in the polytechnics and colleges sector have certainly done this with more alacrity than the universities, a fact that surely owes much to the Council for National Academic Awards and, more recently, to the Polytechnics and Colleges Funding Council, both of which have prompted institutions to produce their own goal statements about themselves as part of their academic planning. Now with the more market-led climate in which all IHEs are operating, and as institutions develop a contractual relationship with their funding body, there has developed more incentive for all IHEs, including the universities, to provide a publicly accessible statement of what they are about.

That, then, is the first distinction concerning institutional purposes: the distinction between the general purposes which mark out the educational territory inhabited by all IHEs (in order to justify their falling under the common description of 'institution of higher education') and the particular purposes which an individual institution might set itself.

The second key distinction is that between the purposes that IHEs fulfil which are set within the academic community and the purposes which are set outside the academic community. In making this distinction, we should not assume that purposes that are set inside the academic community are wholly to the good, and that those that come from the wider community are wholly undesirable. Indeed, it is surely apparent that, ever since their medieval origins, the institutions of higher learning have looked outwards, supplying the state with administrators and other qualified personnel. Purposes that come from outside the academic community are not, therefore, necessarily antithetical to those that the academic community generates itself.

On the other hand, some of those purposes that come from within the academic community are actually of doubtful value, when viewed against the traditional conception of higher learning. For example, the increasing splintering of the academic community by itself into disciplinary sub-cultures (Becher 1989) is clearly a matter of concern to those who believe that higher education should, whatever else it provides, offer a liberal education, and that among the components of a liberal education is a willingness to break through boundaries of thought and to offer a breadth of cognitive perspective (Peters 1980).

So there is a complex set of relationships between purposes set outside the academic community and those set inside it.

Having grasped these two sets of distinctions, we can superimpose them on each other. This generates four kinds of purposes. That is to say, we can talk of general purposes which characterize IHEs as a whole, such purposes being set either within the academic community or outside it. We can also talk of purposes particular to a single institution which are set by that institution or set for it by bodies or agencies in the external community. This conceptual framework raises all kinds of empirical questions about the degree of permeability of institutions both at the local and at the national level (Brennan 1985). In modern society, the area of purposes set outside the academic community is growing; and the extent of those set within it is diminishing. We are, therefore, faced with the situation shown in Figure 5.1.

Over time, the line denoting the division between externally set and internally set purposes is moving upwards, so that the space available for internally set purposes is diminishing.

Earlier, we looked at the phrase 'fitness for purpose' and saw that it was politically suspect. Now, against the background of this analysis of institutional purposes, 'fitness for purpose' inevitably becomes problematic in

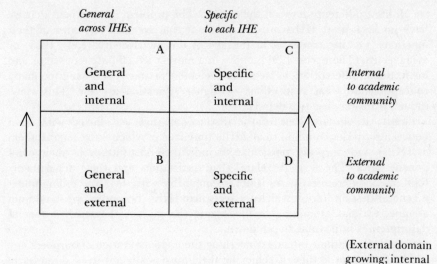

*Figure 5.1* Purposes of institutions of higher education – a schema

terms of its logic and semantics. Which purposes are being referred to by the phrase? Against which of the four kinds of purposes are institutions being enjoined to demonstrate their fitness?

With some justification, it could be countered that the purposes in question are those that are identified within different sectors. In short, polytechnics should stick to their own purposes and not be tempted along the path of 'academic drift' to adopt those of the universities (Pratt and Burgess 1974). If there is anything in this challenge, it actually compounds the problem of institutional purposes since it points to yet a further distinction. The difference in mission between universities and polytechnics would have to be superimposed on the distinctions I have already made; it would not supplant them.

For the moment, let us return to the diagram where I want to focus on its left-hand side; namely, on those purposes that are characteristic of IHEs as such (as distinct from those that individual institutions might set for themselves). In the next few sections of this chapter, I shall argue that, in demonstrating their 'fitness', IHEs cannot neglect their internal purposes, however much they are required to fulfil their external purposes.

## Elusive purposes

What might be meant by general purposes, internal to higher education? Are there any, in fact? Is not one of the characteristics of higher education that everybody knows what IHEs are in business for, but that, unfortunately, we all have different views on the matter? The problem is not, then, that we have no idea what IHEs are for; it is not that we lack any idea of their functions. On the contrary, in the age of the multiversity (Kerr 1963) or megaversity (Thompson 1991), and – in a market-led climate – of sector and institutional differentiation, we suffer the embarrassment of having too many conceptions of what institutions of higher education are for. This view, though plausible, has two defects.

Firstly, it obscures one of the distinctions that we started with, that between purposes common to all IHEs (in virtue of which we recognize them *as* IHEs) and purposes particular to individual institutions or their component parts. The fact, therefore, that institutions and their departments fulfil many different purposes is not incompatible with their also falling under a general description by which we recognize IHEs. Secondly, we should not assume, without attemping to investigate the matter, that such a general description is impossible to pin down.

Other observations intrude concerning the implementation of purposes.

The first point is that, if achieving their purposes is not to be a matter of luck, the members of an academic institution need to have a reasonably informed and uniform idea of what the purposes of an IHE are. Whether or not such senses of institutional purposes need to be written down in precise detail is a further matter.

Some believe that written statements of such general purposes are neither here nor there (Oakeshott 1989). Oakeshott's somewhat organic conception of academic life could, it is worth noting, find support from one current of the modern age. For a market-oriented institution, it might be felt that mission statements are likely to produce inertia, freezing a particular self-conception held at a moment in time. Instead, each segment of an institution should be free to play the market and develop its services in response to its sense of what the market might support.

The counter view – which I share – is that the formation of a mission statement can aid the common sense of purpose across an institution if an attempt is made to identify the services and activities on which an institution wishes to concentrate its efforts. Such an exercise is likely to have internal benefits, especially if the faculty is engaged in the formulation of the mission statement and if the resulting statement is neither a bland résumé of the trite nor a flight of the collective imagination to produce distinctive claims about the institution's purposes.

Either way, it does seem to be an uncontroversial – almost logical – point that the members of an academic institution need to share a consensus of attitude and belief on what those purposes should be; and they need to have a high degree of commitment to them. It seems clear that our modern IHEs, complex and large as many of them are, and faced with increasing demands and limited resources, are hardly likely to meet their purposes effectively unless their members – in particular, their academic staff – are collectively committed to the achievement of those purposes.

So clarity, commitment and a reasonable degree of consensus over purposes seem necessary requirements. But these reflections present problems. For IHEs, by and large, have a pretty hazy idea of what the essential purposes of higher education might be. This is understandable because (as we have observed), other than in the moment of their being founded, UK institutions have not, until very recently, been obliged to think them through. In other words, IHEs tend, unless challenged critically to review themselves, just to assume that they are remaining faithful to the essential character of higher education. It is a case of 'We exist, therefore we are worthwhile'.

## 'Fitness for purpose': an example of instrumental reason

Let us leave the notion of 'purposes' there for the moment and return to the larger term 'fitness for purpose'.

I want to suggest that there is a yet further and a more profound problem with the whole idea of 'fitness for purpose' as a way of understanding IHEs and their effectiveness. In one sense, the key word in the phrase is the smallest: the linking word 'for' is actually very powerful. It both links *and* separates the two terms on either side of it. As a result, the idea of 'being fit for a purpose' is two ideas brought together. The linking word *for* acts to bridge the conceptual gap between the two ideas of being fit and the purpose for which the IHE is fit, or is striving to become fit.

What follows from these apparently pedantic points? Simply this: unpacking the notion of 'fitness for purpose' reveals that, in this terminology, the institution's purpose is tacitly seen as separate from its fitness; in other words, the purpose is extrinsic to the fitness. The fitness is achieved in order to be able to do something else. 'Fitness for purpose' turns out to be a coded form of educational instrumentalism.

It would be wrong to imply that this instrumental way of looking at higher education is irrational. In a sense, it is utterly rational. It posits an end, and asks if the means – our IHEs – are so organized that they will achieve that end. It is the rationality of a technological society; it is, to use the terminology of critical theory and, in particular, that of Jurgen Habermas – a splendid example of instrumental reason (Held 1980).

What, though, is so problematic about this style of thinking? At least, so it might be thought, this approach helps to promote an informed evaluation of the performance of IHEs. If we have a clear idea of their purposes, we will surely be in a better position to assess how well they are doing in achieving them. What could be wrong with that?

The answer is that, from an educational point of view, this style of thinking all too often misses the main target. The trouble with the intrusion of instrumental reason into higher education is that the actual value of institutions – as educational institutions – is all too frequently bypassed. It is bypassed not as a result of some conspiracy, but as part of the logic of this kind of thinking, a style of cognition which has three components. Firstly, as we saw (see

Chapter 3), instrumental reason imports into higher education values and objectives from the mainstream culture of the host society. So, for example, institutions come to be assessed in terms of their financial efficiency through their so-called unit costs and analogous measures. But these are the approaches of the accountant and the bureaucrat rather than the educationalist. Using approaches of this kind, we come to judge institutions in terms of values dominant in the wider society rather than those at the heart of the enterprise of higher education itself.

Secondly, instrumental reason in this domain encourages the use of performance indicators. Examples we have already encountered (see Chapter 3) include the numbers of applicants with good A levels, non-completion rates, the proportion of graduates with good degrees, the numbers of graduates moving into different sectors of the labour market, and the economic rates of return (supposedly an indication of the extra human capital generated by students' higher education).

But this style of thinking goes further: there develops all too easily a focus on the size of institutions and the numbers of different aspects of them come to be predominant. Quantity comes before quality. For example, the number of a lecturer's publications becomes more important than their quality: the imperative on academics is to publish; and implicitly, issues of the quality of the publications are to be addressed later (but somehow, 'later' is usually some way off). Correspondingly, the number of books in an institution's library becomes more important than their quality. And when it comes to choosing who shall gain access to higher education, A-level points scores gained in past school examinations can paradoxically be more telling (as we have seen) than applicants' potential to succeed in the future on a degree course.

Those who want to defend this way of looking at institutions might feel inclined, in response to this line of attack, to point to the way in which such measures of evaluation are becoming more sophisticated and are being developed so as to incorporate indications of quality as well as quantity. For example, in theory, simply looking at a list of an individual's publications could give way to a citation analysis, and that analysis could be weighted so as to reflect the most important refereed journals in the field (Colman, *et al.* 1992). Or, picking up the concern with the throughput of students, an effort could be made to weigh students' qualifications on entry with their degree classifications, and so generate an index of 'value added'.

The problem with these attempts to get at quality is not that they are not worth while; they are. However, so far as higher education is concerned, they offer no insight into the central matter, namely the quality of the educational processes within IHEs. In short, numerical descriptions of inputs and outputs tell us nothing about the educational character of our separate IHEs.

Again, to exemplify this general statement, a disinterested observer coming to higher education solely through a perusal of such performance indicators would have no clue to indicate that a crucial issue is, or should be, the quality of the student's learning. Much lip service is paid to this notion but, in reality, very little attention is given to it (Sizer 1982; CVCP 1986–89). The former University Grants Committee considered that there was no way available to it to assess the quality of teaching (UGC 1985); its successor University Funding Council has been largely silent on the matter. At least, though, teaching quality is on the public agenda. Student learning, on the other hand, the quality of which cannot be expressed in numerical terms, is hardly anywhere to be seen within the public debate over the future of higher education (DES 1987).

This brings us to the third point about the presence of instrumental reason in public discourse about higher education. It is that talk about higher education all too easily focuses on the means, rather than on its purposes; so much so, that the means become purposes in their own right. For example, unit costs become not just a measure of an institution's performance, but also a guiding light by which the institution steers itself. Or, to take another example, the generation of research income becomes seen as worth while in itself, irrespective of the value of the research project to the community that finances it or the consequent downgrading of those scholarly efforts in the humanities which do not depend on large running grants.

Performance indicators are not, therefore, just measures which those on the outside of the academic world use to judge institutions. They also become the means by which institutions organize and direct themselves, and judge their own performance (CVCP/UGC 1988). And the intrinsic character of performance indicators is such that they will tend to divert institutions' attention away from their essential purposes, values and continuing processes (Williams 1986).

## How rational is quality assessment?

If this analysis about the growth of instrumental reason is correct, we might ask why such a style of thinking should have found its way into higher education, looking as it does for external justifications. 'Accountability' is often called up at this point; but the term supplies no explanation, only further questions. For accountability is a code word for the wider society exerting claims on its institutions. Why, sociologically speaking, has such a claim arisen? The answer is, surely, not hard to find. The accompanying preoccupation with facts and figures rather than purposes and values is part of the general form of instrumental reason which is a signal feature of modern society. It springs from, as has been suggested, a motivation within society 'to control and dominate, and to exercise surveillance and power over others' (Gibson 1986). It is not coincidental that this style of reasoning about IHEs comes at a time when the state's interest in planning higher education, and in continuing to reorchestrate its planning agencies, is paramount.

A consequence of this concern with getting the means right is that the need for institutions to be 'managed' takes on a particular slant. If institutions need to be managed, then they need to be managed by 'managers'. We see this thinking coming through not only in higher education – in the Jarratt Report, for instance (CVCP 1985) – but also in our public services in general (for example, in the health service, where managers who are not themselves members of the health professions are now managing the service; and where talk of managing the service all too easily gives way to talk of managing the system).

At the end of the first section, we examined the applicability of the idea of management to higher education. There we observed that, while management has a definite place, it also has real limits in higher education. This is not a plea for professional *laissez-faire*. It is a salutary lesson for many academics to remember that they are the beneficiaries of what, when viewed from other parts of the educational system, and even more so when viewed from the position of other public services, seems to be a well-provided level of resource. Nevertheless, it surely makes good sense to work towards a situation in which members of an institution are not simply managed, but feel themselves to be actively participating in its evolution. This is especially the case for IHEs, in which – as we saw in the last chapter, quite apart from the activity of research – the key activities of teaching and the promotion of effective learning require a particular level of personal involvement and commitment on the part of the teaching staff.

The instrumental style of thinking is not confined, we can note, to one side of the political spectrum. It is also to be found, for example, among those who believe passionately in widening access to higher education. In itself, this aim is surely uncontroversial: if higher education is a 'good', then in principle it should be open to all those who can benefit from it. Indeed, since it is part of my argument that higher education has an intrinsic worth, it follows that higher education is a 'good' in its own right. Therefore, unless there are sound reasons to the contrary, the academic community should endeavour to reduce any unnecessary restrictions on access that lie within its power. This means, for example, developing admissions procedures that go beyond applicants' formal entry qualifications so that an effort is made to assess their potential for future success on the course of their choosing. It also implies that we need to take part-time higher education more seriously, and orient institutional offerings (including the library) much more around evening work and distance learning.

But this line of thinking requires a prior identification of the intrinsic good represented by higher education, and the *internal* benefits to be drawn from it. The problem with unqualified pleas for wider access is that, all too easily, wider access is conceived in such a way that it becomes an end in itself, without its proponents stopping to ask 'access to what?' or 'access for what?' In other words, the means has again become an end, and the actual end – the purposes of higher education – is lost sight of, or (more often) is simply never raised as an issue.

By way of summary, then, we can observe that although the surface structure of the idea of 'fitness for purpose' is that of a general interest in the maintenance and development of standards (which those who use the term are intent on protecting), its deep structure turns out to have little to do with the quality of what is going on in IHEs and more to do with legitimating an institutional hierarchy and an instrumental control of it.

# Two counter-models of purposes in action

## *Institutions of higher education as academic communities*

But how else might we get a purchase on the effectiveness by which our IHEs fulfil their purposes? One of the problems is that, in our modern society, we are trapped into the kind of discourse I have been describing, for it is the discourse of a technological–bureaucratic society with its associated form of rationality. What we need, therefore, is another vocabulary with which to characterize our institutions (Rorty 1989).

As a start, we might usefully return to a conception of what an IHE is – in essence. From their medieval origins, IHEs have always been associations of individuals who have come *voluntarily* to study and learn together. The term 'universitas' originally referred not to the university as a place where all scholars could gather and work together, but referred to 'the self-government of students or masters or both in the conduct of the affairs of' their institution of higher learning (Cameron 1978). In other words, IHEs have been from the start essentially collaborative institutions; and the nature of interpersonal relations between individuals in those institutions is, therefore, highly significant. The idea of democracy is misleading here with its overtones of formal decision-making and representation. What is at stake, rather, is the opportunity for everyone to be able to express his or her point of view, both within his or her own disciplinary field *and* on those academic matters of general interest. What is characteristic of IHEs is that their accredited inhabitants are willing to engage in a critical dialogue with their peers.

Translating this observation into the conceptual framework of the social theorist, Jurgen Habermas (1979), we can talk of an institution's communicative competence. This might be seen in an institution's ability to break down barriers between different subject areas, or the collective ways in which its particular purposes are defined by its members of staff, or – and of particular significance – the extent to which individual staff collaborate in framing the curriculum for their students with their attendant teaching and learning methods. At a more basic level, is every member of staff given a handbook, setting out the institution's academic policies, its committee structure and key procedures (on promotions criteria or for making significant curricular changes) so that all members of staff work with a common understanding of the institution, or are they left to find it out for themselves?

In other words, do individual members of staff by and large 'do their own thing' or do they work together, identifying with and feeling that they are engaged in a common enterprise across the institution?

It will also be a matter of concern how far the students are treated as members – albeit junior members, whose full academic development has some way to reach maturity – of the academic community. What is the character of the relationships between the staff and the students? How far is the individual student's point of view respected? How far are students encouraged to form a view of their own?

This, then, is a view of purpose which looks to the internal life of institutions. It is a view which is essentially concerned with meaning and understanding amongst its participants. Can an IHE promote a sense amongst its members – staff and students – that all its activities are in some sense united by a corporate conception of those activities? Or are we to accept the contemporary sense that the modern IHE is simply a motley collection of interest groups with contrasting and even competing agendas, conducting distinct activities with varying underlying purposes (Kerr 1963; Becher 1989)? After all, as departments warm to the task of testing their attractiveness in the market place, and realize *that* kind of value, so the surface divisions within institutions are likely to increase (Schuller 1990a).

Against these trends of the age, therefore, is the question of whether it is possible to recover a conception and a practice of institutions as academic communities with ties, forms of collaboration and interrelationships which transcend departmental and disciplinary boundaries (McIntyre 1985). Yes, individual careers and patterns of personal development matter – at the levels of both staff and students – but the institution (which is to say, the members of the institution together) can support that process of personal formation.

This, then, is a concern with purposes which focuses on the structures of meaning – for both staff and students – and the ways in which individuals within our IHEs feel themselves to be participating in those structures of meaning, in their negotiation and development. It is, to draw again on the terminology of Jurgen Habermas, a *hermeneutic* conception of purposes (Habermas 1965). We can also conceive of an institution evolving in this dimension (Thompson 1984). The institution as an academic community can go on developing the degree to which members of staff and individual students feel themselves to be part of a common community. These characteristics are not in any sense 'given'; an institution can always go on improving its effectiveness in these areas of its internal life.

## Institutions of higher education as critical centres

So much then for the instrumental and hermeneutic conceptions of purposes. But there is, after all, a third idea of purposes which is related to the hermeneutic conception and which is central to the modern *mission* of higher education in the democratic state. This is the notion of the academic community as residing in a particular *form* of discourse. To pick up again the terminology of Alvin Gouldner, it is a view of the academic institution founded on a 'culture of critical discourse'.

This way of capturing the character of academic life reminds us that the most significant aspect of the critical attitude lies not (as is sometimes assumed) in a direct frontal critique of society's beliefs and practices, but in the critical dialogue as such. It is literally a culture; it is a form of life, singularly characteristic of academic institutions.

This form of internal life is exhibited in a number of ways. Obviously, it is expressed in the extent to which academics are prepared to commit their knowledge – whether in books, journals or conference papers – to the critical scrutiny of their peers. Peer review has, too, a place within the efforts of students themselves, and we are seeing across western institutions peer-assessment among students not just of coursework but also of formally assessed pieces of work (Boud and Prosser 1985).

But the critical outlook can and should come through in the character of the internal life of institutions. For example, it comes through in the way in which the purposes of the institution are kept under review themselves. It is also evident in the extent to which staff allow their own activities to be evaluated – whether it is the work of an individual participating in an appraisal of his or her teaching methods and the learning experiences to which students are exposed; or whether it is a course team or the members of a department submitting themselves, or the courses they offer, to a review by their peers from other departments or from other institutions. It also comes through in the ways in which students themselves are encouraged to develop critical perspectives towards their learning and are given the conceptual apparatus to allow that to happen.

Ultimately, then, this critical conception of the purposes of higher education looks, whether at the level of the institution, the course team, the individual members of staff or the student, to the continuing development of autonomy and independence, though aided by the constructive critical comment of others. This is, therefore, to use an appropriate shorthand description, an emancipatory conception of purposes (Habermas 1965).

## Institutional purposes and performance indicators

To review the position reached so far, the instrumental view of purposes lends itself to a conception of education framed by inputs and outputs, and assessments of achievement in terms of numerical performance indicators which have their home in criteria external to what IHEs are ultimately about. The two alternative conceptions of purposes (the hermeneutic and the critical) are different in both these respects. They look to purposes as they are exemplified in the institution's continuing and learning processes, and they are concerned with the internal life of institutions. In short, *they* are concerned with the intrinsic character of what it is to be an IHE (Moodie 1986b: 7).

The deficiency with numerical performance indicators is not just that they are only indicators and do not illuminate the character of the performance. It is their more pernicious nature in that they never could say anything about the internal life of institutions. Capturing that would require a quite different approach to the evaluation of institutions' achievements. For they are achievements not realized in any end-point which can be pinned down by performance indicators but require, instead, a sensitive insight into participants' intentions and interactions on a day-to-day basis. The illumination of a process, whether it is the learning approaches encouraged of students or the way in which staff collaborate to offer a course, cannot be achieved by a judgement of outcomes, no matter how sophisticated.

In summary, then, I am suggesting that – whatever sectoral or institution-specific purposes they may have – IHEs have to adhere to certain aims, principles and processes by virtue of which they can justifiably be termed IHEs. Those general purposes, which hold for all IHEs, have to do with the development of the mind through a critical but collaborative interchange, among staff and among students, and across students and staff. There are, therefore, general criteria which any institution has to fulfil in order to warrant the title (of 'institution of higher education'). The fulfilment of those criteria is not achieved in a particular moment in time (like scoring a goal) but, rather, is achieved through the continuing internal forms of interaction within an institution. (To continue the sporting metaphor, the quality of the passing between the players is *more* important than the number of goals scored and recorded in the end result.) Consequently, in any evaluation of an institution's effectiveness, we would need, if we were serious about it, to find ways of getting at and illuminating its processes.

# Four intrinsic purposes of institutions of higher education

So what, ultimately, does it mean to be an institution of higher education? Is it possible to specify the conditions that institutions have to satisfy in order to justify the title 'institution of higher education'? I want to suggest that whatever else an IHE does – in the way, for instance, of providing highly qualified manpower, pursuing important lines of research, attracting a student intake from disadvantaged groups or securing high levels of income from contracts with international foundations – whatever its own purposes or those enjoined on it by society, there are four intrinsic purposes that all IHEs must fulfil.

The four essential purposes (which follow from the argument of the book so far) are:

1. A concern with the development of each student's autonomy, self-critical abilities and academic competence. Evidence here would include higher order intellectual skills such as identifying problems, marshalling evidence, seeing connections and forming tentative judgements.

2. The institution being self-determining, taking corporate responsibility for the maintenance and improvement of its own standards and its future development; here, the internal life would promote a self-critical and a self-learning academic community, based on a common understanding of the institution.
3. An institution in which the life of research is important in the sense of a 'culture of critical discourse'; that is, critical and collaborative inquiry amongst members of staff (this sense of research would not necessarily require large research grants or massive capital equipment).
4. A concern to make this form of higher education – essentially one of collaborative critical inquiry among staff and students – available to all who can benefit from it and who wish to have access to it.

These four are, I want to claim, essential purposes of higher education. Any IHE, worthy of the name, must be able to demonstrate that these concerns are built into its internal processes. Simply asserting that its teaching and/or its research is of high quality will not do. Evidence would have to be available that these four conditions – of what it means to be an IHE – are being met. Collectively, then, these four conditions amount to a statement of the purposes of higher education, against which each institution should be obliged periodically to demonstrate its fitness, in order for the external world to be able to accept that genuine processes of higher education are being conducted. 'Fitness for purpose' turns out, then, to have point, provided we also remember that there are general purposes that *have* to be met as well as individual institutional purposes that *might* be met.

To stress the point: the essential purposes of IHEs and their fitness in relation to these purposes are *not* going to be demonstrated through particular achievements; and 'achievements' includes the establishment of a new internationally funded research centre or the success rates with non-traditional students or the provision of a wide-ranging credit accumulation programme. Ultimately, we shall only properly know our IHEs by the character of their internal forms of understanding and interaction. In short, what are the daily experiences of students and of staff? Is it a collaborative, exciting, critical, alive institution in which to develop intellectually? Does the institution draw on all its intellectual resources in monitoring and in improving the quality of the student experience? Do staff talk to each other across departments or even across units within a department?

Although these four conditions are binding on every IHE, they are not absolutely binding because they leave open to each institution how far and in what way they are to be met. Institutions will, quite properly, vary in the importance they give to each of them. Some will give particular importance to access, to ensuring that their admissions procedures are genuinely open. Others will want to give particular attention to the student experience, perhaps encouraging staff to try innovative forms of teaching to foster the student's conceptual understanding. Still others will want to build up the corporate aspects of the institution, communicating its policies and decisions effectively, and encouraging interplay across departments whether in research or in course design and review.

Any of these is a legitimate course for an institution, as an autonomous self-directed community, to take in response to the four conditions bearing on it. But all four conditions would have to be met to some degree.

## IHEs are not ivory towers

It has always been one of the functions of higher learning to supply cohorts for the professions, a function that has grown rapidly across the western world over the past 40 years. Indeed, if an institution designs a course to fulfil certain professionally oriented objectives, its effectiveness must be tested against *those* objectives. Such extra-mural considerations come into account in appraising institutional effectiveness, not as an *ex cathedra* requirement, but because the institution has chosen to fulfil its fundamental purposes in that way.

Similarly, it is not being said here that IHEs, which are in receipt of public monies, do not need to concern themselves with the efficient use of those monies; performance indicators such as unit costs, non-completion rates and pattern of degree classifications do, therefore, have a part to play in assessing the performance of our institutions. But it is only a part. And it is only a minor part. For the elements of the institution's performance that they focus on – largely matters of the institution's organizational efficiency – do nothing to illuminate the nature of the internal processes and interactions which are the real exemplification of an institution's claim to be an IHE.

IHEs will demonstrate their fitness for purpose, therefore, by the ways in which they can show their adherence to the four fundamental conditions of their internal processes (set out above), and by their success in implementing them and the different weight they give to each.

If this analysis is sound, it should be reflected in any methodology by which we evaluate our institutions. It is not enough to say simply that an evaluation methodology needs to reflect an institution's purposes, for – on the analysis here – purposes will ultimately be reflected in the character of the institution's internal processes. It is clear that externally applied assessments of numerical indicators cannot play a dominant part. Instead, an in-depth examination of an institution's internal character would seem to be a necessary condition, perhaps involving external evaluators, but who are so much on the inside of the institution's purposes that the evaluation is conducted as a collaborative exercise with the institution (Adelman 1984; Adelman and Powney 1986).

The conclusion is obvious. If we are clear about an institution's purposes (both general and specific) and if we have an appropriate evaluation methodology, the results of the evaluation will stand as a guide both to the institution itself and to any third party to which the institution is accountable.

Admittedly, the likelihood is that an evaluation of this kind will be problematic for external agencies concerned with national planning and funding, since such an institution-specific evaluation is unlikely to facilitate cross-institutional comparisons. In that case, there will be – as some have recognized (Bevan 1984; NAB 1987) – a responsibility on those who proclaim the virtues of performance indicators to embrace the more qualitative evaluation of IHEs as a distinctive component in assessing institutional worth in addition to the numerical information at their command.

# 6

## Inside the Black Box

### Introduction

One well-acknowledged limitation of numerical performance indicators is that any numerical indicator in itself is literally meaningless, unless it can be placed in some kind of context. In evaluating institutions of higher education, the most favoured context is the corresponding set of data for *other* institutions of higher education. But such data are only 'corresponding' if the institutions being compared are themselves similar. There are certainly overlaps in function and in character across UK institutions, but there are very real differences too. The boundaries of the variations are obvious enough: All Souls has no undergraduate students; Birkbeck College in the University of London has no full-time undergraduates. But precisely because these differences are so obvious – being part of the overt function of each institution – they are unlikely to trip us up. It is much more because institutions of higher education vary in subtle ways that the informational content of their arithmetical indicators cannot be taken at its face value.

At its core, I have been arguing, an institution of higher education is an *educational* institution, having as a necessary aim the education of its students. I have further argued that higher education is (in part, at least) a process of continuing personal engagement. Within this view of institutional purposes, I have been urging caution against reading too much into the information supplied by numerical performance indicators, since the quality of an educational process is ultimately only verifiable in the character of the educational process itself rather than in a numerical description of inputs and outputs.

To this, the advocate of numerical performance indicators might well respond by pointing to degree classes. Are they not an attempt to convert assessments of quality (of individual student performances) into the numerical descriptions of 1st, 2 : 1, 2 : 2 and 3rd? There is nothing new about numerical performance indicators, it might be said, for they have been in use by the academic community for over a hundred years. And, so their advocate may continue, some performance indicators may be able to convey something more or less directly about the quality of the process that the students are experiencing. There are severe problems, however, with this line of thinking.

The first point is to reiterate that a single numerical indicator – even if, as with degree classifications, it is an apparently direct measure of quality – has to be put into some kind of context. Large or small, high or low – these assessments of figures are only possible if we have a sense of the typical range of figures. This reflection leads us again to the issue of what counts as a 'corresponding' institution. Institutions of higher education do not correspond sufficiently for degree classification data to yield uniformly informative insights. Part of the context of interpreting degree class figures is that of the starting point of the students as they embark on their degree course. If institutions have entrants who vary in their preparedness for higher education, it is hardly surprising if they differ in their patterns of achievement as reflected in students' attainment on graduating.

Let us assume that a 2 : 1 honours degree obtained by a student at one institution is equivalent to a 2 : 1 honours degree obtained by another student at a separate institution, as a measure of the quality of the two *students'* level of intellectual achievement. (There are major difficulties with this assumption, which I shall avoid here (Bee and Dolton 1985).) As a measure of their *institutions'* quality, however, the meaning that attaches to the two awards of 2 : 1 may well differ, if the general level of their students' accomplishments on entry is unequal. Consequently, as a measure of the quality of course delivery, a 2 : 1 at one institution may not justify the same interpretation as a 2 : 1 at another institution. The same exit figures do not yield similar insights into institutional performance. Exit figures in themselves have limited informational content.

It is partly for this reason that, as we have noticed, recent years have witnessed moves to derive a measure of 'value-added'. The term is a shorthand for the attempt to put degree performance data into a legitimate and robust relationship with entry qualification data. The attempt to derive a measure of 'value-added' is a recognition that single numerical indicators by themselves are devoid of informational content. This particular attempt to generate extra meaning in these performance indicators is a blind alley. The target is illusory.

## The black box

Between the moments of entering and leaving higher education, the student is on the receiving end of, and participates in, an educational process. The intention underlying that process – provided by an institution of higher education – is to modify the student from his or her state of intellectual maturity at the point of entry. Clearly, there are different viewpoints (as we have seen) as to the kinds of modification in the student that the processes of higher education should bring about. Nevertheless, many things take place between the stages of entry and exit. The so-called black box of the institutional space (between entry and exit) is not neutral: it is a collection of intentional, and unintentional, happenings oriented towards changing the student in various ways.

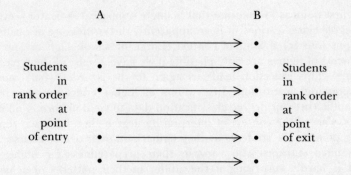

*Figure 6.1* Students: their development and relative achievement

If this is so, why should there be any reason prima facie to expect that there should be any relationship between the student's accomplishments at the moment of entry and at the moment of exit? Why should it be thought that the two states of mind and accomplishment might be related in some way?

Students undergo a developmental process in which they progress in various ways. Putting it schematically, they start at point A and move to point B (Fig. 6.1).

But if this is so, does it not seem surprising to think that there might be a positive relationship between the two points, which can be captured in terms like 'correlation' and 'value-added'? Such an assumption only makes sense by building in a number of additional hypotheses. These include:

1. That the process of higher education simply moves everybody forward more or less equally.
2. That what is assessed at the point of entry is roughly the same kind of entity that is assessed at the point of exit; the logic is that higher education simply develops further the skills that enabled the student to gain entry. Higher education, on this view, is a form of further education, just more of what has gone before rather than the development of higher order skills.
3. That students, despite being adults (of varying ages, from different economic backgrounds and with different social responsibilities), are likely to develop at the same pace.
4. That the educational process itself – the way in which the educator organizes the learning experience – is unlikely to affect individual students differently.

Each of these assumptions is extremely odd; and they all run counter to many findings on student learning and student development. Yet all these assumptions are required to make sense of the expectation of a stable relationship between students' performance at the points of entry and exit.

The corollary is even more disturbing. If we do find a positive relationship between the two, we should not just be surprised. We are entitled to wonder if the intervening processes (the black box) have really justified the title of higher education, and if the assessments for the degree have really focused on the student's newly acquired skills. If the educational processes and their assessment as realized by the student have justified the title of 'higher education', there is no prima facie reason at all to expect that there will be a positive relationship. For the skills that essentially characterize higher education, be they higher order cognitive skills and/or skills related to the student's intending profession, are unlikely to be simply more of what has gone before in the student's life. They are complex and demanding skills, calling for intellectual and personal maturity, and there is no reason to believe that the student's performance at an earlier stage of his or her life is likely to be a good guide to his or her likely accomplishments in higher education.

To emphasize the point, the concept of higher education (see Chapter 2) points to an intellectually emancipatory process, designed to make students self-reflective, to be able to put forward a case of their own and to substantiate it, or to act with their own responsible professional judgement, aware all the time of the essentially contingent character of their knowledge claims or actions. But to say this is to recognize that higher education has a *raison d'être* of its own, and that comparisons with what students achieved beforehand can be misleading.

## Two models of 'the black box' (Fig. 6.2)

In the first model (A), students receive in higher education basically an education with objectives similar to that experienced earlier, and – in the absence of any extraneous factors, such as the trauma of moving from home or personal maturation – might be expected to finish in the same order as at entry. In the second model (B), students are moving towards end points of a quite different order: in educational terms, they are acquiring new kinds of educational competencies.

The point can be pushed further. Not only might we expect fundamental differences in the kinds of demand placed on students as between higher education and their previous educational experience; what students carry away from their higher education experience will vary, even between students on the 'same' course. For students are adults, developing their own stance and capacities, according to their own personalities, preferences and value-orientations. Consequently, the same class of degree awarded to two students on a single course will be gained through the demonstration of admittedly overlapping but somewhat differing achievements. The value and meaning extracted by the two students will not be identical. The informational content provided by a single degree class, therefore, will be limited, even if the course objectives have been specified and are known.[1]

The general point is clear. The placing of students in those final assessments – the extent to which they have taken on the new accomplishments

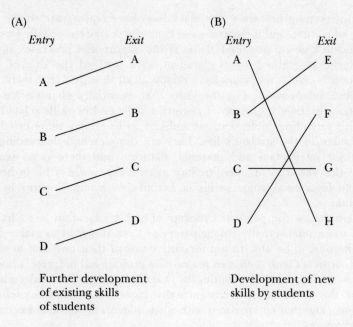

(A)

Entry          Exit

Further development
of existing skills
of students

(B)

Entry          Exit

Development of new
skills by students

*Figure 6.2*    Two models of the black box

and are able to use them to effect – may not bear any relationship to their relative placings on entry; nor should we expect there to be.

## The idea of value-added

This line of reasoning has implications for the application of certain policy ideas. Clearly, care needs to be taken over the use of the term 'value-added'. It seems to promise the possibility of calculating arithmetically the relationship between entry qualifications and degree performance. But such a relationship, even if it can be produced, is misleading if it is taken to imply that the attributes (the student's skills and achievements) at the point of entry are the same as those being assessed at the point of exit.

It is not that comparisons between the two stages cannot be made (CNAA and PCFC 1990) but, rather that their statistical representation cannot easily do justice to the complexity of the student's achievements at the different stages. One immediate response to this reflection might be: very well, let us then employ student 'profiles' to back up degree certificates, providing more information about the competencies actually gained by each student.[2] A key question remains, though. If higher education is intended to attain certain kinds of higher order aims and if we want to assess the quality of our higher education institutions in assisting the students in reaching those aims, can those achievements be fully understood in numerical terms, however complex

the statistical relationships that may be revealed? Is the statistical relationship not a starting point such that, in the end, we are obliged to give a
description of the abilities and competencies of the students on entry and at
the point of exit? 'Value-added' would then take on a new and more informative meaning, namely the degree to which the student has acquired or developed higher order competencies.

It may be objected that we do have at our disposal known correlations
between students' degree results and their performance in A-level examinations. But the extent to which we can, in practice, predict individual students'
degree results on the basis of their performance in earlier examinations
is highly limited. The evidence is that the correlations between A-level
performance and degree results are strongest in those subjects – mathematics
and the natural sciences – which, in higher education, go on building on a
framework of concept and theories acquired at the earlier stages.[3] Even there,
the correlations *are* merely correlations, and not particularly strong ones at
that; accordingly, no definite predictions can be made about the likelihood of
success of an individual student on the strength of his or her A-level grades.

All this has implications for our understanding of entrants' 'ability to
benefit' (DES 1985), to use another term in the contemporary quality debate.
On the argument here, it is hardly surprising if the performance of students
in their school or further education examinations is inconsistent with their
performance in higher education examinations. The kinds of ability that
schools and further education colleges are trying to develop (in getting their
pupils through the public examinations) are unlikely to be identical with
those that higher education institutions are trying to foster in their undergraduates. It follows that the 'ability to benefit' from a programme of study
in higher education may require the assessment of qualities and experience
other than those developed within the school system.

Efforts have been put in hand in the UK to establish ways of assessing
entrants' 'experiential learning' (as it is termed) for the purpose of admission
to courses (Evans 1992). Whether these methods of assessing applicants'
potential to benefit, which have been devised for mature students lacking
formal entry qualifications, can be generalized across applicants remains to
be seen. This initiative has wider implications for the value-added debate,
however. Even if the earlier objections (to placing entry qualifications and
degree results in a tight relationship with each other) can be set aside, there
would still remain the problem of the value on entry that is to be ascribed to
those lacking formal entry qualifications on admission. To say that it is nil –
at one extreme – would produce an *overestimate* of the additional value that
accrues as a result of their higher education experience. They would, after
all, only have been admitted on the basis of some evidence that they were
likely to succeed on their chosen course; they would, therefore, start with
some kind of value.

These reflections suggest a need, first, to identify in broad terms the kinds
of general and higher order aims that higher education is intended to achieve
in its students; and, secondly, to design and apply tests that assess such

capacities on entry *and* on exit. In this way, both 'ability to benefit' and 'value-added' could be calculated for every student.

## Non-completion rates

Non-completion rates form another performance indicator which may appear to be saying something directly about the education process. But there are problems of interpretation here, too. At least, over the past decade or so, we have become accustomed to seeing the phrase 'non-completion rates' rather than, in the UK, its predecessor of 'wastage rates'. The tendentiousness of value-judgements hidden within 'wastage rates' are well understood. It is recognized now that where students do not complete the degree course on which they embark, many reasons might be called up in explanation and some of them may have no element of the failure implied by the term 'wastage'. A student may, for example, simply have transferred to another course in another institution or to a different kind of course in the same institution; or, increasingly in the future, may have just run out of cash.[4]

As that example implies, students may quite legitimately decide – having embarked on a course – that it is not for them. They may not be lost to higher education, but they may choose to take a year or so out of the system, before returning to take a course in another subject. This is to be expected, since students (particularly those who enter higher education straight after school) are undergoing a process of maturation, in the midst of forming their self-identities and intellectual interests. In addition, as we have seen, there may be a gap between the kinds of intellectual and personal demands that higher education makes and their earlier education. It may be an entirely rational pattern of personal decision-making, therefore, that leads some students not to stay the course. Far better, indeed, for them to come to such a realization, than to plough on in a spirit of apathy and indifference to their studies. Such a decision is a sign of maturity and intellectual advancement, and is inadequately described by the language of 'wastage'.

There are three specific points to be made here. Firstly, where students have completed parts of a course but choose to leave it mid-way, systems of higher education should be so designed as to enable them to carry away a certificate verifying those parts of the course they have successfully completed. Secondly, the non-completion of a course is not, in itself, an indication that a student has not gained anything of benefit. On the contrary, as we have just observed, a student may well have gained significantly in self-understanding and may have acquired a more secure basis for a renewed interest in higher education, albeit in another subject or profession and perhaps after an interval of a year or more.

Lastly, no judgements about the quality of a course can be read off directly from a non-completion rate of x per cent. If a course has been so well designed and delivered that its students are brought to form a disinterested view of their studies, and if the total institutional environment is such as to enable students significantly to develop their personal maturity (so that a proportion of students form new ideas about their personal life projects and identities, and opt for other forms of self-realization), a relatively high non-completion rate may be a sign of high quality rather than of poor quality.

Some seem to think that just that situation is especially likely to occur where entrants are being drawn into higher education from backgrounds lacking a culture of easy association with higher education. If an institution of higher education makes a concerted attempt to attract entrants from non-traditional groupings in society, its non-completion rates are likely to rise. Since there is a consensus to the effect that current UK participation rates in higher education are unduly low (compared with other advanced countries), we should be prepared to see non-completion rates drift upwards as access becomes easier. If there are grounds for concern over current non-completion rates, it is not because they are too high but too low.[5]

There are a number of question-begging assumptions with this line of thinking. For example: what is the evidence that those institutions, such as the Open University and some of the polytechnics, which have made it part of their mission to attract non-traditional entrants, actually experience high non-completion rates, compared with other more conventional institutions? Is it necessarily the case that increasing access will lead to increased non-completion, provided adequate systems of student support are developed? The point remains, however, that sense can only be made of non-completion rates by adding other evidence about an institution's entry policies, its student support systems, its approaches to assessment and its attitudes to students. For example, does it deliberately admit a large number in the first year, with a view to conducting severe progression tests to sift out those unable to complete an honours programme?

## Do indicators even indicate?

Neither non-completion rates, nor entry qualifications, nor data on the pattern of degree classes awarded, nor even value-added data can therefore tell us anything definitively about quality. But if the informational content of *these* performance indicators is limited, then even more so must there be limits on the value of other numerical performance indicators. For degree results, measures of value-added and non-completion rates are limit cases. It is there, if anywhere, that we have performance indicators that seem to be able to tell a direct story about the quality of higher education on offer. If these indicators are in trouble, as they must be, then so are all numerical indicators.

To say this is not totally to disparage performance indicators as such. Statistical data *can* be helpful in making assessments about quality or in improving quality in higher education. Interesting statistical patterns can emerge: whether positive or negative; whether as a result of an internal relationship (between entry qualifications and degree performance on the same course, or a time series of data on non-completion for the one course or the one institution); or whether as the result of an external relationship (comparing the performance of a course with comparable courses across the country). In that case, it would be foolish to ignore such data. In making assessments about quality, let us gain our evidence from wherever we can find it.

The question is: what kind of inferences can we make from the evidence? I repeat: numerical performance data tell us nothing in themselves about quality. *Even to say that performance indicators merely 'indicate' is to suggest too much.* They may prompt us to ask: what is going on here? But even the further questions cannot in any sense be read off from the data. We might be tempted to discover what, if anything, is going wrong here. (Is this apparently high failure rate really high? Why are so many students failing?) But the data may equally prompt the question 'what can we learn from this achievement?' (How is this institution able to produce such a low failure rate? Why is this apparently high failure rate so low given the mission of the institution to attract non-traditional entrants?)

Very often, those further explorations will be complex, not easily lending themselves to fruitful outcomes. As we have seen, statistics become meaningful when the context that gave rise to them is filled out. This means examining not just the formal policies on paper, but trying to get an informed view of the way in which a course or, indeed, an institution operates in practice. What, in reality, is the mission and strategy of the institution? What is the ethos? What are the dominant values, and how are they reflected in teaching styles, in student support, in assessment procedures and in resource allocation priorities (between research and teaching, for example)? Filling out the context behind performance data and gaining some insight into what is going on in the 'black box' is no straightforward task, therefore. But only by turning the numerical data into analytical and qualitative investigations, with all their technical and conceptual demands, can we begin to use such arithmetical accounts of quality in a legitimate fashion.

## 'The student experience'

Those who are sensitive to this approach to quality may be inclined to believe that what is needed, in getting behind numerical performance indicators, is to tap into 'the student experience'. This is yet another term being used with increasing regularity in the quality debate; we see many institutions – both universities and polytechnics – claiming to take 'the student experience' more seriously in their course review procedures. It is an attempt to gain insight into the character of the student experience and is an expression of the developmental approach we identified in Chapter 3. But 'the student experience' is yet another ambiguous term in the discourse of 'quality' and is more complex than it might appear.

Firstly, it could refer to the conscious experience which the student has, which might be articulated in course committee meetings or (more likely, because of their less vulnerable setting) in student questionnaires. Or it could refer to the quality of the total curriculum on offer; the kind of thing that a validation panel might want to form a view about.

These are quite different kinds of student experience. There would be nothing inconsistent in students sensing that they had had a good experience and indicating as such in a student evaluation questionnaire, while, at the same time, a review panel might legitimately judge that the total curriculum provided an inadequate student experience. Correspondingly, the validation panel might judge that the curriculum was likely to impart a valuable experience to the students, but the students might, without any inconsistency, feel dissatisfied with their experiences as a student. (Perhaps their expectations on entering the course were particularly high, or they thought that the course was intended to cover ground other than that encountered.)

That is one and a relatively obvious component of the ambiguities in the phrase 'the student experience'. But there is an added and more serious aspect of the complexities hidden in the phrase. Where there is a systematic attempt to form a judgement about the 'quality of the student experience' (through a formal course review procedure, for example), it is all too easy to fall into the trap of forming an impression of the curriculum on offer, *minus* the students. This is, perhaps, what happens sometimes in validating new course proposals. There is no set of students around, but there is a set of intentions, a statement about the staff and the resources available, and so on. Talk of the student experience in that situation – even the intended or the expected student experience – is quite illegitimate.

It is also dangerous, because it implies that students can be discounted. The underlying educational model is that the student experience is something handed out to students which they merely assimilate. It also implies that the student experience is similar for all the students going through the 'same' curriculum.

On the conception of higher education which I have been urging, this way of looking at things is quite wrong. For the student is – or should be – an active participant in his or her own learning. The curriculum is not something we do to students, but is a process in which they are partners with us. This is often said to be the case by the staff responsible, but the students do not always see it that way.

There is then a range of different meanings we can give to 'the student experience':

1. A set of intentions held by the course team.
2. The overt happenings to which students are exposed (whether in the classroom, the laboratory, or other forms of exchange between teacher and taught).
3. The totality of situations in which students are likely to find themselves during their course, both on campus (including the library and the refectory) and off it.

4. The inward experience of individual students as they struggle to make sense of all they encounter, accommodating with their current under-standings and attitudes the myriad of intellectual and emotional demands of the formal and of the hidden curriculum.

But the key distinction that I want to insist on here is that between the student experience as a set of intentions held by the course team and as it appears to the students; and it is well understood by the students themselves. As we have observed, they can distinguish between the experience they are being offered and the experience they frame for themselves.

This does not mean that everything students put down in their responses to course evaluation questionnaires has to be swallowed wholesale. Even in a market-sensitive system of higher education, students should not be felt to be necessarily the best judge of their experience. They may, for example, feel that their course has put all sorts of interesting experiences their way. But novelty does not necessarily require the exercise of the higher order abilities characteristic of a true higher learning. So again, we see a difficulty with the idea of the quality of the student experience.

Can we give, then, positive meaning to the term, or should we just acknowledge that it is intrinsically ambiguous, without any cash value in assisting our efforts to appraise quality? We should not, at least, surrender too easily to linguistic anarchism. I would suggest this, admittedly stipul-ative, definition:

> The student experience is of high quality where there is a process of student development designed to enable students to advance to the higher order capacities (of independent and cautious judgement, of self-criticism, of rational action, and of collaborative inquiry) which typify a genuine higher education.

This definition reflects the definition of quality I offered towards the end of Chapter 3.

## Towards an educational audit

So far, in this section of the book, I have made a number of cautionary comments about performance indicators, both in general (Chapter 5) and about performance indicators thought to reflect student achievements (this chapter). Let us now try to move forward, on the basis of these ideas. At the institutional level, how might we establish a basis for assessing the quality of higher education?

There are two key questions: what is to be assessed and by what criteria? To the first question, there are two kinds of answer (Chapter 5): those aspects of institutional provision that are common to all institutions, and those that distinguish institutions from each other. To the second ques-tion, criteria can be distinguished that prompt a numerical assessment of performance, and those that more typically require a non-numerical assessment of educational processes. It will have become apparent that any serious appraisal of institutional quality has to work at all four levels (commonality and individuality; numerical and non-numerical assessments).

That is to say, the methodology should take account of what it is to be an institution of higher education and take as its starting point those aspects of provision that are universal, but also be sensitive to the different missions of institutions. The methodology should draw on such useful numerical data as are available to see what questions are thrown up, but it should also allow for (non-numerical) judgements about the quality of provision to be offered.

What might be called up as universal aspects of institutional provision? Are there any? Is this not another sign of misleading essentialism? Admittedly, institutions of higher education have a wide range of purposes; that much was acknowledged earlier (Chapter 1). But we should not jump prematurely to the assumption that there are no unifying features. All institutions of higher education have students of their own who invest much in the institution and with whom they have a legal contract and an implicit educational contract. Those students are registered on courses, and have a legitimate expectation that their courses have been professionally designed and are being professionally delivered and examined so that there can be a reasonable presumption that the overwhelming majority of the students embarked on a course will be successful. Success, though, can never be guaranteed (Chapter 2).

These observations (which I take to be relatively uncontroversial) yield the following four strategic aspects of institutional life, which any assessment of institutional quality should embrace:

1. *Teaching and learning*    Indications that the institution encourages and promotes effective teaching and effective learning;
2. *Quality of examining processes*    For example, is there an institutional central committee which reviews degree performance data against national data? To what extent are staff encouraged to improve their professional understanding of examining processes, including the design of an assessment regime against the course objectives, and the marking and grading of students' assessments?
3. *Staff development*    Not just are there policies in existence, but how are they implemented? What is the balance of allocations on staff development expenditures? Is there a system supporting and improving staff's teaching effectiveness?
4. *Quality assurance processes*    Has the institution established procedures for keeping the quality of its courses under review? How rigorous are they? Do they allow for face-to-face dialogue between a course team and a panel of 'peers'? Do they include external members? To what extent are students' views sought and acted on?

These four aspects of internal processes would appear to constitute an irreducible core of any appraisal of institutional quality.

# Institutional missions

It may be responded that that list of 'essential elements' of institutional operation does not do justice to the self-definitions which many, if not most,
institutions have of themselves. There are those institutions that see themselves as heavily committed to research, others that are particularly keen to
offer accessibility to non-traditional groupings, and still others that want to
develop links with the world of work as a defining characteristic of themselves. Even if it is accepted, therefore, that the four characteristics of
institutional life just picked out are inescapable and central (and deserve to
be addressed in any quality appraisal), institutions justifiably will feel that
these four elements are inadequate indicators of their own performance, as
they jostle to establish their own market position.

The necessary adaptation to the general schema is simple enough. All that
is required is that, for each institution, we supplement the core elements
of appraisal with those that reflect an institution's self-perception. Two
demands follow, though.

Firstly, institutions need to clarify for themselves those activities in which
they are going to invest special effort. This points again to the desirability of
each institution producing a mission statement. A bland statement of general
aims (an institution could claim to be concerned about research, access *and*
links with industry) will not be sufficient here, however. The statement has to
be sufficiently specific about the institution's priorities to provide a basis
for evaluation *and* judgement about the institution's performance. Where,
precisely, is the institution attempting to position itself, with respect to its
central goals?

The second demand is that, having specified its own goals, each institution
should be prepared to evaluate itself with appropriate thoroughness against
the elements it specifies, employing assessments of relevant institutional processes supplemented by appropriate numerical indicators (that is, both qualitative and quantitative evaluations).

For example, an institution which sees itself as a front-rank 'research institution' would need rigorously to assess its research performance against
national criteria (taking into account the opportunities available to it). Both
soft and hard indicators should be employed and might include:

1. Applications for research funding against grants awarded.
2. Research income, in terms of both amount and sources, across different
   subject areas.
3. Outcomes of research projects.
4. Institutional processes designed to encourage staff to conduct research,
   irrespective of their other commitments.
5. The support and guidance given to inexperienced members of staff in
   putting research proposals together.
6. The way in which any internal funds for research are allocated, and the
   priorities they represent.
7. The extent to which research outcomes are disseminated or marketed.

Irrespective of the actual indicators employed, the purpose of the assessment is to take the institution's claim about itself seriously, and enable the institution to conduct a searching self-inquiry into its research activities. Assessment cannot rest, therefore, with numerical indicators. The effort has to be made to make judgements about the quality of the work being conducted *and* the character of the institution's internal culture, so far as it can be seen to support and encourage research.

In addition, the self-appraisal might attempt to form a view about the relationships between these research aspects of an institution's internal life and its teaching activities. For if (as on the argument here) teaching, and more specifically the character of students' development, lie at the heart of higher *education*, then every institution should be interested in determining the relationships between teaching and the other central activities that it has defined for itself. The institution in our example might, for instance, find that the national use of research-oriented performance indicators as a measure of institutional worth influences staff to spend more time on income-generating activities (preparing research submissions, for example) and less on teaching-related activities. *Or* it might find that real attempts are being made to incorporate research problems into the curriculum as problems for the students themselves, so enhancing the quality of student learning.

Equally, an institution that perceives itself as centrally involved in national efforts to widen access should want to ensure that the relevant aspects of its work in that domain are assessed. Again, indicators employed should include qualitative assessments and might embrace, for example, the following:

1. The training given to admissions tutors (Fulton and Ellwood 1989).
2. The provision for and the use made of assessing applicants' experiential learning.
3. The attention paid to the quality of interviewing.
4. The extent to which non-traditional entrants are admitted in practice, especially to courses that are oversubscribed with conventional applicants (Fulton 1981).
5. The support given to mature students once admitted (and others from social groups with low higher education participation rates).
6. The monitoring of students recruited from access courses and other non-traditional routes.[6]
7. Income from national and other agencies to assist with recruitment, assessment, counselling and other activities designed to make the institution more 'open'.

As with research, efforts should be made to go behind the numerical data. In this case, to get a sense of what it is like to be, perhaps, a person in the local community wondering about what this institution has to offer him or her, and following through the experiences of such a potential student entrant as he or she tries to elicit information from the moment of inquiry, through the application process to the interviewing, admission and subsequent induction processes. Attempt could be made, too, to assess the links between efforts on this front and the institution's teaching activities. Are the non-completion rates assessed within the context of recruitment policies? How far has curriculum content and (more importantly) curriculum delivery been modified to take account of the changing intake?

## Profiling performance

I have suggested that there are four core activities characteristic of any institution that takes seriously the quality of the higher education it offers: (1) teaching and learning; (2) student assessment; (3) staff development; and (4) quality assurance processes. These domains of activity, too, lend themselves to both qualitative and quantitative assessments: how well is the institution performing in each domain? Where is there room for improvement?

I have also said that institutions deserve to have their own self-definitions taken seriously and that if they claim to be investing effort in particular kinds of activity, and want to be thought of as market leaders in them, those aspects should be subjected to critical assessment. Here, as we have seen, assessment will draw on numerical performance indicators, but will need to go beyond the data to gain an insight into the relevant aspects of institutional life. Even formal written policies are no more than a start; the question is, how are they implemented on a day-to-day basis? What is the perception of the policies held by the junior lecturer and the student at the sharp end?

What is emerging, therefore, is the idea of an institutional quality audit, tailored to some extent to the specific character of the institution as it sees itself. 'To some extent' because, as we have seen, there are surely some elements of institutional life that are common to all institutions that take quality seriously. Judgements can and should be made in every case about the quality of an institution's care for teaching, for assessment, for staff development, and for its courses (as reflected in its course review procedures).

We can illustrate the ideas emerging in this discussion as indicated in Figure 6.3.

At the centre of the diagram lies the essential activity of student learning and his or her educational development. In contact with it are those core educational activities that directly and immediately affect the quality of the student's development: the quality of the teaching, the quality of the examining process, the quality of the courses (as revealed in the institution's course review processes), and the quality of the staff development programme (in so far as it is aimed at improving the staff's teaching effectiveness). These four activities constitute the 'protective belt' of institutional elements safeguarding the quality of the student experience. They are common to every institution of higher education and should form inescapable elements in reviewing the performance of any institution.

Beyond that circle lies a ring of auxiliary institutional activities, which have an important – though less direct – bearing on the quality of the student's educational experience (cf. Lakatos 1977). In contrast to the four

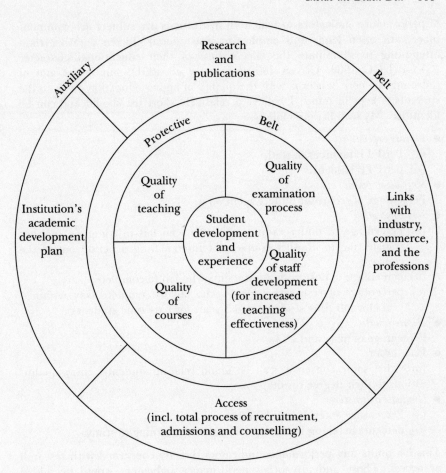

*Figure 6.3* Structure of institutional activities affecting the quality of higher education *('Protective belt': necessary and common activities; 'auxiliary belt': more indirect and variable activities.)*

elements constituting the protective belt, these constituents may vary between institutions. Accordingly, those elements that appear in the outer ring in the diagram – the staff's research activities, the institution's policy towards access and recruitment, the institution's envisaged programme development, and the links with the wider society that the institution is forming, especially with the business and professional communities – are simply indicative of the kinds of activity into which an institution may be putting particular effort and by which it wishes its performance to be judged.

It follows from this discussion that some numerical performance indicators are going to be common to all institutions, since there are some which seem to bear directly on the quality of the core activities I have specified. Lists of performance indicators to which all institutions are subject are common-place, are often long, and emphasize institutional efficiency rather than attempting to illuminate the effectiveness of their educational character (CVCP/UGC 1988; CNAA 1990a; Cave *et al.* 1991); but if the aim of reflecting the core concerns with the quality of higher education given to the students is kept in mind, I believe a relatively short list should and can be identified. My own list is as follows:

- *Library expenditure*
  (a) Per FTE member of staff;
  (b) per FTE student.
- *Staff development*
  Percentage of recurrent budget spent on it.
- *Non-completion*
  (a) Percentage of undergraduate students who fail to complete (neither transferring to another course, nor intercalating a period out of the course);
  (b) percentage of postgraduate students who fail to complete;
  (c) percentage of research students who fail to complete (say within 4 years for full-time students and 5 years for part-time students).
- *Degree results*
  Percentage of firsts and 2 : 1s.
- *Value-added*
  (provided some consensus can be found relating students' entry qualifications to their degree results)
- *Graduate destinations*
  (a) Percentage entering employment;
  (b) percentage taking further qualifications/returning to study.

This list omits any performance indicators directly concerned with research or access. Those and any other performance indicators would be added where an institution claimed to be devoting particular attention to such aspects of its mission. This is merely a minimalist set of indicators, on the dual belief that data should not be sought unless they are demonstrably linked to the evaluation in hand; and that institutions should be free to specify the additional indicators by which they wish to examine their performance.

It should be clear from this discussion that *any* specification of performance indicators is problematic. So the above list is offered with some hesitation. Once performance indicators come into play, they are likely to dominate proceedings, and in two senses. Firstly, being available, weight is given to the data they yield rather than to qualitative assessments. Secondly, judgements are read off from the data, quite illegitimately. The tenor of the argument here has been that they have a part to play, but in a residual role; and, again, in two senses. The weight accorded to them should be limited. And, even more importantly, no assessments should be read off from them directly. Their use is to prompt questions for additional qualitative explorations.

In other words, I am suggesting that numerical indicators be granted an *appendix status*. Include them, but as interesting background to a fuller inquiry and set of institutional assessments. If at all, it is in the body of a report in appraising an institution – in the non-numerical evaluations – that real insight into an institution's performance is to be found.

## Conclusions

There are two key drawbacks with performance indicators as a means of assessing the quality of higher education.

Firstly, the character of performance indicators – as they have developed in practice – is that they are numerical. But there has to be a continuing query over whether quantities (even expressed as ratios) can ever in themselves tell us anything of substance about qualities. Is there not (as Gilbert Ryle might have called it) a category mistake in running these two different kinds of concept – qualities and quantities – together? For the identified quantities even to begin to tell us anything about qualities, judgements have to be applied to the data themselves. So the numerical indicators cannot provide us with the firmness and robustness they may seem to supply.

Secondly, those performance indicators that could be said to be addressed to quality focus on the inputs and the outputs to higher education. What goes on inside the black box is neglected. But that continuing internal life of institutions – their ethos; the character of the interpersonal relationships between staff at different levels and in different departments and between staff and students; the extent to which staff are prepared to reflect seriously about the educational character of what they are doing, to be self-critical and to take possibly dramatic remedial actions – all that is of the essence, in understanding quality. Unless we find some way of illuminating and evaluating the character of the educational processes of institutions and the procedures-in-practice that bear on them, we cannot expect to understand the quality of our institutions of higher education.

Institutions of higher education will have some characteristics in common, since they are all trying to educate students to a high level and advancing their students' autonomy in the various disciplines they offer. But they have legitimate differences too, as they develop their own mission and market niche. In evaluating the quality of our institutions, we should try to do justice both to their common elements and to those aspects in which they differ.

The evaluation of institutional quality should draw upon and seek to utilize the fullest range of information and evidence that can reasonably be accumulated. Numerical performance indicators may be helpful in raising questions for further examination, and I have suggested a limited set of indicators applicable to every institution and bearing directly on quality. With them has to be coupled explorations, analyses and judgements on the character of institutions' internal procedures and educational practices (and those will not be captured by a numerical treatment). Those indicators and process inquiries should, *for every institution*, embrace four key aspects of institutional life: teaching and learning; student assessment and examining; staff development and appraisal; and course review. To those universal four elements of appraisal should be added any particular elements of institutional mission in which an institution claims to have particular strengths. And again, evaluation of an institution's performance in any such additional domain (such as research, links with industry or access) should contain but go beyond numerical performance indicators to include an inquiry into the relevant institutional policies and their day-to-day operation.

For every institution, therefore, we should end up with a *profile* of quality covering a range of domains of institutional activity, some of which are common to all institutions and some of which are particular to the institution in question. For every activity, the evidence will be both descriptive and numerical, leading to questions for further inquiry and to subsequent judgement and recommendations for future action. The weight of any evaluation of an institution's quality, however, should lie with the institution's performance on the four core aspects, since they are the paramount criteria of quality.

Placing such institutional profiles of quality alongside each other and making comparative judgements of them will not be an easy task, if indeed it is possible. For that, further value-assumptions about the relative importance of domains of institutional activity might have to be employed. It might also emerge that some institutions with international research reputations turn out to perform less well in other important domains – such as the quality of teaching and learning or staff development – than some less-favoured institutions. But the bar charts of institutional performance may vary quite considerably, with the bars standing – if only to some extent – for different aspects of institutional life or achievement, depending on their importance for each institution.

This chapter has tried to sketch out the elements of quality at the institutional level. It has left unexplored how any institutional evaluation might be conducted and how any institution of higher education can, qua institution, improve the quality of its work. Those two topics form, in turn, the subjects of the next two chapters.

# 7

# What's Wrong with Quality Assurance?

## We are all responsible for quality

In the modern debate over quality in higher education, the term 'quality assurance' has come to be seen as more helpful than 'quality control' (Frazer 1991). Both terms have been taken from contexts of industrial processes but reflect slightly different aims. 'Quality control' inspects products in a more or less finished state and those which do not come up to scratch are rejected. It is a method of ensuring that quality is maintained after the event. 'Quality assurance', instead, looks to developing processes so rigorous that imperfections are heavily reduced and ideally eradicated. 'Quality assurance' reflects the hope that error can be eliminated. That, at least, is the theory; and attempts are now being made to translate that thinking, and the industrial models accompanying it, to higher education.

'Total quality management' (TQM) represents a development of the concept of quality assurance, being an attempt, a strategy, to produce an institution-wide commitment to quality assurance. There is a new realization that every person involved in an institution of higher education, from the porter through the teacher and researcher to the senior manager, has a responsibility towards the overall quality of work of an institution. By bringing home to all members of staff their responsibilities over 'quality', so that every action is undertaken with the utmost professionalism, it is intended that a high quality of service will permeate the whole of an organization.

On the face of it, there can be little quarrel with this thinking. For example, it is readily understandable that, as the first point of contact with an institution of higher education, the telephonist should answer incoming calls speedily, have a courteous manner, and not leave a caller stranded while an extension rings in vain for a staff member not at her desk. Even that might be thought to be inadequate as a measure of quality of service. Ideally, the telephonist knows sufficient about the departments, the various units within the institution and the courses for real help to be given to a caller who is not certain exactly which person or unit he should be put through to. A caller might be interested in talking to the head of the staff development unit, but not be sure whether the institution even possesses such a centre. If it does, it might be called 'Educational Development Services' or the 'Teaching Methods Unit'. The really helpful telephonist will not be satisfied with looking down the internal telephone directory under 'S' (for Staff Development) but will be so well informed about the institution and its constituent parts that other possibilities will occur, and the telephonist will be able to give real assistance to the caller.

This kind of example can be multiplied into hundreds of examples, occurring every day at all levels of an institution:

- The departmental secretary typing and laying out a research proposal.
- An admissions tutor counselling and interviewing an anxious mature applicant, who is uncertain of the nature of a course in higher education.
- A teacher offering comments on an essay.
- The assistant librarian helping research students understand the resources available to them.
- A chairperson of a departmental meeting, working efficiently but amicably through an agenda.
- A vice-chancellor, welcoming a group of visitors from overseas.

In all these and many other instances, there are opportunities for individuals to have an eye to the sheer professionalism of what they are doing and, in that way, to have a positive and significant effect on the general quality of the work of an institution.

In so far as quality assurance implies a determination to develop a culture of quality in an institution of higher education, so that everyone is aware of his own part in sustaining and improving the quality of the institution, there can surely be little amiss with the idea. However, quality assurance does not always rest there. For alongside this devolution of responsibility arises the sense that placing the responsibility for quality on individuals is too risky an approach. The hoped-for error elimination that quality assurance is supposed to bring is not going to be won purely by giving staff a heightened awareness of the significance of their day-to-day actions; for what guarantee is there of individuals, however well-motivated, translating that awareness into new and appropriate forms of action?

## The check-list culture

All too easily, therefore, 'quality assurance' can lead to a parallel wish to see in place procedures – at all levels of the organization and in all spheres of activity – which will offer a real 'assurance' of quality. We see this development most strikingly in the willingness of some institutions to demonstrate their fulfilment of BS5750, a British Standard for quality systems, a set of specifications originally designed for application to industrial processes (TEED undated; Ellis 1990; Major 1990). By itself, quality assurance as the implementation of systems, regulations and procedures – of which the search for a BS5750 accreditation is simply a signal example – constitutes a check-list approach to maintaining quality. In higher education, whatever its validity in other contexts, such a single-minded check-list approach to safeguarding quality is misguided, ineffective and pernicious.

It is misguided because it springs from the belief, however plausible in industrial processes, that error can be eliminated. In a service sector enterprise, activities are conducted to a very large extent by people and not by machines. People make mistakes; and learn through their mistakes (Popper 1975). So 'right first time' is an entirely inappropriate slogan in educational and truth-seeking transactions (TEED undated).

Equally, in many educational settings, correcting mistakes is not central to the improvement of quality. More usually, it calls for doing things with care, sensitivity, accuracy, aesthetic taste, judgement or helpfulness. Educative situations have literally an infinite variety of possibilities open to those engaged in them. It is more a matter of imagining and then discriminating between a range of alternative actions; *and* then having the personal capacities to put the chosen action into effect with aplomb, daring, subtlety or delicacy. It is less a case of right as against wrong action than a case of being continually thoughtful, resourceful and capable. The idea of error elimination is almost always neither here nor there.

But it is also irrelevant for another quite profound reason. We saw in an earlier chapter that – again, unlike an industrial process – the ultimate 'product' in higher education is rather unpredictable. The language of 'products' and 'outputs' is itself indicative of a quite misguided approach in evaluating effectiveness of higher education institutions. If real higher education is going on, students are inevitably actively involved in their own education. That, indeed, is part of what we mean by a *higher* education: that students emerge with a mind literally of their own, able to put forward a point of view of their own or act on their own account and defend what they are saying or doing in the critical company of others. But, if students really are to have minds of their own, or to act in their own way, then there have to be large elements of unpredictability about the outcome of the educational process. The student's 'engagement' (in Oakeshott's terminology) has to have a significant degree of open-endedness about it.

This point about the essential open-endedness of higher education also gives the clue to substantiating my second claim that the check-list approach to quality assurance is ineffective. Rules of procedure can certainly be established for many activities, even in higher education. In the UK, the extension of such rules is one area that differentiates universities (which are relatively free of check lists or conditions governing academic activities) from polytechnics and colleges (which are used to working by them); though we are now seeing codes of practice – for example, over external examiners or research students – coming into use in universities too. These lists or notes of guidance are *not* to be disparaged; they can be very useful as *aides-mémoires*, as a means of establishing a culture of care about important areas of academic life, and in gaining a reasonable uniformity of approach across a single institution. And, at the end of the book, I offer a check list of check lists; a specification of quality assurance systems against which institutions can conduct an audit and against which institutions *can* usefully develop their own guidelines (see Appendix).

There is, though, a problem with codes of practice and check lists as a dominant means of securing quality. The problem is that it is easy for the assumption to develop that the procedures in themselves are indications of quality. Both among those charged with evaluating an institution's perform-ance – perhaps in a process of academic audit – and among the staff at all levels of the organization, it is understandable that a sense can arise that the procedures, codes of practice and internal regulations are testimony to the character of what goes on. The assumption has *some* logic to it; for the procedures and regulations have been agreed – it is to be hoped – after some debate, often quite protracted and at times difficult. What was the point of all that committee work and consultation throughout the institution if the agreed procedures were not in themselves of value? The thinking is under-standable but neglects the simple point that there is always a gap between formal procedures and actual practice.

The gap is parallel to that identified by Argyris and Schon in professional life in general, between espoused values and values-in-practice (Argyris and Schon 1974). Even to see this gap as one of implementation, of carrying over the procedures into action, is too simple an explanation. For all rules, pro-cedures and guidelines have to be *interpreted* before, or as, they are imple-mented. If rules are really to become part of the fabric of institutional life, directly impinging on quality at all levels, then every member of staff has to internalize those rules. No matter how much effort is made to ensure a uniformity of interpretation, there will inevitably be differences according to the different values of departments or the differing interests of staff at various levels of the organization.

Rules in themselves will remain inert, unless efforts are made to develop general understanding *and* to allow a flexibility of interpretation across the institution. It follows that a rule-governed approach to maintaining quality or to evaluating the quality of work in an institution is misguided. In them-selves, check lists are an ineffective means of achieving quality.

I turn to my third charge against the check-list approach to quality, that it is pernicious. Part of the reasoning has just been brought out. The check-list approach to quality is pernicious because it contains an anti-humanistic ideology. The implicit assumption in the approach is that the participants in the institution are simply followers of rules existing outside themselves. It neglects the point that human beings, if they are to be fully involved in and committed to their work, must be permitted to invest something of them-selves in it. This means that they must be given the freedom to interpret and colour their role in their own way.

Even the analogy with service industries is misleading. The activities which go on in an institution of higher education are not like the production of a hamburger in a fast-food restaurant, where every ingredient and the manner of its display – including the counter staff's form of interaction with the customer – are strictly controlled. In particular, the academic staff are performing actions every day which, *necessarily*, are open-ended and do not lend themselves to tight control (whether it is deciding on a teaching method, refereeing a journal manuscript, or putting together a research proposal or simply interacting with students in an individual manner).

The check-list approach to quality is pernicious because its hidden function is to reduce the area of spontaneity, originality and creativity. Indeed, continuous creativity is anathema to the check-list approach, for that approach is one of control, prediction and uniformity. Continuous creativity of the kind that should characterize an institution of higher education is in tension with the check-list approach, and so the check-list approach should be kept *in* check. If unchecked, this approach to quality with its in-built elements of prediction and control could end up as obliterating part of the essential values of higher education which offer, within society and against the dominant images of the day, a countervailing source of ideas and open-mindedness.[1]

Arising from this discussion, we can see that the term 'academic audit' deserves to be treated with a certain amount of scepticism. For not too far under its surface, too, may lie a check-list approach in evaluating the quality of an institution's work. Tell us what procedures you have in place for course monitoring, course review, staff appraisal and external examiners, and we will tell you the quality of your institution. Admittedly, academic audit can be oriented by a wish to bridge this gap between procedures and practices. The gap cannot be leapt. *No* assumptions about the actual quality of work of an institution can be made from an inspection of its written procedures, however thoroughly worked out. And it is certainly insufficient to listen, however attentively, to the expositions of senior managers to the effect: this is how we do things here.

For example, there might be a rule that for every course there is a course committee; and that that course committee includes student members. Or this might be an expectation or understanding on the part of senior managers. An audit might establish that. But to what extent is the rule or expectation fulfilled in practice? And how does the institution know whether its rules or expectations of this kind are implemented? Even if a rule such as this one were known to be implemented across every course in the institution, what would follow from that understanding on the part of the auditors? Further questions should then arise, such as: what is the character of student involvement in such meetings? Are the meetings held at a time when students can attend them? Do students always receive the papers? Which items (if any) are counted as reserved business, from which debate the students are excluded? In practice, to what extent are students encouraged to make their contribution at meetings (a daunting opportunity for most, surrounded by their teachers)?

So real evaluations of quality cannot be satisfied with enumerating codes of practice, regulations and procedures. Instead, they have to find ways of identifying and illuminating the character of the internal life of institutions.

But even that is problematic, owing to the special character of higher education.

## The ineffability of validation

In an industrial setting, it may be doubly plausible to think in terms of eliminating error in the production process. First, because the products are inert, and do not possess a consciousness and a will of their own; they are therefore relatively plastic and malleable to a pre-specified formula or description. Secondly, because it *is* possible to lay down by fiat the desired character and properties of the finished article. Senior management may wish to keep that specification under review, but at least – for the time being – a decision of that kind once having been made, there can be no argument that that set of objectives is what is required. In the previous section, I tried to show the inappropriateness of transmuting the first set of ideas to an educational setting. I now wish to tackle the second set.

Far from being determinable in any final way, the objectives of a course of higher education are essentially contestable. In saying this, I am not concerned with the point that a curriculum should always be kept under review and that it is always possible to ask of a course tutor or the course team: why are you doing things in this way? That *is* the case; but I want to offer a stronger thesis.

Higher education is irrevocably bound up with knowledge; not, though, knowledge as such (in the form of collections of facts), but open claims to knowledge offered in such a way that they can be appraised by others. Whether one takes an essentially objectivist or a relativist approach to knowledge, formalized knowledge (of the kind favoured in the academic community and higher education) is essentially dynamic: the temporary outcome of continuing debates. So the base on which higher education stands is always shifting. But more than that, that base of formal knowledge is understood to be open to critical assessment.

The lesson to be drawn from these observations is quite sharp. In higher education, in determining and evaluating those activities which are bound up in the knowledge enterprise, there can be no final authorities. Not only over particular claims to know that might be uttered – whether by a teacher or a student – but also over all related activities, there has to be an element of openness about them. Whether it is the character of a curriculum, the types of teaching method employed, the links between the practical and the theoretical elements, or the nature of the student assessments: accompanying each of these activities is, in effect, a hidden invitation to the wider world, namely 'This is valid or worth while, isn't it?'

It might be said, in response, that this state of affairs is no different in industry, where manufacturing processes have to be kept under critical review (or else international competition will overtake the quality of the finished article). But there is a fundamental difference. That determination to keep an industrial process under continuing critical review may or may not exist; it would be a matter for the management team of each organization in that sector. Here, though, in higher education, critical appraisal is of the essence. It is part of what we mean by 'knowledge'. While there are no final judges in determining what counts as knowledge, it does not follow that 'anything goes'. Anyone (or any research team) can put up whatever view they wish in principle; but it will only count as knowledge once it has withstood some kind of critical gaze of the individual's (or the group's) peers. There is no resting point, however. Claims to knowledge remain contestable and are contested. The debate can be joined by anyone at any time: the most junior lecturer can have a go at the most respected professor, and the first-year undergraduate at the teacher (provided the customary houserules of academic life are respected).

Evaluation by one's academic peers is, therefore, part of the academic enterprise. It is built into the character of knowledge, not as a supporting plank but as its very foundation. Academic knowledge simply does not count as knowledge without it having been subjected to some kind of peer evaluation. Habermas, indeed, has erected consensus arising out of an open argument amongst equals as a formal definition of truth. It is entirely proper, therefore, that peer assessment has been extended from its central place in truth discourse as such to its occupying a strategic function in activities critically associated with academic life. For a long time, fairly systematic procedures have been in use in the research domain. Over the past generation, peer review has been further extended in the UK to play an increasing part in assessing teaching and course provision, firstly in the polytechnics and colleges and more recently in the universities.

In short, legitimacy in higher education is derived through peer evaluation. Popularity or income may be derived through the market, by means of the entrants who come through the front door, but authoritative assessments of and approval for academic activities lie with one's peers, with those who are authorities (whether or not they are in authority).

There is a problem with this account of legitimacy in academic affairs. For if there are no final arbiters, who guards the guardians? Even if we establish systematic and sophisticated methods of course review, what faith can we invest in the judgements of the review panel, however 'authoritative' its members? For what has just been said is tantamount to saying that the panel's judgements are not absolute. Indeed, if another panel of 'peers' was to be assembled, it might well be that another judgement might emerge. And just to make the counter-point even more forcefully, might there not be some tendency in any peer review system – where the roles of defendant and judge may be reversed tomorrow – for the really critical comments to be softened? Precisely because those in both roles are all members of the same academic community, is it not the case that there is an in-built tendency for assessments (particularly where they are made in public) to be couched with due deference to their likely impact? Or, alternatively in a market situation, perhaps the inclusion of external members drawn from rival institutions will be avoided, for fear of non-impartiality; and so safe externals are invited to participate.

Such scepticism is justified up to a point; but no more. That there is no end point to a debate, that it has no absolute answers, and that questions can always be raised about the composition of a review panel are no justifications for not undertaking the debate. It is worth while for a course team to engage in a critical dialogue with a group of its peers, even if the judgements and decisions that result cannot be said to be definitive.

In a sense, 'critical dialogue' is all we have in the academic community. It might not provide absolutely sure knowledge but its virtue lies elsewhere. Its justification lies in its calling to account those who see themselves as part of the academic community. It requires those who hold views or who conduct academic activities to reflect on their own beliefs or actions. It helps to examine the validity and soundness of those beliefs and actions. And, through the dialogue, new possibilities of thought and action are likely to arise. Critical dialogue is, therefore, a vehicle for both change and improvement (Pratt 1983).

Such a critical dialogue also does justice to the sense of the idea of accountability as a calling to account of actors for their actions. 'Accountability', therefore, is an idea of value so long as we read into it giving an account through a *process* of collaborative critical inquiry with one's peers in a quasi-public setting, rather than a means of coming up with judgemental *outcomes*.

## Into the secret garden

So far, in this chapter, I have argued two points. Firstly, that a check-list approach to quality assurance is, in itself, inadequate. Procedures do have important functions to perform: helping to raise awareness of issues of quality, giving guidance to members of staff, and developing a reasonable uniformity of approach across the departments and faculties of an institution. However, procedures, written policies, notes of guidance and internal regulations can be, at best, only an element in assessing the quality of work of an institution.

Secondly, I have tried to show that 'peer review' has a legitimate and valuable part to play in maintaining the quality of an institution's courses, including its teaching. Polytechnics – which have had such a system for some time – are concerned about its costs, both financially and in staff time. Universities are thinking about introducing it, but are also nervous about its costs. Financial considerations are not to be downplayed. Nevertheless, I have tried to make an argument, in principle, for the use of peer review on the teaching side.

There is a link between these two points – the limitations of a check-list approach and the value of peer review for courses – but it may not be entirely apparent. I can, perhaps, best make the link by making a further point.

What goes on in the teaching situation – whether in the form of a lecture, a seminar or a genuine interaction between the participants – all too often has a degree of privacy to it. Particularly in universities, but even in other institutions (where visits from Her Majesty's Inspectorate are increasingly commonplace), there is within the culture of higher education a sense that the transactions between teacher and taught are quasi-private. They have something of the character of an interaction between the doctor and the patient. Yes, the professional is always accountable for what takes place; but the substance and manner of the transaction remain under the control of the professional. Those elements of control and responsibility, and of immediate interactions with one's patient, are constitutive of being professional.

It is considerations of this kind, perhaps, that have generated the sense that the curriculum – as it is experienced by the students – has the character of a 'secret garden'. In Basil Bernstein's graphic imagery, the student may adopt a hands-around sensitivity towards his work; but so too, we may observe, teachers in higher education all too readily adopt a similar approach to their own work. Even the head of department will think twice before asking to enter the teaching domain of the most junior member of staff (or perhaps would similarly see it as unprofessional behaviour on his or her part and betraying signs of a lack of confidence in that individual's teaching competence).

There are good reasons for supposing, therefore, that there will be difficulties in getting a direct insight into the teaching situation. Where it can occur, either through external visits of HMIs or through an internal colleague sitting in and offering constructive comments, it can certainly play a valuable part in a total system of quality development. But its role is limited.

Quite apart from ideological and practical matters, there are issues of principle here. Even if such access to teaching in action were entirely open, even if the teacher could always be viewed in that situation (like the surgeon in the teaching hospital), that still could not provide a sufficient means of illuminating the quality of the teaching and the curriculum. Firstly, much of the student's work is accomplished outside the formal teaching setting.

Secondly, the teaching – whether in the lecture room, the laboratory or the studio – is only a small part of the total set of activities in which the teacher interacts with the student. Some other activities are relatively public and are open to assessment, such as the quality of handouts, the up-to-dateness and informativeness of bibliographies, and the existence and coverage of course guides. Others, though, are relatively private activities, such as counselling students on options, the quality and detail of a tutor's comments on an essay, and the numerous informal interactions that occur on an *ad hoc* basis where students are seeking advice. So much of the most valuable aspects of 'teaching', broadly considered, are not easily susceptible to observation and assessment by a third party (whether an external inspector or even an internal colleague).

Thirdly, the individual teaching situation is one sub-unit in a larger whole, and its purpose and value can only be fully appreciated in that wider context.

Lastly, the individual teacher is usually working together with other colleagues in offering a course, and questions need to be raised about how the staff members work together, and about the degree to which there is a team approach to the student experience and a collective understanding about the purpose of the course and its delivery.

The members of staff teaching on a single course can profitably be invited, therefore, to give an account of their collective efforts. To pick up the earlier points, the only people to whom they can sensibly give 'an account' are their peers (although there are questions to be raised about who constitute their peers). Since such a meeting will be one between peers, the exchange ought to take the form of a dialogue (neither side having any clear superiority). The dialogue becomes an open critical dialogue, in which a mirror is held up to the course team for it critically to review aloud the quality of its achievements. In the process, insight can also be gained into the internal life of the institution, both that of the student experience (assuming suitable evidence is available) and about part of the academic community of the institution.

In addition, the form of the dialogue will tell the institution something about the character of the institution itself, as a total academic community. If the dialogue does draw in members of staff from across the institution, if academics recognize a responsibility to assist in course reviews even if not in their own subject area, and if the dialogue is conducted as a genuine interchange which is helpful rather than being judgemental, and in which real communication takes place so that the whole process is one of mutual interchange, then we have indicators that a real academic community exists which transcends subject boundaries.

## Being explicit about quality

Let us now take these very general ideas into the context of evolving patterns of quality assurance across the UK sectors of higher education.

The first point to make is that, while many universities are making rapid efforts to develop their quality assurance systems, there remains (if only temporarily) a difference in the culture between universities and polytechnics. While any university will be able to point to a wide range of activities and processes which help to maintain quality, they are – in comparison with polytechnics and colleges – relatively unsystematic. Under the encouragement of the Council for National Academic Awards since its inception in 1964 (and its predecessor, the National Council for Technological Awards), polytechnics and colleges have been obliged to reflect on their quality assurance systems, to make them explicit, and to go on continually refining them.

When we look at the two sectors, it is too easy to be diverted by overt differences in approach. For example, few universities have yet instituted a systematic procedure of periodic course review, in which course teams are exposed to a face-to-face critical dialogue with their peers. Such a system is universal in the polytechnics and colleges sector, even if it is now being reviewed by many institutions. This is a significant difference, but it is the contrast in the internal culture of quality which is reflected in the greater explicitness of policies and procedures. (I need, perhaps, to repeat an earlier point, that policies and procedures are in themselves no indication of quality *per se*. I am making sociological observations rather than expressing a comparative judgement.)

So, in a typical polytechnic, we might find written policies or procedures, adopted by the Academic Board, on:

1. The elements of proposals for new courses (which, when completed, might produce a substantial booklet).
2. The precise path that a submission for a new course has to undergo.
3. The likely schedule and timespan.
4. The composition of panels established to conduct periodic reviews of courses.
5. The elements of an annual course monitoring exercise.
6. The responsibilities towards course quality of course committees and faculty committees.
7. The responsibilities of a committee established under the Academic Board with oversight of academic standards.
8. The responsibilities of course tutors (often seen as a key group in maintaining quality).
9. The rights and duties of external examiners.
10. Criteria for upgrading MPhil research students to PhD programmes.
11. Appeals procedures, both for taught courses and for research students.
12. Staff development.
13. Staff appraisal.
14. The involvement of students in different aspects of quality assurance.

Typically, too, all these and any other general statements of policy or procedure will be collected together in a handbook produced by the institution which is given to all staff. This apparently bureaucratic point is actually quite crucial. For putting these institutional statements together in a public document performs a number of important functions.

Firstly, such a handbook demonstrates publicly and explicitly the institution's commitment to quality care. Secondly, both through their collective presentation and in their separate texts, the statements will impress on all members of staff their responsibility in helping to maintain and to improve the quality of courses. Thirdly, such a handbook is a useful *aide-mémoire* for staff members. They do not have to memorize any of it; but, if every member of staff has a copy, they have readily to hand an up-to-date summation of the institution's agreed policies on any quality topic. Lastly, being public and visible, it is at once apparent how far the Academic Board has considered particular matters of quality and how recently it has reviewed its policies. The sheer publication of a handbook of this kind becomes, therefore, a spur towards general debate in the institution about quality issues.

## Patterns of convergence?

The UK polytechnics and colleges are familiar with explicit and highly codified systems of quality assurance (Harris 1990); but they are continuing to review their systems and the institutions accredited by CNAA are showing understandable signs of wishing to simplify their systems. For example, one move taking place among those institutions is for course-specific reviews to give way to subject reviews. The universities, on the other hand, are beginning to systematize their efforts at quality assurance: one significant development is that of departmental reviews, often involving some external membership within the review team (Gregory 1991).

So we are witnessing some degree of convergence between the sectors in patterns of quality assurance. That observation, though, deserves to be carried a little further. Within the group of institutions accredited by the CNAA (40 institutions in 1991, including all the polytechnics and some of the major Scottish central institutes), there are several emerging patterns of course review, some of which are in tension with each other.

One shift is that of a renewed desire to take the voice of the students and their experience more seriously. All major institutions in the sector make some use of student questionnaires, but some have reviewed their usage, have recast them for institution-wide use, and have systematized the use made of the information gained so that it contributes to course review processes.

Course review panels have long been accustomed to having a meeting with a group of students and, where practicable, have seen the students engaged on their day-to-day activities. The latter is easy to do in a non-threatening way for laboratory or studio-based work. Now, more efforts are being made to enable the character of the student experience to come through. Thought is being given to the meeting with students, to hold it at a time convenient to the students and to orchestrate it so that they feel at ease. Members of a course review team might even visit students on placements (student teachers, for example). Correspondingly, course leaders, in giving a presentation to the review panel on behalf of the course team, might be invited to present the course in whatever way they wish; and that invitation might be taken up through a video or other ways in which the day-to-day character of the course can be demonstrated.

Alongside shifts of this kind, we are also seeing efforts by some institutions (possibly even the same institution on occasion) to adopt a 'performance indicators' approach. Here, student 'performance' data on a course (entrants' qualifications, non-completion rates, degree results and first destinations in the labour market) are placed against comparative data for other courses. The comparative data might be of other courses in the home faculty or the institution, or – and perhaps more significantly – they might be national data for similar courses. Through this approach, assessments can be made of courses in the light not of subjective feelings but of evidence about corresponding courses.

I discussed and indeed cautioned against a 'performance indicators approach' to quality assessment in the last two chapters and will not do so at any length here. There is, though, a commentary to be made bearing in mind the two sets of shifts in course evaluation that we have just observed.

## Clients and consumers

The pull towards taking the views of the students more seriously and the move towards a performance indicators approach are, on the surface, radically different. The first builds on the assumption that the perceptions of those engaged in higher education matter, and that quality in higher education involves getting on the inside of people's experiences. The second is an attempt to derive supposedly objective data on which judgements can be made. The two approaches might be termed soft and hard. Yet, for all their overt differences, they actually have an important aspect in common. They both reflect the willingness of the higher education sector to respond with more sophistication to the claims of its clients. The difference is that, in the first approach, the client is the student with personal preferences and attitudes towards her experience as a student; in the second approach, the client is the state, insisting among other things on value-for-money, and generating a desire on the part of institutions that, pound-per-student educated, they are at least as cost effective as other institutions.

So higher education is showing clear signs of responding more deliberately to its clients, although there are alternative views over who its clients are. That is why we can see these contrasting approaches developing even in the same institution. However, institutions employing the two approaches could perhaps reflect with profit on the disparate nature of these approaches. It is not just that one is a quantitative approach, while the other illuminates felt perceptions of quality. If that were the only difference, we might feel that the two approaches should be run together to give a balanced overview of the course, programme or department under review. The main difficulty is that the two approaches are logically at odds with each other. One seeks to give greater influence to the student as consumer; the other says, in effect, that the state has a legitimate interest in the character of what is on offer.

As a result, there may be moments when these two approaches give rise to opposed views of what counts as a high-quality course or department. The students on a course may demonstrate, through the most sophisticated form of student feedback, that they are entirely happy with their experience as students; they may feel that the course is well planned and delivered, that they receive sufficient information about the course and assessment arrangements, and that the quality of feedback given on their own development is entirely helpful. The course data, however, may tell another story. Against comparable courses nationally, the course turns out to be recruiting poorly because it is situated awkwardly in an inner-city institution. Many are mature students and cannot always see the course through to its conclusion.

Hence the non-completion rates, while not spectacularly high, are above the normal threshold of acceptability. The two sets of evaluations perhaps lead to different conclusions and actions because they spring from contrasting ideologies and motivations.

## Evolving patterns of course review

The performance indicators approach and the student perception approach are not the only developments taking place in the evaluation of course quality. The two key issues are, firstly, on what is evaluation to focus? And secondly, where is responsibility for the evaluation process to lie?

An institution's strategy in response to the first question is important because the answers reveal the balance of values held at any one time. Members of, and institutions within, the academic community can be placed somewhere along a research–teaching axis. Scholarship, consultancy, services to the community, widening life chances and many other functions are performed by modern institutions. But research and teaching remain the dominant activities. There is, too, a tension between them in the sense that institutions and individuals – while they may be active in both spheres – typically favour one or the other to some extent. It is hardly surprising, therefore, that evaluations of quality will also tend to give more prominence to one aspect than the other.

In the past, within polytechnics, the greater (though not sole) weight of value was accorded to the teaching enterprise, with the major focus of systematic evaluation being the single course. Attention was paid to the research enterprise, but as a support to the teaching and the character and quality of the curriculum. Where evaluation has taken off in the universities, with one or two exceptions, it has been largely concerned with research. Courses are given cursory attention, it being assumed that the quality of the research endeavours has (I commented earlier) a direct carry-over into the quality of the related courses. The assumed relation between the two has been reflected in the form of universities' evaluation exercises which have tended to be departmentally based.

However, as we also noted, polytechnics have begun to alter the focus away from individual courses to departments. Partly, the move has come about because of institutions' sensitivity to the costs of quality assurance exercises. But partly, too, it has come about because of the linked belief that evaluation of courses in contiguous subject fields must go over much of the same ground, in assessing the competence of staff, their ability to frame valid curricula, the quality of their research and other activities, and the quality of the related institutional resources. Admittedly, the overt agenda is one of focusing on the 'health of a subject' within an institution, as it is often called, rather than research *per se*. Nevertheless, this is prima facie evidence of a convergence in approach between the sectors. Such convergence is perhaps indicative of much common ground in the UK between the interests of the

Council for National Academic Awards and the Academic Audit Unit and offers support for the recently announced intention of a move towards a unitary academic audit body for the whole sector (DES 1991).

On the second point, that of the distribution of responsibilities for quality assurance, each institution has to decide where the balance is to lie between the institution's centre and local units across the institution. We can see alternative models in both sectors of UK higher education. The universities are perhaps happier to accept a system of devolved responsibility, expecting departments to fulfil their duties, even to the extent of arranging periodic self-reviews or reviews of their own courses (involving external members of review groups). Partly, this approach reflects an earlier state of affairs when quality assurance was observed in universities 'more in the breach than in the fulfilment'. Now, however, with the advent of the AAU, universities are systematizing their quality assurance systems, and are at least beginning to lay down a framework of expectation within which their departments are expected to work.

In the polytechnics sector, we are seeing evidence of a move in the opposite direction. When CNAA was pressing institutions fairly hard, and mounting visits to some of the major institutions every week (some polytechnics having upwards of fifty courses), it was understandable that institutions in that sector would develop a well-oiled central capacity for coordinating, directing and controlling all their validation work. Typically, an assistant director would be working almost fully on such activities, with a hands-on approach to overseeing the course validation process, and establishing good links with CNAA. Now, with that pressure lessened in the wake of gaining accredited status (conferred by CNAA), institutions are releasing much of the internal control and justifiably placing it much more with departments and local centres. In one polytechnic, indeed, the centre is heavily engaged in the early stages of course review, actively supporting faculties in their initial discussions of new or existing courses, but then places responsibility with faculties for arranging and handling the formal review itself. Again, therefore, we are seeing a convergence in outward processes between the sectors.

## Systematizing quality assurance

Course review, however, is only one aspect of quality assurance in higher education. For institutions looking to systematize their quality assurance systems, I offer the following 10-point code of guidance:

1. Give a *senior manager* a 'quality assurance' remit, and the time seriously to provide institutional leadership in the matter.
2. *Ownership* – At the local departmental and faculty levels, allow staff a real measure of control over the shape and execution of the emerging quality assurance systems.
3. Establish a regular *cycle of review*, with a published timetable, covering all courses and departments.

4. Use *trusted intermediaries* to act as a filter of communication between the departments and the senior management in shaping the systems.
5. Involve *students* in the design of the systems.
6. Begin with a dynamic *group of interested and motivated members of staff* to propel the new ideas out across the institution, both informally and formally.
7. Seize opportunities and create them to give the ideas *exposure* across the institution.
8. *Disseminate good practice* and give publicity to interesting developments.
9. Enhance individuals' sensitivity to and capacities for improving quality through forms of *staff development*.
10. Develop the *reward structure* in the direction of those who take explicit care over the way in which they maintain and enhance quality at the unit level.

## Conclusion: towards total quality care

Higher education, as an enterprise, is centrally focused on knowledge. Knowledge is more a process than a product, a structured conversation conducted by those seriously interested in getting at truth. There are no end points in the quest for knowledge; only temporary resting stages, before the conversation is joined again. Such observations constitute no apologia for a relativist view of knowledge. On the contrary, they underline that what counts as knowledge depends on an engagement between those seen as authorities in the matter. Becoming educated in that context necessarily implies an exposure to, and a personal engagement in, continuing processes of open-ended and critical conversation.

Any such account of knowledge should be reflected in some way in evaluations of activities founded on knowledge. It would be inconsistent to do otherwise. And, indeed, this has long been the case in evaluations both of research activity and of courses of higher education. The quality of work in either sphere, as with knowledge itself, cannot simply be proclaimed by those on the inside of the activity or measured in any absolute way. It has to be *judged* by those who are competent to do so. The critical dialogue that characterizes the production of knowledge has also to characterize assessments of activities (research and curriculum delivery) which hinge on knowledge.

Seen in this way, the question 'Should course review contain an external component?' is wrongly put. For an assessment by those seen as competent authorities is not external to the activity in the sense of being outside the academic community. Such members of review teams may be external to the department or institution or even to the subject in question. But providing they have relevant expertise to offer, they should be seen as internal to the academic community.

There are bound to be questions about the working out of the details of such an approach to curriculum assessment. Who is to count as a peer? How far, within an institution, should course review be devolved to departments or other local centres? How far can course review take the form either of a joint review of a number of related courses or of an assessment of the teaching and research activities of a department, rather than being confined to individual courses? These, though, are procedural questions. The point of principle is that a critical dialogue should take place between those responsible for delivering a course and another group of those judged competent to form a view. Placing weight on such a critical dialogue also dissolves the question of whether course review should be summative or formative, for it will inescapably be both. That is the character of a critical dialogue.

Giving a central role to critical dialogue also dissolves a final question of whether responsibility for quality should lie with those delivering courses or with some other superior agency. A genuine critical dialogue demands that each of its participants be self-critical; it is the internal dialogue of individual professionals made public. The critical dialogue prompts and makes permanent the internal dialogue. The quality of courses has to be sustained by those immediately responsible for the delivery of those courses. As professionals, they have to go on keeping their own efforts under continual self-critical review.

Quality in higher education demands the establishment of an institutional culture, not so much a matter of total quality management but rather one of *total quality care*, in which each professional is seized of his or her responsibilities and takes care over all his or her own professional efforts. The critical dialogue held periodically with peers in order to review a course systematically cannot itself deliver quality. And neither institutional procedures nor processes can *assure* that quality is attained and maintained. But a carefully orchestrated process of critical dialogue, in which a course team feels that it has an appropriate degree of ownership, and which is organized so as to illuminate the educational processes in which the students are engaged, can be a most positive force in identifying problems, offering possibilities for improvements, and implanting a self-critical culture of continuing care for the students and the quality of their course experience.

# 8

# Institutions for Learning

The central claim of this book is the twinned assertion that higher education is essentially a process of student development, albeit a special kind of development, and that our notions of quality in higher education should begin with this acknowledgement. Where this point is taken seriously in institutions of higher education, there arise two questions. How is the effectiveness of an institution in promoting high quality student learning to be *appraised*? And how is an institution to discharge its responsibilities in *improving* the quality of the learning that goes on under its auspices?

Putting these questions in this way implies that, quite apart from any responsibility that there might be on individual teachers and course teams, there is a responsibility at the institutional level for maintaining and enhancing the quality of student learning. That is to say, we can talk quite legitimately about institutional effectiveness in these matters, just as we can talk about the effectiveness of individuals or specific groups of individuals. Without unreasonably distorting the language, therefore, we can talk of an institution's responsibility in ensuring and improving the quality of its teaching.

If that point is valid, then we are entitled to ask of any and every institution: what is it doing – at the institutional level – to improve the quality of student learning? Also, what kind of an institution, as distinct from what kinds of curricula or teaching practices, might we expect to see where student learning receives a high – perhaps the highest – priority (Wright 1989a)? I shall try to offer some answers to these questions in this chapter. But first, there is a prior question to tackle which I implied at the outset: how can we assess the quality of teaching at the institutional level?

## Assessing the quality of teaching within an institution

There is a general sense that performance indicators, as they have so far developed, are insufficiently refined to illuminate teaching quality in any satisfactory way (Sizer 1989). It is as if, at the moment, there is a barrier

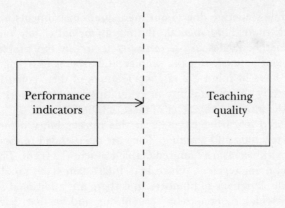

*Figure 8.1*   The impenetrability of teaching quality to performance indicators

between performance indicators and teaching quality, so that teaching quality is something of a mysterious entity (Fig. 8.1).

The implication of much of current thinking is that, with a little more effort, our indicators can be made more sensitive and teaching quality will be more transparent.

I want to argue to the contrary. The difficulty in assessing teaching quality is not easily overcome. Indeed, given our present preoccupation with numerical context-free indicators, this elusiveness of teaching quality is of the essence. This does not mean that we should give up the hunt for measures of teaching quality, but it does mean that our strategies for assessing teaching quality should be sensitive to the nuances of the activity of teaching.

From another perspective, difficulties in getting at institutional teaching quality were also voiced by the University Grants Committee (in its final days), as it developed its range of performance indicators. Indeed, it was often said by its Chief Executive that, whereas it was possible to assess the quality of research performance, it was very difficult, if not impossible, to assess the quality of teaching. Putting the point in that way, however, tells us more about the values of the academic community, or at least part of it, than it does about our ability to assess different activities in higher education. In some quarters, research productivity matters; teaching effectiveness is relegated to an inferior position.

Consequently, we get into a vicious circle. The more we believe in the value of research as the defining activity of the academic community, the more we are likely to look for and spend time in refining our methods for assessing research performance. The continuing work in developing citation indices is just one example of the way in which effort is being spent on appraising the quantity and quality of research. In turn, it is hardly surprising if we end up with what appear to be more sophisticated instruments for assessing research than those we have for assessing teaching.

Still, there are real difficulties in assessing the quality of teaching and learning. While some are due to our inadequate instruments, others are due to something more fundamental. Putting it formally, our unsophisticated evaluation methodologies are a *contingent* factor in the problem; they are capable of being refined. But the problematic aspects of teaching and learning which I have in mind are *necessary* features of their being human transactions. There is an intractability in evaluating teaching and learning which is rooted in the intrinsic character of these activities.

I have hinted in earlier chapters at this intractability of uncovering the character of teaching and learning. They are open-ended processes of human interaction, with necessarily unpredictable elements to them. Those processes of open human engagement (Oakeshott 1989) cannot be taught – with any justice – in the language of numbers. But there are additional aspects of this intractability which deserve to be brought out; and for that, I wish to turn to the work of Karl Popper.

## Worlds of learning

Throughout his work, Popper has been a staunch defendant of the idea of objective knowledge (albeit adopting a sophisticated version of it, for in his insistence on the importance of 'falsification', we never reach truth but continually approach it) (Popper 1975). The problem arises, though, of where objective knowledge lies. Popper's answer is by means of a threefold classification of knowledge. World I, as he calls it, is the external world, that of nature and of objects. (This includes human beings, considered as part of the external world.) World II is the world of human consciousness, and World III is the world of objective knowledge. Popper places objective knowledge in a world of its own because, as he sees it, objective knowledge does not reside in the external world; we cannot see it or smell it or touch it (even though we gain it partly through our senses). But neither, he insists, does it inhabit World II, the world of human consciousness. The contents of World II, our concepts, theories, bodies of knowledge and claims to truth, have certainly been produced by human minds. However, they only count as knowledge when they have been subjected to public and critical assessment, and for that they must have an independence of human consciousness. Objective knowledge is the outcome of a process of continuing critical examination; indeed, it is as much a public process as it is an outcome. In so far as the World III of objective knowledge resides anywhere, it is to be found in libraries, in books and journals, and increasingly on computer tapes.

What bearing does this have on my claim that the evaluation of teaching and learning has an intractability about it which research does not? Research, I want to suggest, is a human activity which takes place in World III, in the world of objective knowledge. Because the products of research have an independence and an externality of their own – they have to be expressed in a durable form (in books, journals and so forth) in such a way that they can be carefully scrutinized, acted on and evaluated – it is comparatively easy to conduct some assessment of the quality of the outcomes of research activity.

Teaching and learning, by contrast, take place in World II. Those activities are centrally concerned not with the advancement or refinement of public knowledge, but with the development of the minds of students. Certainly, teachers often invite their students to engage in quasi-research activities such as working on projects, on library research, on surveys and on problem-solving. But these teaching and learning methods are drawn on because they offer vehicles for the development of the student's mind. The point can be taken one step further. Often, students are given a problem or are faced with an issue which researchers have confronted in the past, but not in the belief or hope that the students will emerge with some original finding. On the contrary, it is assumed that the students will come up with a finding or solution that others have produced before. On this occasion, however, the fact that others have come to the same conclusion is immaterial; for the students are not engaged in the task of widening human knowledge or understanding, but are embarked on a process of 'mind-stretching'. It is the World II of their consciousness, and its development, that is at stake; providing that development occurs, the fact that others have been over the same path in the past and reached precisely the same end-point is immaterial.

But if, then, the effects of teaching and learning are to be found in World II, the domain of the individual student's mind, there is bound to be a difficulty about assessing the quality of these activities. We cannot peer directly into students' minds to see what changes have taken place in their consciousness; still less can we directly judge the character and quality of those changes.

Two objections might be raised against this argument. Firstly, it could be said that in our curricula in higher education, we are interested precisely in objective knowledge and in bringing students into contact with it. What is more, we call upon students for quasi-public display of their learning, through some kind of assessed performance (whether in the written language or in action, as in a professional placement). The students' achievements, it could be argued, only count in so far as they stand in World III of objective knowledge (Phillips 1987).

This line of argument, though, is a misreading of what is going on. For we remain centrally interested in students' cognitive achievements, in the state of mind that they have advanced to (whether expressed in thought or action). The semi-public displays we ask them to give in the formal assessments are not demanded as a means of adding to the world of objective knowledge, but as vehicles, as indicators, of the students' state of mind. We, therefore, find instruments that allow us to make plausible judgements as to their state of mind. And the performances remain, for the most part, only semi-public; they are not genuinely open for all the world to criticize. That is not their function. On the contrary, they are semi-private transactions between the student and those responsible for considering the performance and coming to a judgement.

The second objection that might be lodged against my claim about higher education and objective knowledge residing in different worlds of knowing is that, in examining student performances, we can and do produce marks. Those marks can be expressed in or converted to numbers. In turn, we can produce performance indicators on the pattern of degree classifications achieved on a course, and across a whole institution. So it seems after all as if hard, objective indicators can be produced on the basis of student perform- ances. The quality of student learning can be expressed in a way which inhabits World III of objective knowledge. The difficulty of getting at the quality of student learning disappears.

But this will not do, either. I pointed out in an earlier chapter that difficulties in interpreting degree class results have led to a demand for students' performance at the moment of exit to be put into the context of their abilities at the moment of entry so that a measure of 'value-added' can be computed and an apparently objective means of interpreting patterns of degree results can be derived. That move seems to offer us a re-entry into World III of objective knowledge; we appear to be in the realm of making seemingly robust claims (and in numerical formulations) about the character of degree results and the students' achievements which they reflect.

However, I also argued that that move could not be relied on to carry us very far. Quite apart from the technical problems of relating entry and exit performance indicators (which, arguably, could be solved), there remain stubborn logical problems over the legitimacy of even trying to put scores of entry and exit abilities into a relationship with each other, for we might not be comparing like with like. The move towards value-added computations itself springs from a recognition that exit scores may tell us something about the states of mind reached by students on graduation but tell us very little about the educational process they have undergone. But if my earlier argument was valid, value-added scores have to be put in parenthesis; their apparent sophistication is illusory. Value-added scores do not offer us the firmness they pretend. They are not real examples of the World III of objective knowledge.

My central claim remains undented by arguments which are likely to be brought against it, therefore; and it is perhaps worth repeating it. The claim is that the world of higher education is located in the world of personal knowledge of the individual student (Popper's World II), and it is the quality of students' development and their final state of understanding that matters.

## Bridging the gap

It is possible to make observations and judgements about those states of mind and intellectual achievements (whether expressed in thought or action by the student), and such judgements will lie in the world of objective know- ledge (Popper's World III). But as we try to make assessments about the quality of the achievements of increasing numbers of students, so the gap grows between our World III judgements and the students' states of mind to which they refer (in World II). By the time we reach the numbers of students (typically thousands) and courses (perhaps over a hundred) in an institution, the gap between the students' personal knowledge (World II) and the temptation to say something about them *en masse* in 'objective' numerical statements (World III) is so great as to be unbridgeable. The changes and developments in understanding, in the state of mind of each student, can only be represented in numerical scores for whole groups of students at the cost of failing to do justice to what is going on. Identifying the character and the quality of the state of mind of a single student is complex enough; running together that exercise for, say, the students of an institution as a whole and expressing their achievements in global numerical scores is likely to render much information but little real insight into the situation.

Given this analysis of the character of the acquisition of knowledge and learning in higher education, and the essential invisibility of the development that takes place in our students, the following thesis presents itself:

> We cannot assess directly the quality of learning across an institution. Therefore, we have to find ways of doing so indirectly by assessing the value that an institution of higher education attaches to teaching *and* learning.

There are two points embodied in this formulation which are worth bringing out. The first is that it contains an implicit acknowledgement of the point that institutions as such have a direct responsibility for the quality of the teaching and an indirect responsibility for the quality of the learning that goes on under their auspices. These observations have real force, and have implications for our assessment of *institutions*.

Just as we can ask of a teacher: what is she doing to improve the quality of her teaching? Or similarly of a course team: what is it doing to achieve improved quality of student learning on its course? So we can ask of an institution: what is *it* doing to facilitate the quality of student learning? It will be no defence on the part of senior managers that that is the responsibility of individual teachers, course leaders, course teams or heads of department. An institution, and its senior managers too, has a responsibility towards the quality of student learning. Just as there are actions that individual teachers, course leaders or heads of department can take, so there are actions that can be taken at the institutional level to address the issue. It is not just a question, either, of vague proposals such as developing an ethos, or setting the right climate, important as those ideas are. There are specific actions that an institution, *qua* institution, can take to help maintain and improve teaching quality.

The responsibility at institutional level is particularly important because it is the institution that can set the framework of rewards, establish certain kinds of institutional expectations and offer incentives that have a direct impact on both the value and the attention accorded to teaching quality. The institution is perhaps the most influential actor, for its policies and activities (at the institutional level) show through in the approach and attitudes of hundreds of staff. At the same time, in comparison with the funding bodies, the validating bodies and other national agencies, it is also close enough to the teaching situation to have a real effect. So the institution has major responsibilities which cannot be shirked if the quality of teaching in higher education is to be continually improved.

The second point embedded in the formulation I have just offered is that it looks to uncover definite evidence that an institution is taking the quality of its teaching seriously. In other words, evaluation in this sphere looks to go beyond numerical data (for we have seen how open to interpretation that is), seeking instead specific examples that an institution can point to which are testimony to its determination to improve quality. This, in itself, is important. For even *if* incontrovertible data were available to indicate a high quality of teaching (a logical impossibility, I have argued), it would still be open to us to ask of the institution: but what are you doing to improve teaching and learning still further? It is the evidence that an institution can muster to back up its claim that, as an institution, it is doing much to maintain and *improve* its teaching quality that is important here.

## Promoting teaching quality

In the following sections, I shall sketch out some actions in which institutions, *as institutions*, might be engaged which would help to promote teaching quality. They would also, *ipso facto*, be the kinds of activity that might be looked for if an institution were to evaluate its own success in improving teaching quality, either on its own initiative or as a prelude to an institutional audit by an external agency. I claim no originality for them; they are all to be found in the system, some being employed by many institutions, though others perhaps by only a few.

In what follows, too, I deliberately identify questions that an institution, perhaps in collaboration with an external agency, might wish to pose of itself. They are questions that not only look backwards at an institution's performance, but also indicate policies and actions that an institution might wish to adopt in the future. They are much more powerful, therefore, than numerical performance indicators which are – in that respect – impotent, as we have seen; for numbers and ratios give no guidance as to how an institution *ought* to conduct itself.

### Research activities of teaching staff

The interests of a large proportion of the academic community continue to revolve around its research. This is such a dominant part of the life of the academic community that it is likely to be with us for the foreseeable future, even if the drive to separate teaching and research funding continues, and even if steps are taken to divide universities into research and non-research institutions (Shattock 1991). The incentives, rewards and reputation structure are so weighted that the drive to conduct research will not be dissipated. But the issue remains: what kind of research should be conducted? A concern with the quality of the teaching might reasonably be expected to form one (if only one) motivation so that lecturers' professional teaching responsibilities are reflected in their research activities.

A key debate in UK higher education is over the vexed issue of the extent to which research has any carry-over into teaching. But, the traffic might be the other way in that, in the institution which gives high marks to teaching, teaching can come to influence research.

For example, if an institution is seriously interested in student learning, presumably it should be making some effort to see that the research activities of its staff do bear a proportionate relationship to the courses that it offers. Polytechnics especially will claim that they do this, but perhaps even there those connections between research and teaching – where they occur – are more *ad hoc* than they might be. Even if there is a connection between an academic's research and teaching activities, there are further questions to be asked: are the research activities driving the curriculum, or is the curriculum prompting research projects? Where the findings of an academic's research activities find their way into the curriculum, are they simply bolted on or are they integral to the topics being tackled by the students? Are those findings taught disinterestedly or are they offered as if they were the only way of dealing with the issue in question?

These are questions that a head of department or a course review panel might pose of individual teachers or of the course team as a whole. They are not questions that can easily be asked of an institution. But they point to questions that can be so asked. For instance, to what extent do the institution's committees for research and for staff development (if such committees exist) actually look at the connections between staff's research activities and their teaching commitments when it comes to disbursing resources for research? Is the Research Committee – or the Pro-Vice Chancellor or Assistant Director responsible for research – engaged in any way in encouraging positive links between research and teaching, whether in promoting or supporting research proposals? Does the Research Committee encourage staff to shape their courses, whether through student projects or case studies, to conduct the groundwork useful for future full-blown research proposals?

A further set of institutional possibilities springs from the sense that staff might be encouraged to undertake research into their own teaching activities. This does not have to be especially technically informed; teachers in higher education (in chemistry or law, say) do not have to become skilled social science researchers. Rather, what is at issue is whether teachers in higher education are prompted to reflect rigorously on their teaching activities. This could be felt to form part of a teacher's professional responsibilities: as a teacher, rather than as a researcher, each teacher should – it might be thought – be interested in evaluating his or her teaching methods.

More to the point is the related consideration that to gain an informed insight into the quality of students' learning will require some kind of systematic investigation on the part of the teacher. The teacher cannot assume that the students are generally gaining a deep level of understanding of the material which has been assimilated, or have gained a sense of the ultimate contingency of what they are thinking, doing and saying, or have gone beyond to a position of personal 'authoritative uncertainty' (Goodlad 1976). That knowledge of the students' intellectual development has, in the end, to be grounded in a structured inquiry; and the person best placed to carry it out is the teacher.

More generally, teaching staff – either by themselves or in collaboration with a central unit in the institution – could conduct research into the student experience. One polytechnic, for example, has tested a number of evaluation instruments aimed at eliciting the student experience, ranging from a general questionnaire to 'tracking' the students on a class-by-class basis, following their activities through a typical day (Birmingham Polytechnic 1989). However, knowing how students spend the time available to them, even if backed up by personal logs or diaries, could only be a beginning of this exercise. What is really required is a phenomenological insight into the learning challenges as they are seen by the student, the conceptual apparatus that the student has to bear on the topic in question and the choice of coping strategies that results (Marton *et al.* 1984).

## Course monitoring and review

I argued in the last chapter that institutions have a particular responsibility in promoting the quality of student learning by ensuring that it is explored in systematic processes of course review. In any such event of consequence, the course team should be required to give, at the very least, a statement of its 'philosophy' in relation to the student experience. For instance, how didactic are staff/student interactions? How interactive are lectures? What opportunities for independent learning are there? Are students encouraged to work in groups? Are students required to assess their own work? How much initiative are students expected to take in determining their own learning? To what extent, in courses of professional education, are the professional elements integrated with the theoretical units? And are students' achievements in those professional domains sensitively and rigorously assessed?

Such questions will not necessarily appear on the agenda of a course review. If the ethos of the institution is centred on research, any questioning about curricular strategies may be thin on the ground. Where it is to be found, it may well be questions about resources for teaching and for a course, and nitpicking over the content of a syllabus, rather than searching self-questioning about the aims of the programme, the teaching in the context of those aims, and the curricula themselves. Still less might it involve an attempt to understand the character of student learning and the student experience.

So here, too, we have a domain of quality assurance in which the institution has a role to play: not only in the establishment of sound procedures of course review (see Chapter 7), but even in prompting the kind of self-questioning that should be embraced. This is not a matter of being narrowly prescriptive; it would be entirely possible and legitimate for an institution (which is to say its academic members) to identify the range of questions which might be asked in relation to its particular courses. In a large institution, built on many subjects and professional domains, such a task could be devolved to faculties. There would be no compulsion to follow systematically such a check list. It would simply form a useful *aide-mémoire*, in the first place for course teams to apply to themselves. Its legitimacy would derive from its having been compiled by the academic community (or the relevant section of it) for use on such occasions.

## Staff development

Staff development is a crucial link in an institution's enhancement of the quality of student learning. There is, at least, a suggestion in the research literature to this effect (Ramsden 1983; Badley 1989). Strangely, though, it is doubtful whether – while extolling their support for staff development – institutions sufficiently orchestrate their staff development activities so that they do lead to more effective learning.

Staff development generally fulfils four functions. Firstly, it is used to allow teaching staff to gain further qualifications related to their subject field or to retrain for a new subject area. Secondly, it is deployed to enable staff working in professionally related areas to gain experience in the working situation or acquire other related skills. Thirdly, it is used to pump-prime research or consultancy activities. Lastly, it is deployed to improve staff's teaching effectiveness.

These four functions of staff development can be represented diagrammatically (Fig. 8.2). Any institution's or department's staff development policies could be placed at a particular point in the space of the tetrahedron, depending on the weight attached in practice to the four elements.[1]

There are, though, some qualifications to be made to the apparent tidiness of this analysis. Firstly, staff development practices – as distinct from institutional policies – are the result of a tacit negotiation between the perceived wants of the institution and the individual staff members. Consequently, they take on something of an *ad hoc* character. Secondly, staff development practices will reflect both the institutional mission and the values of the academic staff. So the emphases given to any of the four aspects will vary between institutions, and between departments within institutions.

Thirdly, the last function, that of using staff development explicitly to enhance teaching effectiveness, is – across the system – perhaps the least developed of the four; and in some institutions is virtually absent. Just recently, especially among polytechnics, it is beginning to become more

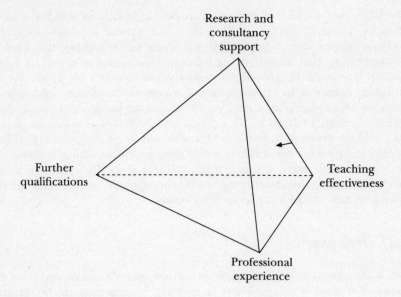

*Figure 8.2*    Institutional staff development policies (staff development devoted to improving teaching effectiveness especially vulnerable)

evident, as the quality of teaching comes higher up institutional agendas (with larger and more diverse student populations). In some institutions, too, with the dominant values of faculty oriented around their research profile, such a function is likely to be overlooked.

But if the use of staff development to improve the quality of teaching has suffered neglect in the past, perhaps a more subtle and almost paradoxical reason can be identified. It is that much can be accomplished in this domain of staff development relatively inexpensively. It does not require costly equipment or year-long staff sabbatical leave. Encouraging self-supportive networks among staff, or running occasional in-house workshops on teaching and learning, does not demand the kinds of resources needed for many of the other forms of staff development. Consequently, for an institution's staff development committee which sees itself primarily in business to disburse staff development funds, such low-cost activities can be easily neglected.

## Institutional ethos

The report of the Committee of Inquiry chaired by Mary Warnock on *Teaching Quality* (PCFC 1990a) talks of 'institutional ethos' as a significant contributory factor. Unfortunately, the report fails to spell out what 'institutional ethos' is, or how it can be recognized or developed. Since 'ethos' is an important dimension of quality, there is a responsibility to spell out the cash value of the term.

We can perhaps get started by identifying questions that might be asked by an institution engaged in a self-appraisal. Is the ethos one that accords high priority to student learning and to the student experience? Very often, this kind of statement is expressed by institutional managers, but how can it be given cash-value? Which is to say: what kinds of activity would be testimony to an institution's seriousness in this domain? How might an institution go about developing an ethos that reflected this claim, and promoting an institutional culture in which teaching and learning, and education in the broadest sense, were taken seriously and were given high marks? The following are just some suggestions, taken from existing practices.

## General educational aims

In the USA, a number of colleges have given backing to their claims to take students seriously by identifying – as a collective exercise, across the whole institution – a set of specific educational aims that the college wishes to promote (for instance, the Miami-Dade Community College (Badley 1992)). These aims are usually heavily centred on the student experience and the kind of general educational capacities on which the college places a high value. The abilities identified by Alverno College include effective communication, analytical capability, valuing in a decision-making context, effective social interaction, and taking responsibility for the global environment (Collier 1984). The point, though, is less the specific capabilities fastened on by Alverno, than the fact that the whole college has identified for itself – in broad terms – the kinds of personal capacities that it feels are important in its students and wishes actively to foster.

In the UK, various national bodies (including the Council for National Academic Awards; BTEC; and the former University Grants Committee and the National Advisory Body acting together) have espoused not dissimilar sets of general educational aims (UGC/NAB 1984; CNAA 1990c). But they are likely to remain bureaucratic statements unconnected to the internal life of higher education unless they are actively taken up in some way by individual institutions. One polytechnic has indeed incorporated the CNAA's general aims into an institutional statement on 'quality' governing its own course review criteria (Baume 1990). But that (CNAA-produced) list of aims is likely to remain just a list unless efforts are put behind its incorporation into the general consciousness of the staff. It is difficult to see how that could happen unless the staff are given an opportunity to put their own imprint on it and to modify it in ways that seem appropriate to the institution's portfolio of courses and general mission.

Even if such an institutional set of general educational aims was to be identified and set down (and in a large institution, those general aims would benefit from amplification at a faculty level), questions would still remain about their take-up within the institution. By what means does the institution keep those general educational aims before its teaching staff, and go on encouraging their implementation? How does the institution see that students on all its courses are receiving an educational experience in which these aims are reflected? It might, for example, try to ensure that its chosen aims formed a potential element in every course review exercise that it conducted. It might, from time to time, lay on workshops for all staff, in which its educational aims were re-examined, re-endorsed and perhaps modified, with their character and significance being duly reinforced by the experience.

## Appointments and promotions

Over recent years, if not yet commonplace, it has become a familiar occurrence at conferences and seminars on higher education to hear a call for teaching effectiveness and commitment to play their part within the criteria employed in academic appointments and promotions. More rarely, though, do we hear guidance offered as to how this desirable objective might be accomplished. It is a relatively easy business to add up – or even assess the quality of – a candidate's research record. Identifying an individual's commitment to teaching and his or her competence in that domain is more difficult.

Perhaps the most productive way forward is to place the onus on a candidate to demonstrate the quality of his or her contribution to teaching. In other words, there might be an invitation to candidates to offer, along with their curricula vitae, a portfolio of evidence backing up their claims. It could contain, for example, sample handouts given to students, evidence of the speed, detail and positive character of comments given to students on their essays, overhead slides, examples of innovative teaching methods, software written for students to use computers as learning resources,[2] student questionnaires and the resulting student responses, any course guides produced, and any indications of the way in which assessments or examinations have been so shaped as to promote high-quality learning.[3]

## Learning week

In this initiative – now successfully run by several polytechnics – the staff of the whole institution are encouraged to experiment for a week with a completely new teaching method for one of their classes. The whole exercise can be promoted vigorously in the institution's newsletter, given the public support of the senior managers (quite apart from departmental heads), and assisted by the institution's staff development office. The students' union can be actively involved, encouraging students to play their part (for many experiments might place considerable responsibility on students to be active in or work together on their learning experience). And the particularly interesting or innovative teaching experiments would also be publicized for other colleagues to adapt to their own circumstances.

## *Institutional newsletter*

Many institutions, indeed, do have a newsletter, but how many column inches are given to reporting on teaching and learning? The occasional report of a student having produced an exciting (perhaps an award-winning) project is all too often lost amidst departmental news of a new research contract or the institution signing a consultancy agreement with a major firm, or simply news and pictures of visitors and events.

An internal newsletter is an ideal vehicle for the institution to show, to its staff and the wider world, that it is really concerned about the quality and character of its teaching. What is really required is a regular report, in some depth, of the way in which a member of staff has designed a successful teaching innovation, written in a non-technical way so that other members of staff can adapt it to different subject areas. Students might also be invited to write about their course experiences (and that writing and publishing activity in itself would be educationally valuable for the student authors).

## *Teaching awards*

There is currently in the UK a major open teaching awards scheme where the approach of any course team can be submitted under a number of headings in open competition (Partnership awards 1991). Quite apart from such a national competition, institutions individually might consider how far they could go in introducing something analogous.

In fact, some institutions have established an awards scheme for interesting teaching innovations. The cost to the institution lies not so much in the awards themselves – which can be quite small while still offering an incentive – but in the promotion, organization and operation of the scheme. The assessment of candidates' submissions, in particular, needs to be handled scrupulously and may merit the institution enlisting an external member on any judging panel. In any event, the judging needs to be seen to be independent of the Vice-Chancellor or Director.

## *Institutional reports*

Easily overlooked is the institution's own documentation, particularly that produced for public consumption across the institution and to a wider audience; not so much the course prospectus but the annual reports, development plans, mission statements and the like. Precisely because the delivery of a curriculum is a relatively secret affair, the institution's other achievements are often much more evident and are more easily reported. Research income, new courses, connections with industry and Europe, and student inflows into and out of the institution are easily documented; but the character of the student experience and the effort being made to enhance student learning must not be forgotten if they are to gain centre stage in the institution's internal life. Again, an institution might gain much from a student offering in its annual report a personal statement of what being a student at that institution is really like.

## The work of committees

Committees are easily overlooked in considering institutional *ethos*, for they may seem to be almost private, local and bureaucratic aspects of institutional life whereas *ethos* is public, general and expressive. But, through the signals they give out, through the evidence they collect, and through the policies they promote and the systems of rewards and sanctions they establish, academic committees can have a profound impact on an institution's ethos.

Obviously, committees are differentially placed in the extent to which they can affect the institutional ethos and particularly as it bears on teaching quality and the student experience. But committees involved in staff development, staff appointments, course evaluation, and academic support services can all play an influential part. For instance, in seeking academic plans from departments, do faculty boards or committees always look at the effort being given over to student learning and the student experience, as distinct from teaching? As well as calling for envisaged future cohort figures, is there a request for indications of, say, a shift from teaching to learning, so that more responsibility is placed on the students for their own learning (suitably supported by the department)? Is there positive encouragement given to departments to identify any examples of innovative or imaginative teaching with which they are particularly pleased? Are steps taken to prompt links between departments to develop joint courses or multidisciplinary curricula, where fruitful connections can be glimpsed by a committee?

The suggestions just given are simply suggestions; institutions will be able to supplement them or substitute other activities more appropriate to their circumstances. In Table 8.1, indeed, I have set out the activities just identified, together with several additional possibilities. The table differentiates the institutional activities in terms of *policy* (what kinds of institutional policy might promote teaching quality?); *management practices*; *activities organized centrally* within an institution; and *ad hoc* forms of *institutional support and encouragement*, all intended to improve teaching effectiveness.

## Conclusions

I have been trying to make one central point in this chapter, which is that, in the improvement of teaching quality, institutions matter. Responsibility attaches to individual members of the faculty, as it does to departments; but it also attaches to institutions. The institution of higher education is more than the sum of its individual staff members or its departments. The institution as such can significantly affect the character and quality of teaching across all of its courses.

Table 8.1 Teaching quality: indicators of institutional performance

| Policy | Management (with or without committee support) | Central activities | Institutional support and encouragement |
|---|---|---|---|
| Appointments and promotions criteria | Use of external examiners | Staff development unit | Student guides |
| General educational aims | HMI reports | Learning week | Student feedback |
| PIs: teaching and learning | Review of assessment methods and general quality | Newsletter | Innovative assessment methods |
| Mission statement | Relation between research and teaching | Workshops for deans and heads of department | Research by teaching staff into teaching methods |
| Public documents | Role of key committees | Staff induction | Peer support |
| Staff appraisal (explores staff's teaching effectiveness) | Staff development | | Quality circles |
| | Course validation and review | | Personal tutors/academic counselling |
| | Member of senior management team with responsibility for quality | | |

There are three subsidiary points, which build upon the discussion of this whole section. First, institutions can and should be assessed for the serious-ness which – at the *institutional level* – they attach to the quality of teaching. Secondly, such an assessment cannot be adequately accomplished by the production of numerical performance indicators, or even by an audit of institutional procedures. Instead, an exploration of each institution's pro-cesses orchestrated at the institutional level with a view to bringing off more effective teaching is called for. Thirdly, that kind of assessment not only should be conducted to produce summative judgements but also, and much more importantly, should be aimed at identifying elements of institutional life where improvements and useful developments can take place.

I have tried to show that there are good reasons which prevent us from easily assessing the quality of teaching and of the student experience on an institutional level. In assessing institutional performance, teaching and the student experience *are* more elusive quarries than published research or funded consultancies. Numerical performance indicators may raise interesting and fruitful questions, but they cannot serve as the basis for judgements.

Acknowledging the real difficulties of getting at teaching quality should not, though, lead us precipitately to abandon the assessment of institutional performance in these domains. As well as looking for numerical indicators of institutional performance – which could only be indirect indicators – we should look for indicators which tell more directly about an institution's educational performance (Yorke 1991c). In other words, we should seek to identify varieties of institutional policy and practice which tell in support of an institution's claim to take teaching quality seriously. If an institution is really investing time and effort in promoting teaching and the quality of the student experience, then it will be able to identify aspects of its internal conduct likely to lead in that direction. (I have given a number of such examples.)

Driving the institutional assessment in this direction – of non-numerical rather than numerical indicators, of institutional process rather than per-formance – has the advantage that indicators are likely to be identified which can directly assist the institution to improve its future effectiveness. As well as enabling the evaluators (whether in-house or in partnership with an exter-nal agency) to assess how much institutional commitment there has been in the recent past to teaching quality and to giving the student experience a high priority in the institution's affairs, the indicators serve as markers for ways in which the institution can improve its effectiveness in the future. So an evaluation organized in this way, as well as being judgementally summative about past performance, will almost certainly have a formative character. The evaluation is actually more oriented to the future, offering positive assistance to the institution as to ways in which – *at the institutional level* – it can enhance its teaching quality and the quality of the student experience.

# Part 3

Improving the Quality of Courses

# 9

## Practice makes Perfect?

### Thought and action

Higher education, whatever else it is, is a process in which the language of knowing is central. The terminology of knowledge – intellect, mind, thought, and understanding – is part of the taken-for-granted vocabulary in which we describe our activities and is testimony to the claim. The frame of thinking that generates that terminology is so part of the dominant conceptual structure of higher education that it is difficult to see that it could be otherwise.

Higher education is also, though, a home for the language of doing, the terminology of which includes: action, skill, performance, practice, competence and capability. The terms of profession, occupation and vocation also have clear connotations of doing, and each of them has some affinity with higher education.

Putting the world of action in the context of higher education has a particular contemporary ring to it. In the UK, the Higher Education for Capability initiative of the Royal Society of Arts, the Enterprise in Higher Education programme sponsored by the Training and Enterprise in Education Directorate (formerly the Training Agency), and the work of the National Council for Vocational Qualifications in developing a competency approach to curriculum development: these are perhaps just the major examples of a current general determination to move the higher education curriculum more in the direction of action.[1] These developments are not building entirely on unprepared ground. The growth of courses directly oriented towards specific professions has perhaps been the most significant feature of the postwar expansion of UK higher education; while approximately two-thirds of undergraduates in polytechnics and colleges are taking courses that are to some degree vocationally oriented. So there is an increasing readiness to tie in the enterprise of higher education with the promotion of right action.

But the willingness to assent to a link between higher education and the sphere of action is not new. Ever since its origin in the twelfth century, higher education has offered a professional education to many of its students. This historic reflection reminds us that weighting attention on the side of action as distinct from thought is not in itself reducing higher education to mere technique and training in low-level skills. Where action is accompanied by knowledge, understanding and reflection, action is a justifiable and important element in higher education.

## Reflective openness

At one level, the connection between the higher profile being given to action and the quality of higher education can be made relatively easily. If we want our students, on leaving their courses, to be able to make their way in a changing world, with its unforeseen patterns of demand and expectation, with its shifting relationships between work and non-work activities (Gorz 1988) and with the complexities of global citizenship becoming more insistent (Collier 1984), a narrow acquisition of pure knowledge for the inner delight it offers (Reeves 1988) hardly seems to provide an adequate basis for framing a curriculum for the twenty-first century. Students surely should be given general frameworks of thought *and* action which enable them not merely to cope with the demands of a changing world but also to be able to act with deliberation and with a reasonable degree of predictability of outcome. That, at the very least, is what we have a right to expect of professionals with a higher education behind them.

These complex expectations generate curriculum demands. Students need to learn that such and such; and even more than that, to learn how to evaluate their experiences and to know how to act effectively in the complex situations with which they are confronted. As graduates, they will not be able to act effectively if they are bound to what they have learnt and understood. In a changing world and in unpredictable professional situations, they have to have the ability to discard their learning as such, to leave it behind them, and to take on new experiences with a relatively open mind. Yes, they have to go on learning, both learning that x is the case and learning how to do new things. But those demands in turn suggest that a higher meta-ability is called for: one which we might term 'reflective openness'. That is, the effective professional has to have a predisposition to develop in both thought and action, not unthinkingly but in an evaluative mode of operation. Constructive, but reflective, cooperation with others: something like this disposition seems a requirement of the age, if its global, intersocietal and interdisciplinary problems are going to come under any kind of adequate attack. But to say all this is simply to say that a higher education curriculum adequate to the modern age has to be one of both thought and action.

It follows from these reflections that, if we are interested in improving the quality of student learning, we cannot derive an adequate strategy which is focused only on the development of the student's acquisition of subject-specific, or even profession-specific, knowledge and skills. General intellectual capacities and the student's wider personal skills also have to be developed.

*Table 9.1* Forms of competence

|  | *Specific* | *General* |
|---|---|---|
| *Educational* | 1 Subject-specific competencies | 2 General intellectual competencies |
| *Vocational* | 3 Vocationally specific competencies | 4 General personal competencies |

# Forms of competence

We have, on this analysis, four kinds of competence in which improvement of learning should take place, given that competencies may be either specific or general, and derived from either intrinsic educational motivations or more extrinsic vocational interests. They can be represented by Table 9.1.

## *Subject-specific competencies*

All courses require students to be able to exercise subject-specific skills associated with their home disciplinary culture. A philosophy student should be able to construct a valid argument; a chemistry student should be able to feel at ease in the laboratory without harming herself or other students (or the building); a psychology student should be able to handle statistics in appropriate ways; a historian should be able to find and interpret archive material; and a student studying a language should be able to speak it.

These are not simple skills. Each skill calls for knowledge and understanding if the skill is to be exercised with effect, in appropriate ways, and with due care. Each skill, too, is integral to the form of life exhibited by each discipline. Being on the inside of a discipline is to *know how* to exercise the relevant skills; but even more, it is to be so familiar with the art of deploying the skills that they provide part of the knowledge of the discipline in themselves, albeit a largely tacit form of knowledge (Polanyi 1966). The skills in question are not an adjunct to the knowledge and perspective offered by the discipline but are central in supplying that inner knowledge and understanding. It is the skills, themselves of a somewhat more durable character than the discrete pieces of knowledge that they produce, which are perhaps the true carriers of the traditions associated with the discipline (Peters 1966; Oakeshott 1989).

Skills and techniques, as terms in the educational vocabulary, receive a bad press in the academic culture. This is for good reasons, since they often presage low-level and relatively undemanding routines, all of which – in their unreflectiveness, lack of intellectual demand and finiteness – are the opposite of the claims of higher education. Yet skills and techniques need not be like that. For the skills and techniques of the disciplines are complex and open ended, call for high intellectual demand, and provide the means by which knowledge and understanding are carried forward. Even more than that, they offer the means by which students develop themselves. The skills in question, being so open ended and demanding, require the students to extend themselves in new domains of personal achievement, in interacting with the material or intellectual environment in which they find themselves.

## General intellectual competencies

The term transferable skills has gained some currency in the academic milieu over the past decade or so (Bradshaw 1985, 1989), and has been taken up as a banner for certain curricular development (such as those prompted by the Enterprise in Higher Education Initiative). The term is not used consistently, however. In particular, a confusion exists over whether the transferability (of the skills in question) is between academic fields *or* between the student's chosen course of study and the wider world of employment.

On one view, the main aim is to foster skills which transcend subject boundaries, so helping students in different subjects to recognize that they have aims in common with each other and, in this way, attempting to break down the artificiality of much of the boundary maintenance within the academic community (at least in its teaching activities). On the other view of transferable skills, the major deficit in higher education is the apparent inability of students to be readily assimilable into the labour market, not having the personal (as against the academic) wherewithal to be immediately absorbed into the culture of the world of work. Here, the need is to identify those general capacities which graduates in their working roles are likely to need to carry them through the demands of the professional environment.

Admittedly, when it comes to working out the detail, the distinction between a transferability of skill between academic subjects on the one hand, and between a programme of study and the world of work on the other, is difficult to sustain entirely. Being adept in the use of information technology, for instance, both is useful across disciplines in the academic world and has obvious value in the wider world. Nevertheless, the distinction still has some analytic value as I think we shall see. In this section, I shall therefore concentrate on the first kind of transferability, that between subjects *within* academe (domain 2 in Table 9.1). To help carry this discussion forward, I shall attempt to restrict my explorations in this section to general skills which are narrowly academic ('intellectual') as against those with a more practical aspect.

As we saw in an earlier chapter, various attempts have been made by national bodies to identify a set of general abilities; and some individual institutions have followed suit (Alverno College 1987; Badley 1992). By and large, those efforts have not sought to distinguish general intellectual abilities from general personal skills (of the kind linking the academic world with the world of work), so we have to pick out one set from the other. Typical of the general intellectual skills that are invoked are: analytical skills; being able to integrate ('synthesize') material and see relationships within it; being able to form critical evaluations of the claims to knowledge encountered; and being able to place one's learning in a wider context. Probably, these general aims are so much part of the teaching culture in higher education that almost all teachers, whatever their subject or level, would claim to be striving towards them in their courses.

All these abilities amount to this: that the educated person should be able to form a view of his own learning experiences, and not be entirely caught up by the experiences of the passing moment. Rather than being captivated by first this and then that intellectual experience, students should be able to stand back and place all their experiences under some kind of organizing framework. Being analytical and being able to synthesize material call for a meta-framework of concepts and theories through which sense can be made of the different truth claims encountered by the student. Whether one is making the discriminations, distinctions and evaluations required by the analytical mode of operation, or whether one is making the assessments of sameness, hierarchy and causal connection required by the synthesizing mode of operation: both demand access to higher order conceptual and theoretical frameworks, under which to bring together the student's discrete experiences.

Two points are worth bringing out from these observations. Firstly, it is a common – if implicit – aim of teaching in higher education that students should come to see that nothing hangs on any intellectual experience as such. No solidity or virtue attaches to a single intellectual experience, whether gleaned from the laboratory, the book or the lecture. The experience is free-floating and unworthy of attention unless it can be put into a wider frame of reference. It is the student's ability to do *that* that counts. Otherwise, being a student would become simply a marshalling and recalling of largely discrete facts, in a *Mastermind* kind of exercise.

Secondly, it is the student's own ordering of her experience that counts, not someone else's ordering. The stigma that attaches to plagiarism (reproducing someone else's orderings) and to cheating (producing one's own orderings, but in an underhand way) is testimony to this point. The student is expected to make something of her experiences; literally, to make something *out* of her experiences. Higher education is a process of personal development: a process of individuals becoming more individual, more of persons, in the sense that they become their own person. They do not take up stances, form views and come to conclusions unless they believe in them themselves.

The process of higher education, despite its taking place amidst highly technical codes already in existence and its involving the students getting on the inside of those frames of experience, is *pari passu* a creative process on the part of the student. Creativity is not to be confused with originality; its central feature is that of authorship and ownership. The students have to form their own views and be ready to be judged by them and by the reasoning they advance for holding those views.

## Vocationally specific competencies

Many courses, as we observed in the last chapter, have a definite vocational orientation. Increasingly, courses are designed, amongst other things, to develop particular kinds of skill in the students taking them. In some such courses (for example, in medicine, in teaching, in languages and in some of the health professions), the practical elements are so important that the students are required to demonstrate their practical competence in order to qualify for the degree award. A licence to practise may be separately granted, but the degree itself will not be awarded unless the practical abilities have been satisfactorily demonstrated. In other areas (for example, in engineering, architecture, accountancy, librarianship and social work), students begin their professional training on the course to some extent, but the practical components are completed in a professional environment after the course, and for this the students receive their professional qualifications. In still other forms of professional training, the undergraduate course is devoted to the academic work (for example, in law and pharmacy) and the professional training is begun after the higher learning has been completed.

Whatever the pattern and approach, however, the student's acquisition of professional skills (assuming it forms some part of the programme of study) merits, and is given, attention in its own right. Sometimes, these abilities are developed outside the formal learning situation on a professional placement (as with librarianship and social work); sometimes (as with law moots, for example), professional skills are acquired within a quasi-academic setting. Where supervised work experience is used, placements are themselves far from uniform. There may be several brief periods of supervised work experience or a whole unbroken year may be used in this way. Differences are also to be seen across subject fields over the extent to which work experience is being integrated with the more cognitive course components.

Apart from differences in the placing of professional experience within the curriculum, there is scope for a more profound contrast over the value orientation of the professional skills to be acquired. Are they seen simply as techniques, to be used on a client as an adjunct to the professional's interests and operations? Or is a more reflective approach adopted, where the techniques are elements of a wider repertoire of interactive capacities, with the would-be professional ready to engage with her clients as persons and ready to share her professional knowledge to assist the clients towards greater self-understanding? Skills can be exercised with greater or lesser judgement, be placed in wider or narrower frameworks of interpretation and perspective, and be ends in themselves or the means to the achievement of self-development and client development.

To sketch in the contours of subject-specific skills in this way is to provide a needed corrective to the work of the National Council for Vocational Qualifications (NCVQ) in its sponsorship of a 'competency' approach to vocational education (Burke 1989; Jessup 1991). Recently, there have been indications from that quarter of a realization that overt behavioural competencies cannot in themselves be an adequate criterion of achievement in the professional sphere (Black and Wolf 1990). There is now something of a readiness to acknowledge that knowledge is important in its own right. But this entire way of conceiving of the issue, of knowledge versus competencies or knowledge alongside competencies, is itself part of the problem. For effective professional performance is not adequately captured by that kind of vocabulary. Rather, we need to embrace the vocabulary of reflection, judgement, self-reflection, interaction, exchange, dialogue, tacit knowledge, knowledge-in-use, informed action, empathy, informed listening, interpersonal communication, and so on.

In other words, we have to recognize that educating for professional competence can never be a matter of supplying students with predefined skills and knowledge to be turned on to situations. Professional action, at the highest levels, is unpredictable and presents situations of such complexity that no straightforward solutions (of some mix of knowledge and skills) may be available in predetermined 'outcomes' (Jessup 1991). Instead, the professional has to puzzle matters out for herself, envisaging possible strategies and actions (some of which may work with some clients and some of which may work with others), and negotiate her way through the situation (whether in the operating theatre or in the architect's studio) to formulate and to choose her own solutions.

A hallmark of the activities which find their way into higher education is that they provide literally infinite opportunities for human creativity, judgement and interpretation. It is always possible to say something more or to do something differently with greater discrimination, finesse or insight. And yet, just this seems to be ruled out of court by the NCVQ competency approach, in which a student has either mastered a technique or has not. It is a yes/no situation; no subtleties or gradations of evaluation are allowed for. Either the identified competencies have been demonstrated or they have not. Admittedly, a gradation of achievement in relation to competencies is evident in the hierarchy of levels which the NCVQ is mapping out in different occupational levels. But what differentiates the different levels is less a complexity in skills *per se* as the incorporation at the higher levels of increasing degrees of knowledge, understanding, and general personal qualities such as leadership.

Skills themselves are, as I argued in the last chapter, inseparable from their accompanying cognitive – intellectual, evaluative and affective – elements. In professional education, those purely cognitive elements can never in themselves provide testimony for professional effectiveness. But nor is it the case, as the current insistence by the NCVQ on outcomes implies, that what a person can do is separable from what that person knows and understands.

This is a paradoxical position for the NCVQ to have got itself into. In its efforts to give prominence to occupationally specific skills, it has ended up by diminishing their character, their complexity, and their capacity to provide genuine educational development. Wanting to drive up skill, competence and overt performance (in a wish to see tangible 'outcomes'), and to distinguish them from thought, mind and critical reflection, the NCVQ approach has succeeded in producing an emasculated conception of professional action. The very object in which NCVQ is interested – effectiveness in working life – instead of being lauded for its complexity and its genuine educational virtues, is seen simply as the capacity to perform. An education for working life, on this analysis, is largely a matter of being able to produce certain kinds of routine on demand.

Central to the NCVQ's notion of competence is that of predictability, the idea that the required performances can be specified and that a programme of study consists of enabling the student to reproduce those performances in appropriate settings. But neither a genuine higher learning nor the heart of professional life is like that. A defining characteristic of both lies in an open-endedness, in the infinite etceterations of response that they invite, and in the opportunities for continuing redefinition of the presenting problems. The task for a higher learning oriented towards professional fields lies not so much in developing predefined responses but in enabling the graduates to cope with uncertainty. It is the student's ability to form adequate strategies for coping with such open-endedness, her ability to put such strategies into effect, and her ability to evaluate them that matter.

## General vocational competencies

These go on under various headings: personal transferable skills (UGC/NAB 1984); enterprise skills (TEED – Higher Education Branch); generic occupationally derived skills (Training Agency – Occupational Standards Branch); and capability (Royal Society of Arts). There is, as we noted earlier, some overlap here with general educational abilities. Typical of the skills that appear in the various lists are: interpersonal skills, the ability to work in a team, decision-making, problem-solving, communication skills, risk-taking and leadership. But some of those, such as problem-solving, communication skills and even the ability to work with others, could also be found in a list of intellectual transferable skills.

To what extent can this distinction, between general intellectual skills and general vocational skills, be sustained? So far as communication skills are concerned, we might try to make a distinction between clear and effective expression in writing (an intellectual skill, perhaps) and in speech (a personal transferable skill, of wide application in the world of work, it could be said). The distinction is far from watertight, however. Any higher education course, even a course of 'distance learning' such as that fostered by the Open University, will provide some opportunity for students to meet and explore their ideas with tutors and other students. Oral interchange, putting a point of view and being able to back it up in the company of one's peers, and being able to listen and contribute appropriately to a conversation, are part of what is meant by higher learning. Through such oral interchanges, through such critical dialogue, opinions and beliefs are tested and the individual student is allowed to mature. Correspondingly, graduates in commerce and industry are increasingly having to make themselves understood in writing. Their control and deployment of the written word is becoming crucial to their professional effectiveness.

So there are definite overlaps between the sphere of intellectual transferable skills and of personal transferable skills. In this sense, there is no sharp boundary between the demands of the academic world and those of the world of professional work.

There are, then, problems of definition of personal transferable skills, and of their connotations. What is meant by the term and what is to count as a personal transferable skill? Different agencies come up with contrasting lists, and it is unclear how much attention ought to be paid to them by course designers. The idea of their being 'personal' poses problems, too. If they are really personal, what is the likelihood of their being transferable? For a person's skill in one social or professional setting may be highly developed; and yet, just on that account, through the personal style and aplomb that goes with it, it may not be easily transportable to another kind of situation. What is socially or professionally acceptable in one setting may receive the cold shoulder elsewhere. Different professional milieux carry their own cultures and value sets; the assumption of professionals that their adeptness in their own professional setting will carry them through other kinds of professional situation may lead to the most unfortunate social blunders and insensitivity.

If there are problems over what might be termed the metaphysical reality of personal transferable skills – one group's clarity of expression may be another group's brusqueness – there are also more mundane problems over their incorporation into the curriculum. Even if genuinely transferable skills can be isolated, and even assuming that agreement can be obtained on the identification of those with overriding value, hard decisions await over the relationship to be achieved between the personal transferable skills and the core curriculum, dominated as it will be in higher education by disciplinary concerns.

It might be thought, for example, that the ability to speak a foreign language is one that should be encouraged amongst all undergraduates. Or again, it might be felt that all undergraduates should acquire some hands-on skill at the computer keyboard. Both could be said to be key examples of transferable skill, valuable to the graduate in the modern world. But even if there were agreement in principle over such objectives, awkward questions arise over the character of the skills to be developed and their link with the student's main programme of study. Indeed, need there be any link at all? Would it be educationally justifiable for higher education students to go off to a language laboratory or to a room full of personal computers simply to acquire a certain range of skills? Is it French for the student's holidays that is to be on offer, or wordprocessing to assist her with her essays? Should there not be some organic link between the transferable skill and the main course of study?

Loosely connected to these questions are two distinct points of view which are not new, but have a legacy stretching back over at least 150 years. On the one hand, there are those who believe that higher education should take as its starting point the world in which its graduates will find themselves, as professionals developing their careers. On this view, curriculum designers should begin by identifying the capacities that graduates apparently are called upon to deploy in posts of high managerial or cognitive or skill demand. The curriculum is essentially to be derived by a sense of the demands of the world external to higher education, which are imported into and translated into curriculum experiences.

On the other hand, there are those who believe that higher learning should take its point of departure from the theoretical and conceptual structures of academic disciplines. On this view, skill development with obvious application in the outside world is justifiable only if there is an internal link with the demands of the disciplines. So gaining hands-on familiarity of computers can be justified provided it fulfils a definite educational need related to forming an understanding of the traditions of the discipline, and not because it is provided for the occupational skill it might offer.

This, in itself, is a nice example of one of the claims I have been making in this book, that ideas of quality are essentially contested. There is no absolute way of deciding between these viewpoints. Both have a merit, a defensible logic, of their own. And improving the quality of student achievement will lead to quite different views, depending on the original set of assumptions about the dominant purposes of higher education.

## What's transferable about transferable skills?

I said a moment ago that the two viewpoints I have just sketched out are loosely connected to the discussion of personal transferable skills. Let us now try to bring these two sets of reflections closer together.

The idea of 'transferability' has gained currency at the present time, as a result of a number of extramural interests colliding. The economy, the demand for high level capacities in society, and the growing complexity of social problems together being what they are, there is a general sense that graduates are not sufficiently fitted for society. In spite of, or indeed because of, the high-quality experience they have had, students are on the receiving end of a certain degree of scepticism of their capacity to make an effective contribution to society. The claims of personal fulfilment and social responsibility seem to be in tension with each other (Barnett 1989).

The UK system of higher education is generally considered to be of high international quality, indeed among the highest, but there remains this suspicion about the suitability of its graduates for the world of work. The high quality is, indeed, part of the problem. For high quality is a synonym partly for specialization: precisely on account of its narrow disciplinary focus (coupled with its selective basis of entry), the UK higher education system is felt to be both extraordinarily successful in terms of the academic worth of its graduates and of limited effectiveness in producing graduates able and willing to take their place in the world of work.

There are two senses of narrowness underlying this angst about the higher education system. Firstly, there is a sense that courses of study are too narrow in disciplinary terms. There is a belief that the knowledge enterprise has been so professionalized by the academic class (Scott 1984), with knowledge having been so differentiated into separate sub-cultures, that graduates are blinkered in academic terms. How can they take an objective view of their own academic interests if all they have studied is one discipline?

The other sense of narrowness springs from a belief that, despite the undoubted links that have been formed over the past thirty years between higher education and the wider work of the professions, commerce and industry, there is still a gap between them. They still retain something of the appearance of two worlds, businessmen (it normally is men) and professional people not fully comprehending higher education in its present form, while many disciplinary fields are driven (entirely legitimately) by their internal demands and interests. And so the sense arises that graduates are 'products' of the academic community and are, therefore, academics *manqué*, rather than persons fully integrated into the values and culture of the world of work.

'Transferability' is inevitably, therefore, a confused term because it is playing several roles and is reflecting many hopes. It does, though, in all its manifestations, derive from a view that higher education in the UK is too narrow, not only in its cognitive content and in the practical demands placed on students but also in the values and attitudes that they are acquiring, albeit tacitly.

The call for transferability is a plea, in other words, for a broadening of content and, more importantly, of purpose. It contains the presumption that academic development, especially at undergraduate level, cannot be left to the academics. The internal logic of the disciplines alone cannot be sufficient in working out an adequate curriculum for the modern age. That approach is doubly deficient. Firstly, it reduces the ability of students across different subjects to speak to each other in academic terms. Their discourse is otherwise limited to the disco; to discussion of worldly events in the coffee bar but in a fashion hardly more informed than that among the passengers on the number 10 bus; or (perhaps even more rarely today) to the gamesfield. Secondly, the disciplinary approach downplays wider social and, indeed, intellectual skills of general value in the labour market, so reducing graduates' effectiveness in contributing to the economy.

There are, as we have seen, problems about the assumptions within these criticisms, problems of identification, of transferability and, indeed, of the very existence of the general skills that are being posited. And there are issues too, as we have also seen, about the similarity or difference between skills which will carry students across subject domains (that is, within the academic world) and those which will carry them from their higher learning into the generality of experiences which the world of work is likely to throw at them. 'How general is general?', we might be tempted to ask. These are real questions to which those advocating the development of transferable skills ought to be able to give a coherent answer if their pleas are to be taken seriously. However, in these closing paragraphs of this chapter, I want to broaden my discussion even further. There are, perhaps, even larger issues at stake.

## How skilful are skills?

I start from the observation that the term 'skills' is frequently brought into use in the current debate. Weaning students away from the narrow technical and intellectual demands of their home discipline is seen by some to be a matter of changing the character of higher learning, so that graduates acquire the kind of high level skills that are needed by an advanced technological society competing in world markets. The language of skills comes through repeatedly in government reports, and in those of its agencies such as the Training, Enterprise and Education Directorate and the National Council for Vocational Qualifications. 'Knowledge' is less evident and is a 'problem' (Jessup 1991), and 'understanding' virtually never appears in the documents issued from the national bureaucracies. The term 'skills' is also frequently coupled with 'industry', though 'commerce' is sometimes used, and so too 'the professions' are acknowledged (now, more frequently, as the NCVQ begins to turn its attention to identifying competencies above level 4).[2] The tendency to employ the term 'skills' is not limited to the national bodies; the academic community has been very willing to embrace this vocabulary.

As we have seen, this language and the initiatives that have accompanied it have been represented as an attempt to overcome the narrowness of higher learning. But this movement is in danger of supplanting one set of narrownesses with another.

The narrowness of the prevailing counter-approach is evident on a number of levels. Firstly, there is an all-too-ready assumption that the world of work is synonymous with that of manufacturing industry.[3] Secondly, there is an assumption that the world of work is the destiny of graduates, in the sense that it is the world of work which gives value to their higher learning. Thirdly, there is the taken-for-granted assumption that activities in the world of work are adequately captured by the description of 'skills'.

These are serious enough charges, but rather than develop them I want, as a fourth charge, to develop a point I have made already. It is that the idea of skill has its home in contexts which are relatively predictable, and where the appropriate response can be specified in advance. The belief that the educational process lies in the acquisition of such 'skills' has two connotations worth bringing out.

First, there is the associated assumption that assuring 'quality' in the world of work lies in the elimination of error (see Chapter 3). If only nasty errors can be eliminated from the production process (the 'Friday afternoon syndrome') then, by definition, a high-quality product will emerge, in which the customer can have confidence. Even if this is a plausible assumption in the manufacturing process, it is entirely bogus in the education business. For error is not just gremlin-like an awkward feature of educational activities, but is intrinsic to them. Even the language of 'error' is somewhat otiose, since it carries punitive and pejorative overtones. In higher education, to the contrary, we want to give academics and students (as researchers and as learners) the freedom to try things out in an open-ended process of experiment. Researchers and students should have the freedom, without fear of punishment, of getting things wrong. In education, people learn through their mistakes. The outcomes are often a matter not of right or wrong, of truth or error, but rather of 'could do better'.

The second reason behind my suggesting that ideas of predictability are misplaced in education (especially higher learning) is that unpredictability is of the essence. If, as many say, one of the defining features of higher learning lies in its promotion of intellectual autonomy, then we have to be prepared for students to form views of their own; and some of those may never have been heard before. In some courses, such as those of mathematics or of logic, or where human safety is at stake (as in medicine or engineering), there are difficulties with this view – though even there, students may be asked to engage in projects or solve problems where there is no one right answer. Indeed, it is one of the conditions of an activity being offered in higher education that there is no one answer that can be known in advance. If there were not such an open-endedness about an activity, it would soon lose its intrinsic interest and fall out of use. Intellectual openness and the development of real intellectual independence demand a degree of unpredictability.

There are, then, a set of reasons why we should be mistrustful of the terminology of 'skills' forming a dominant place in the language of higher learning. The dominant interests behind its recent upsurge are drawing on its usage in other spheres of human activity which are intrinsically unlike higher learning, and its incorporation into the mainstream of higher learning carries an impoverishment of perspective and implementation. It betokens predictability, routine endeavour, non-reflection and finiteness of human action. Higher learning, on the other hand, stands for unpredictability, complexity, critical self-reflection and an infinite range of human action.

To say this is *not* to pour disdain on skills as such. Perhaps all the activities in higher education, whether of a disciplinary, a research, a pedagogical or a learning character, call upon some kind of skill. Returning to our opening observations – whether in the laboratory, in the design studio, at the computer keyboard or at the blackboard working out an equation, or whether producing a philosophical argument, assessing a historical archive or writing an essay in literary criticism – all these activities demand the deployment of skills, often of a high order. That is to say, being effective in a discipline is built on being on the inside of certain modes of action and communication particular to the discipline. Tacit conventions in one sense, they are habits of thought and activity which the practitioners of a discipline learn as the building blocks of being practised in the discipline. The demands built into the acquisition of these skills, certain ways of going on in particular contexts, justify indeed the title of 'discipline'. And the symbol of their acquisition in the form of a degree has, until recently, been a sign to employers that graduates had demonstrable achievements to their names.

The difference between acquiring skills in this way, *pari passu* with getting on the inside of a discipline, and acquiring skills incorporated into the curriculum *because* they are felt to have employment currency is profound. The disciplinary skills are a necessary means to the higher order end of human enlargement, albeit in a narrow area of human thought and endeavour. The skills are simply the tools that enable students or lecturers to drive their thoughts, understanding, arguments and critical reflections forward. The skills are irrelevant in themselves; it is the use to which they are put, the consequent effect on students' own mental progress, and the achievements that result which matter.

In the industrial sense of skill, matters are completely inverted. The effect on the user's mind and the contribution to human understanding are irrelevant. What matters is producing a product to a given formula or specification. Human individuality is either repudiated altogether or permitted within tightly drawn limits, amidst talk of 'leadership', 'teamwork' and 'the ability to work in groups'. Critical reflection, similarly, is tolerated only so far as the boat is not rocked. Kuhnian revolution is not on the industrial cards; still less is Feyerabend-type anarchy (Kuhn 1970; Feyerabend 1978). (In other words, this view of skill would hardly serve even the growth of scientific knowledge, let alone the incommensurability and general mayhem of the rival paradigms in the human sciences and in the humanities proper.)

## Conclusion

Higher learning is being enjoined to come out of the ivory tower, being too confined both as an academic enterprise (the academics cannot even understand each other, *even* within individual disciplines) and as a preparation for the world of work. In different senses, *both* charges are right, but this does not mean that they should carry similar weight.

In the UK, higher learning *is* too narrow. One of the forgotten recommendations of the Robbins Report of 1963 was a plea for the introduction on a wide scale of general degrees (along with the assertion that the fostering of the 'general powers of the mind' was an underlying principle of higher education planning). Despite the introduction in the then new universities of interdisciplinary courses built around cognate areas, the subsequent development of multidisciplinary programmes in the polytechnics and colleges, and the general growth of interdisciplinary studies built around professional education, UK higher education remains by international standards a narrow affair. Not surprisingly, the idea for a general degree has recently resurfaced (THES, Jan 1991).

This is, though, a problem of intracommunication within the academic world, of communication across the disciplines. Neither academics nor their students in different disciplines recognize each other as having anything intellectually in common. This situation is understandable as a result of a divide-and-rule mentality on the part of the state, in which each discipline is encouraged to carve out, defend and fight for its own territory. The upshot is that the disciplines as sub-cultures with their own agendas fly off, centrifugally, without any common sense of purpose.

The other charge is one levelled at the intercommunication problem between the academic world and the wider society. The plea for skills is an inadequate approach to the matter, when what is required is flexibility, a readiness to try new courses of action, and a mobilization of all our intellectual resources, imagination and creativity. The demands of a complex national set of problems and a world order faced with global ecological disaster and famine are not going to be met by a vocabulary of skills and outcomes. Even problem-solving (another of the catchphrases of the pedagogical times) is inadequate, when what is needed is the ability to re-conceptualize issues and problems in quite new ways, rather than taking as given the definitions of problems in common currency.

Practice, by itself, will not then make perfect. To 'practice' has to be coupled insight, understanding and critical acumen. A call for 'wisdom' has recently appeared on the fringes of commentaries on the state of higher learning, and that is a term worth bringing back into play (Maxwell 1987; Midgley 1989). If we put the two together, we re-emerge with something like 'practical wisdom', where practical accomplishment and insight come fruitfully into a relationship with each other. The old distinctions between theory and practice, and knowledge and skills, are no longer helpful. On the contrary, they serve to erect boundaries between human endeavours which have to be brought together if higher learning is really to achieve its potential in contributing effectively to the improvement of the wider world.

# 10

# Communication, Competence and Community

## Theory and practice

In this third section of the book, I have turned from looking at quality at a national and an institutional level to looking at quality at the level of the curriculum and the student experience. In the jargon, I have moved from a macro to a micro level of analysis. More specifically, in this section, I am engaging with some of the current debates and issues which, in part, take their bearing from a sense that the quality of higher learning could be better than it is. Some consider that higher education has, for example, become too much an acquisition of theoretical knowledge and ought to be more oriented towards the wider world if graduates are to be sufficiently effective (see Chapter 9).

In the last chapter, I tried to show that the underlying presumption of these contemporary attacks, that practice and theory are separable, is misguided. Effective and enlightened practice should be reflective and self-critical as well as being based on knowledge. Even 'knowledge' in educational settings is complex, for it calls for a personal appropriation of knowledge ('understanding'), along with critical self-awareness and forms of action, through interpersonal communication and self-projection. An approach to higher education through competence and outcomes – as advocated by the NCVQ – is bound to neglect these dimensions of personal development.

It is worth observing that there is nothing new in these debates. They are the modern forms of the central debate over the character of higher education for the last 150 years. That debate, which fell to Newman to inaugurate in the 1850s, asked the question: what does it mean for higher learning to be liberal? The strength of Newman's reply lay in his emphasis on the significance of higher learning as *higher*. Its centrality lay in the formation in the mind of higher order states of cognition, the acquisition of a 'philosophical' view (as he put it), through which an independence of intellect was acquired. The weakness of Newman's view lay not so much in the repudiation of the claims of the wider world, for he saw that graduates were going into the professions and he wanted an education which would help them to be effective. Rather, the weakness of Newman's argument lay in the tight distinction he drew between theoretical pursuits, from which the higher order perspective was to be derived, and the world of action as such. The world of work was one which higher order learning and reflection could illuminate; it was not, for Newman, a vehicle for deriving that higher order learning itself.

The previous two chapters have carried the discussion forward at a fairly high level of generality. The general proposition that has been examined can be summed up in this way. Higher education is both too theoretical and too locked up in individual disciplines; higher education should incorporate, therefore, curricular elements derived explicitly from the demands of the world of employment in which the graduates are going to find themselves. As I said a moment ago, this contemporary attack contains the assumption that theoretical and practical curricular elements are distinct forms of experience, and it is the paucity of that assumption that needs rectifying. Whether or not certain kinds of practical element are notable for their neglect in higher education is one matter; the assumption that theory and practice are entirely separable is another. It is that latter assumption which I have been trying to attack and undermine.

In brief, as we have seen, academic theory has practical elements; and informed practice in the world of work and of professional life contains (or should do so) not just informed understanding but higher order reflective capacities, analogous to those found in – and sometimes derived from – academic life. Indeed, if professional, industrial and commercial practices are not simply to become ideologies, unreflective carriers of entrenched social interests, then they have to be open to examination by the armoury of intellectual critique. The world being as it is, we need all the intellectual resources at our disposal if its global problems are to come under any kind of control. This means, in turn, that our taken-for-granted practices should be scrutinized, and that we should so order our creative capacities that we are able to intuit new problems, as well as new ways of seeing the old.

To argue, as I have done, that no sharp distinction can be drawn between theory and practice, is not to say that there are no distinctions between them. On the contrary, I have earlier pointed to the tendency to introduce practical elements into the higher education curriculum simply because they are felt to have a useful instrumental value (such as skills in handling information technology or in foreign languages), irrespective of their relationship to the core elements. Without wishing to repudiate those developments as such, I have suggested that there might be a consequent likelihood of the curriculum fragmenting and the higher order promise of higher education being lost. Equally, I have suggested on the other side of the argument that the higher education curriculum, when driven predominantly by the academic interests of a disciplinary culture, can become too narrow in its character. All too easily, in higher education especially, students can be exposed to an

*Table 10.1*   Forms of curriculum objectives

|  | Specific | General |
|---|---|---|
| Theoretical | Subject-based objectives | General educational aims |
| Practical | Specific professional objectives | General transferable objectives |

overnarrow range of intellectual demands, if their programme of studies is confined both in content and in form.

On this analysis, the higher education curriculum can be understood as in Table 10.1.

This is a modified version of Table 9.1 (see p. 155). The main difference is that of now depicting the curriculum in terms of the objectives it is intended to fulfil, instead of the competencies that are likely to emerge. The point of the earlier table was to bring out the different ways in which students are expected to develop a range of capacities, the abilities to be able to do things as well as to know things. Now, the table shifts its focus to the intentions behind the design of a higher education curriculum. And while I have been arguing that the distinction between theory and practice can be drawn too tightly, the table is meant to bring out the point that the balance of the curriculum can be tilted towards propositional knowledge (knowing-that) or towards action (knowing-how).

The table also makes a separate distinction between curriculum objectives that are specific to disciplines or areas of professional life, and those that are said to hold across different domains; but that is an even more debatable distinction, as I have tried to show. For it hinges on the belief that there are human capacities that are subject or context specific, and that can be distinguished from those that are transferable across a range of quite different contexts.

## The changing curriculum

I want to come back to the theory–practice distinction, as conveyed in Table 10.1. My comments here should be put firmly in the context of my argument that the theory–practice distinction can be too tightly drawn. Nevertheless, I want also to point to a development which depends precisely on the distinction. It is that, in higher education over the past 30 or so years, we have witnessed a movement in the character of the curriculum from one that is theory based to one that is centred much more on the world of practice and action. In other words, the curriculum has tended to shift from the top half of the table to one that is located much more in the bottom half. Or to put it another way, the language and conception of curriculum design have so shifted that the horizontal line separating the two halves has moved upwards; and the space for curricula organized mainly around forms of intellectual insight and understanding has diminished. In this sense, the table is an interpretation at the level of the curriculum of Fig. 5.1 (see p. 85) which depicted the ways in which institutional purposes are shifting in post-industrial society.

As the state and its authorized sub-agencies (including the professional bodies) have taken a closer interest in the design of the curriculum, it has been increasingly taken for granted that the curriculum should be oriented towards the worlds of action and commercial intercourse. (I make this observation in a spirit of value neutrality. Nothing sinister should be read into this change alone.)

At the same time, we have witnessed a further move from the left-hand side of Table 10.1 to the right-hand side. There has been a general movement to the effect that subject-specific abilities, whether in the domain of propositional knowledge or in the domain of professional competence, cannot be sufficient for effectiveness in the modern world. Instead, the world of increasing change and uncertainty (whether the cognitive world of the academics or the wider social, commercial and professional world) requires the 'flexibility' – as it is put – to move comfortably across disciplinary boundaries.

Consequently, there has been a readiness to develop curricula which transcend the confines of particular disciplines. This shift has worked at both levels. Academics, as we have seen, are increasingly ready to employ the vocabulary of general educational aims which carry across subjects; there is frequent resort to justifying curricula in terms of such aims as analytical or synthesizing skills, critical skills and communication skills. Correspondingly, curricula organized around objectives derived from the world of work are justified not just in terms of specific skills relevant to particular forms of occupation, but also in terms of much more general abilities, such as working in groups, communication skills (again) and being self-motivated.

So while no curriculum was ever perhaps confined to one of the corners of the table, what we have been witnessing over time is a steady movement by which the weight of curricula has shifted from the top half to the lower half, and from the left-hand side to the right-hand side. This evolutionary process has, in some disciplinary areas, been far from smooth. In certain areas, a fairly fierce contest has taken place, with the curriculum being the territory on which the battle has been fought out. Indeed, Table 10.1 can be read in this way: as the battleground of contending forces. There are not just two combatants but several, defending and advancing the claims of the territories of the four segments.

In the top left-hand corner are the disciplinary sub-cultures, seeking to protect the objectives and curricular forms of their own disciplines. In the top right-hand corner, we find national bodies representative of the whole academic community. In the UK, the CNAA has been the lead body here, but the former UGC (for the university sector) and its complementary body, the National Advisory Body (for the public sector), also took upon themselves the role of advocates for the curriculum as a whole. The joint statement of the UGC and the NAB, in which the two bodies set out a common view of the general educational aims implicit in higher learning, is a nice example of this function (UGC/NAB 1984). (It remains to be seen whether their successors will develop an educational view of that kind; there are signs that the PCFC may, but the omens for the UFC are less clear.)

In the bottom left-hand corner, we find the professional bodies, who identify with a certain range of abilities and demands found in particular professions. It looks, too, as if the National Council for Vocational Qualifications will move into this segment, identifying itself with an approach to curriculum design which starts from specified competencies supposedly required by individual occupations. In the bottom right-hand corner are to be found the agencies, such as the Council for Industry and Higher Education, and the Higher Education Branch of the former Training Agency, which are attempting to orient the higher education curricula *en masse* towards the development of those general abilities felt to be required of their graduate employees by industry and commerce.

On this analysis, it becomes clear that a curriculum in higher education is typically not just the result of a whim of one or more academics. That may have been not far from the truth, even up to and during the higher education boom of the 1960s. Then, the design of a new curriculum could very easily be predominantly located in the top left-hand corner of the grid, with the curriculum decision-making being mainly under the control of the relevant academic grouping. There may have been some seepage into the other domains; for example, under the influence of the CNAA, some course designers were compelled to think of the way in which their course would address the general education aims identified by the CNAA (and enshrined in various formulations within its Principles and Regulations). By and large, though, with the exception of professionally oriented courses (bottom left-hand corner of the grid), course designers could be comfortable in the knowledge that their recruitment was rising, while the dominant orientation of their course stayed firmly in their own territory (top left-hand corner).

Recent years have changed all that. Course designers and teachers in higher education have had to think carefully about the outcomes that they were striving for as the state and its agencies have taken a closer interest in what goes on within teacher–student interactions. The drive from the TEED (formerly the Training Agency) towards 'enterprise' aptitudes and skills (with the incentive for individual institutions of a million pound tranche of new monies over five years) is the most obvious example. Less vividly, but collectively of similar impact, has been a host of developmental projects, and their associated bidding processes, from the TEED and the CNAA; funding from industry for such initiatives as the Management Charter Initiative; and catalytical documents and conferences from agencies like the Royal Society of Arts and the Council for Industry and Higher Education. All these together have had the general impact of pulling the curriculum into the right-hand side of the grid, by influencing those responsible for the delivery of curricula into incorporating into their undergraduate programmes new elements aimed at developing students' wider abilities beyond the confines of subject boundaries. And so the curriculum has moved across the total territory of the grid.

As I remarked earlier, these shifts have not been without some pain and anguish. What is happening here is a clash of ideologies, of the internalist perspectives of the academics against the externalist perspectives of the state and its agencies; of the discipline-bound commitments of individual teachers against the cross-disciplinary perspectives of their institutional managers; and of the liberal sense that an academically derived curriculum was a good in itself against the more instrumental view that a curriculum which did not at least acknowledge the claims of the wider world was going to render its graduates in some senses incompetent to deal with the challenges facing them through their careers. Consequently, the formation of the modern curriculum is much more the outcome of a negotiation between contrasting viewpoints and group interests. (Not surprisingly, interpenetrations from the wider world have been more marked in some disciplines than in others, reflecting in part the strength of attachments by disciplinary communities to specific epistemological paradigms (Boys *et al.* 1988).)

## Communicating communication skills

On a sociological level, the analysis could be left there in one sense. As a matter of fact, the modern curriculum (in any country in the western world) has become the site of a contest between contending interests; and the resulting shape of the curriculum will reflect the disposition of the forces involved, including the students themselves (as their consumer power grows). But at this point, the educational discussion begins to get a purchase. For there are questions to ask about the character of the changes that are taking place. Do they represent a real improvement (as their adherents would claim) in higher learning? Is the contemporary rhetoric of competence, skill and qualifications (as in 'highly qualified manpower') a symbol of a reaching out for a new conception of higher education; and with it, a sharper sense of what 'quality' means in the contemporary age? Or are we seeing here the transformation of higher education, from a cultural enterprise organized around conceptions of the good life and individuals' personal worth, to its being part of the economic superstructure of modern society?

I want to confront these abstract questions by tackling a specific issue arising out of the current debate about higher education. The issue is quite simple: what do we understand by 'communication skills'? 'Communication skills' has become a key term in the debate over improving the quality of learning in higher education, a term that is employed by all the interest groups I identified earlier. Across the academic community, the professions, representatives of industry and commerce, national educational bodies, and national bodies representative of the state, there is an extraordinary consensus that communication skills are important and should be taken more seriously in undergraduate courses.

Typical examples culled from public statements are the following.

In its paper on *Transferable Skills in Employment*, the former National Advisory Body began with this statement:

> The personal or non-academic skills of students, which higher education is expected to develop, include the general communication, problem-solving, teamwork and inter-personal skills required in employment.
>
> (NAB 1986)

A second example:

In its Notes of Guidance issued to institutions wishing to bid for grants under the Enterprise in Higher Education initiative, the (then) Training Agency asked institutions to propose a plan which will (amongst other things):

> Offer the student the opportunity to develop and apply skills including those of communication; teamwork; leadership; decision-making; problem solving; and task management.
>
> (Training Agency 1988)

It will be noticed that, in both examples, 'communication' comes first in the order of skills to be developed.

A last example. As we noted earlier, under the sponsorship of the Council for Industry and Higher Education, a series of *Partnership* awards were launched in 1988, with the financial backing of a number of major corporations, to encourage and reward examples of innovative teaching. The prizes (which in 1991 numbered 24) include one addressed specifically to 'Communications Skills'. The rubric of this one is carefully worded; it is not just any kind of communication skill that is being promoted under this prize, but:

> a full range of the communication skills needed in industry and generally in the world of work.
>
> (Partnership Awards 1991)

What might we deduce from these selective quotations? The first observation is simple enough: students' communication abilities are important, and should be given specific attention in the undergraduate curriculum. There seems to be something approaching a consensus that the improvement of communication skills should be a definite and explicit part of the student experience, no matter what subject is being studied.

Seen against the background of higher education in the UK, the formation of this consensus has been rapid in the extreme. What has led to the formation of such a consensus? What constellation of interests have come together in society, and what driving motivation lies behind such a development in social policy and educational ideas? For such developments do not just happen; they emerge as a response to an identified social problem or demand. This is not the place for a detailed excursion into the sociology and economics of higher education, but we might plausibly surmise that in the background here is a renewed belief in the capacity of higher education to solve certain key problems of social steerage faced by the modern state (Habermas 1976). Against the interpretation given to communication skills in the various public documents, we might also make the further judgement that the problems in question are primarily economic in nature, rather than sociological, cultural or ideological.

The second observation I wish to make on the emergence of this consensus over the importance of communication skills is tautological but is, I believe, still worth making. In the collective mind of those expounding this viewpoint is the belief that, in giving prominence to communication in the curriculum, what is at issue is the improvement of students' communication *skills* rather than knowledge and understanding about communication. It is their overt effectiveness in interpersonal interaction that matters, not their knowledge and understanding about the arts and intricacies of communication.

The last observation is that the communication skills to be developed in our students are typically taken to be those to be found in and required by the world of work. It is the expression of communication skills in a particular domain of human activity that is felt to be especially important, important enough at least to warrant its incorporation into the higher education curriculum.

Later on, I want to develop these three points about the contemporary drive to enhance the place of communication skills in the undergraduate curriculum. For the moment, I shall change tack by trying to sketch out a somewhat larger canvas against which we might develop further our ideas about students' communication skills.

## Styles of communication

It is, I take it, a commonplace observation that effective communication is not merely a technical matter, one of getting the language or the voice 'right' in some way. What counts as 'right' varies between social groups, professions and disciplines and even between societies themselves. We are aware, perhaps, that the appropriate social space between two people engaged in conversation differs between cultures. But the conditions of appropriateness are seldom formalized and made explicit; they are simply acquired as part of one's socialization into a culture.

This point holds both for the professional world and for the academic world. Each firm or commercial enterprise, we are increasingly made aware, has its own style of communication (reflected in expensively designed corporate insignias and liveries). Whether a uniform is required or not, certain modes of dress are acceptable and others not. It is not a matter of 'smartness'. Dress can be *too* formal; the hair can be cut *too* short (compare the form of attire that is socially acceptable for barristers as against that typically found in an advertising agency or among social workers). Correspondingly, language – written or oral – is also context specific, in whatever range of expression is desirable or tolerated. A linguistic style, taken for granted as appropriate in one professional setting, can be quite *outré* elsewhere.

These observations have their counterparts in the academic sphere. The different conceptual schemes that academics live with are an obvious enough feature of academic life. The fields of thought form boundaries across which there is comparatively little trade. The boundary maintenance and resulting forms of solidarity are so strong that academics may well identify with other academics in their subject on the other side of the world more readily than with other academics in contrasting subjects in their own institution. The use of first names might even come more easily to academics in the first category than in the second.

The pervasive character of the patterns of communication of the disciplines is perhaps not always so easily recognized. The manner of communication that academics employ within a discipline is largely unnoticed as having an intrinsic character of its own, having been acquired as part of their socialization into the discipline. By and large, it is a matter of the use of 'tacit' knowledge. The practitioners simply know how to go on (as Wittgenstein put it); they intuitively know the acceptable forms of address and interchange.

Again, just as with dress in professional life, so with language in the academic world: the most subtle of differences can be important to a disciplinary sub-culture. A textual analysis across disciplines of the forms of sentence construction and the use of words would in itself be revealing. It would be surprising if differences did not emerge in the typical length of sentences and paragraphs, in the complexity of sentence construction, in the extent to which recourse is had to technical terms, in the use of personal pronouns, and in the use of active verbs. Other differences are to be found over the preferences for communication in conferences, in journal papers or in books.

But the differences take on even more subtle hues than that. Philosophy, for example, abhors the use of diagrams (the restriction never being made explicit to students). Such unspoken rules are usually not sensed *as* rules or restrictions on the practitioners of disciplines because they are, as remarked, lived as part of the culture of the discipline. The form of life is not simply a *form* of life, but is lived. It becomes the taken-for-granted life-world of the adherents, and plays a dominant part in the identity formation of academics. It is only when a maverick comes along who wants to break the rules that they are brought out into the open and made explicit. For the most part, they are imbibed as one's admission into the secret society of the discipline.

Precisely because each disciplinary community has its characteristic form of communication, difficulties of communication arise when:

1. Academics find they need to communicate to academics in other disciplines;

or when:

2. Academics wish to communicate to the wider society.

So, rules of communication assist communication between those who know the rules (if only tacitly) and are competent in using the rules. But the rules act to reduce or even prevent communication among those who are not on the inside of that form of life.

## Modes of communication

These reflections may seem to be marginal to the centre of this discussion, which is about the improvement of the communication skills of students and the apparent widespread sense in the UK at the moment that graduates are not as effective as they might be in communicating in their professional roles in the world of work. Going back to my philosophy example, diagrams might be anathema to philosophers but might be just what is required in the world of work.

There is, therefore, a dysjunction – as it appears to many, at least – between graduates' communication skills in the academic world and their communication skills in the wider world. Students may come to be competent in expressing themselves in their chosen discipline, but seem to flounder when cast into the world of work.

As it stands, the argument posits a difference between the demands of communicating effectively in the academic sphere and in domains of human interaction outside the academic milieu. And it suggests that the arts of communicating effectively in the former are not treated with the seriousness they deserve in higher education.

Before we tackle the charge contained in the previous sentence, let us muddy the waters somewhat. I have been suggesting that what counts as effective communication, whether in the academic world or in the world outside, varies considerably. There is no one academic discourse which all undergraduates have to master; nor is there a single form of communication in the world of work. In both spheres, there are different worlds inhabited by disciplines, professions, forms of trade and commerce (in the widest sense), and forms of activity, each marked out in part by its characteristic style of communication.

But communication itself, in whatever context it is practised, comes in many guises. It is multi-dimensional, as Figure 10.1 shows. The first point that emerges from this diagram is, to repeat, that forms of communication are numerous. In fact, they can probably never be captured in any absolute way for, as long as there is human intercourse between people of varied circumstances, ages, cultures and technologies, forms of communication will emerge to serve the purposes and resources in hand.

The second point is that, despite the extraordinary variety of forms of communication available and in use in different milieux, the academic world predominantly uses the forms of communication in one of the four boxes – the written forms. Even there, the academic world concentrates its energies by deploying a limited range of written forms of communication, built around a non-personal form of expression.

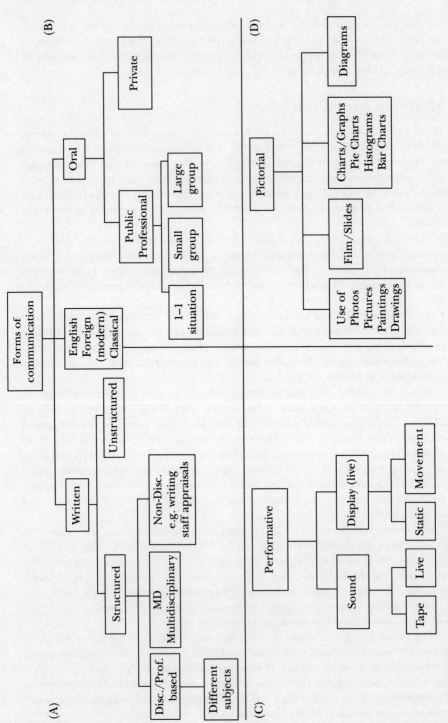

*Figure 10.1*  Forms of communication

From some parts of the higher education curriculum, especially from professional education such as nursing and teacher education, the response to that claim might be that it is an unfair characterization of higher education; and that communication skills from other domains are much in evidence. Even if that were the case (and the counterclaim would need to be substantiated), a further question would remain: how much of the student's communication abilities in all those other areas, including non-conventional areas of written work, is actually assessed? How many of those skills are actually taken into account in determining the student's degree award? For unless such skills fall within the explicit target of the formal assessments, their claimed-for centrality must be in doubt.

So, to sum up the last few paragraphs, we have reached the interim point of saying that, yes, indeed, the academic community by and large operates with an over-restricted view of what communication can be; or, at least, places a set of boundaries around the range of communication skills it expects from its graduates. It is hardly surprising if graduates' communication skills in the workplace are deficient since their undergraduate experience has normally not prepared them to acquire many forms of communication, some of which may be quite valuable in the wider world.

The key question is this. Recognizing the often limited character of the communication demands placed on graduates, is it as a matter of principle desirable that their undergraduate programmes should be so designed as to promote the kinds of communicative accomplishment required by the world of work? Before answering that question, I want to widen the discussion still further.

# Communication and community

I shall move immediately to what I want to say by means of another diagram (Fig. 10.2), in which I try to set out the key structures of communication.

## *Internal to disciplines*

I touched on this earlier in mentioning the way in which individual disciplines have their own quite subtle and complex forms of communication. The educational assumption of a curriculum organized around communication of that kind is that graduates are at least able to communicate effectively within their chosen subjects. This may be true, up to a point.

But even if we have in mind written forms of expression in the curriculum, it remains a further question as to how deep an understanding we expect of our students. Are our examinations always designed to assess and, therefore, to encourage a personal response and a deep insight? Or do they sometimes allow the student to get away with a superficial understanding, a mere reproduction of what the student has come across?

Academic World

| | |
|---|---|
| 1 <u>Internal</u> to<br>*Individual disciplines* | 3 <u>External</u> to<br>*Individual disciplines<br>(multidisciplinarity;<br>interdisciplinarity)* |

Social + Work Worlds

| | |
|---|---|
| 2 <u>Internal</u> to<br>*Social organizations* | 4 Cross-organizational,<br>i.e.: <u>Societal</u> *(Intermeshing of<br>personal, social, industrial,<br>professional and pressure<br>groups)* |

*Figure 10.2*   Communication structures affecting higher education

In other words, at what level of communication do we expect our students to operate? On occasions, it may be quite appropriate for students to have an instrumental understanding of some elements of their course: 'carry out this operation in this situation'. The humanities student that we encountered earlier, using a personal computer with ready-made computer software package, does not need to have an informed understanding of computer science. But perhaps we are not always precisely clear about the level of understanding required of students for every component of their course, and the extent to which we expect them to communicate in those different components.

Consider practical activities that are an integral part of the curriculum, especially in professional education, but also in other areas such as the laboratory or the design studio. How much do we expect students not just to get on and act effectively in those situations – communicating *through* their actions – but also actually to articulate that what they are doing is the outcome of weighing alternative courses of action, and that they are all the time evaluating their own actions as 'reflective practitioners' (Schon 1982, 1987)?

## Internal to the world of work

Most graduates eventually find employment in some kind of organization, whether in industry, commerce, the public services or one of the professions. And, as we observed earlier, it is the students' ability to communicate in that milieu which is at the top of the agenda, in much of the national debate about the development of curricula.

The charge has been accepted by the academic community, at least in polytechnics and colleges. One polytechnic, for example, has been running a competition for its students, in which a dozen students each give a six-minute presentation. As the polytechnic's press release stated, the purpose of the competition is to improve the students' presentation skills; and the incentives are small money prizes offered by a local electronics firm. It is worth noting, too, that in the criteria that the judges have been using, 75 per cent is for presentation while just 25 per cent is for content.[1]

In a further example, another polytechnic, as part of its Enterprise scheme, set up a Communications Unit for the polytechnic. The unit's purpose was to contribute to course design, devise course components, and conduct workshops and simulations to develop skills in speaking, presentations, and interview techniques.

## Societal communication

The main idea here is that of public debate being informed by expert opinion. It is a way of giving expression to the historic idea of a citizenry taking decisions about its fate in a post-industrial society. It is about a genuine participatory democracy where members of the public do not leave matters to the experts but come to an informed view based on the widest range of expert views made available to them.

Examples come readily into view: matters of the built environment, such as the siting of major pieces of new infrastructure (roads, bridges, tunnels and even new towns); of public health, such as the possible dangerous emissions from nuclear power stations, or concerns over bacteria in commercially sold foods; or of the pollution of the biosphere and related matters of personal responsibility (whether through the use of CFCs or of hardwoods from the world's rainforests, or in the emission of vehicle exhausts). These examples remind us that in order to make responsible decisions on many matters of social policy – whether in health, food, or the environment – we need a great deal of information. And we need to be able to communicate that information, both across disciplines and between the academics and the wider public.

There is nothing new, it should be added, in any of this. Intellectuals in mid-Victorian England saw it as part of their role to communicate their ideas, their knowledge and their beliefs to the wider public. For example:

> in the 1830s and 1840s, [Faraday] probably more than any other living Englishman, was the exemplar in the public eye of the scientist. His marvellously clear lectures, beginning with some observations on an ordinary object, proceeding with carefully chosen and staged demonstrations, and ending in remarks on the wonders of science, established the British tradition for popular science.
>
> (Heyck 1982: 55)

In other words, a great scientist engaging in communicating the discoveries of his field well beyond the scientific community.

Men of letters were also conscious of their responsibility in communicating with the public in ways that the public could understand. We find, for instance, John Stuart Mill dissenting from the idea beginning to emerge that an aristocracy of intellect should be developed separate from the public consciousness. On the contrary, he declares that:

> the notion of an intellectual aristocracy . . . while the rest of the world remains in darkness fulfils none of my aspirations and the effect I aim at by the book [his book on Liberty] is, on the contrary, *to make the many more accessible to all truth* by making them more open-minded.
>
> (Heyck 1982: 195, emphasis added)

Admittedly, as Heyck makes clear in his book, *The Transformation of Intellectual Life in Victorian England* (from which those quotations are taken), and which helps to explain its title, that sense of being responsible to a larger public did not last even through the Victorian age. Before it was over, the university system had begun to take form, knowledge was becoming systematized, and intellectuals had framed for themselves a career in the academic world. The academic world could begin to forget about communicating to that wider public.

## Cross-disciplinary

At this point, I need to move back from box 4 to box 3 (Fig. 10.2). I want to suggest that, over the last 100 years, the most significant feature of the academic community has been less its dramatic growth in size and much more its continual splitting off into discrete disciplines and sub-disciplines. Accompanying that development of academic discourse, that professionalization, has been an overlooked introversion, in which the academic tribes have been content to see as their territory simply their own disciplinary discourse and those who inhabit it, rather than the general academic community; and still less the wider society in which that discourse was located (Becher 1989).

And yet, if we are to get to grips with the many profound problems facing us today in society, we must surely find ways of generating a discourse in which participants from many disciplinary backgrounds – or none – can share. If there is to be informed dialogue between the public, politicians, planners and industrialists, a prior requirement has to be that academics from different disciplines talk to each other, and that our students begin to see beyond the confines of their immediate disciplinary interests.

## Conclusions

Institutions of higher education are continually being enjoined to improve the communication skills of their students. Nor is this unreasonable. A student experience which is confined to box 1 (Fig. 10.2) is hardly likely to be sufficient to provide graduates with the wherewithal to operate effectively in the world of work; the curriculum has at least to straddle box 2, if students are to be autonomous and able to fend for themselves.

But that by itself cannot be sufficient, for we are liable to end up by exchanging the narrowness of communication based solely on academic discourse for an equally narrow view of communication based on technique, and technique as defined by particular interests in the wider society. It is the form of communication characteristic of getting things done, of managers communicating their intentions to colleagues and subordinates, and of influencing people. It is the style of communication adopted when one has a clear idea of the outcome one wants to produce, and the object is that of persuading others to see the world as one sees it. It is the communication of people manipulation, of treating people as means rather than as ends, and of strategic communication rather than communication oriented to reaching a consensus.[2]

There is more to communication than that; and I have drawn attention to two specific senses. Firstly, there is the responsibility of academics to accept that their role includes communicating the results of their researches to the public (who largely pay for that research). In this way, the academic community can assist in recovering and promoting a genuine community in society, where there is informed collective debate over the ends *of* society, as well as the means of securing those ends.

Secondly, if we are to bring about a genuine widening of communication, then it has to be institutionalized in higher education in the student experience. Modular programmes of study in themselves will not suffice. We have, instead, to find ways of enabling the student to communicate across subject boundaries. Through the imaginative incorporation of interdisciplinary elements in courses, we have to find ways of encouraging students to reflect on the limits of of their own disciplines, to sense how other disciplines might shed light on what they are interested in, to have some appreciation of the styles of thinking and communication in other disciplines, and to develop a genuine sense of being involved in a larger enterprise of enquiring into knowledge and truth.

Unless we can develop that sense of community within the academic world, we cannot hope to develop community in the wider world. Ultimately, the development of communication – both within the academic community and between the academic community and the general public – is connected with the development of a more rational society, characterized by a genuine conversation, in which communication is used collectively to widen public understanding and the shared identification of public goals.[3] Genuine communication is at least two-way and is open, without any attempt to steer the conversation towards a predetermined outcome. Unless that degree of openness is realized in a society-wide conversation, the society-wide problems which face us will continue to be resistant to solution. For society has both to understand, and collectively to be engaged in, the formulation of strategies of public policy.

What we mean by improving communication skills, therefore, turns on what we take to be the scope of communication, the nature of the public sphere, and the relationship of higher education to society. If instead of skills in specific occupational settings, we think more of assisting in developing a society-wide conversation, in both content and process, the implications for our curricula in higher education are likely to be profound.

# 11

## We're all Reflective Practitioners Now

## Introduction

In this chapter, I want to take up the idea of 'the reflective practitioner' and examine its usefulness for higher education as a whole. The phrase is that of Donald Schon, and was developed by him in the field of professional education (1982, 1987). It arises, therefore, out of a set of curricular problems oriented around the task of producing effective practitioners in professional domains. For Schon, the form of knowledge that characterizes the professional in action is that of knowledge-in-use. An effective programme of professional education should, on this view, build in knowledge-in-use as an integral element of the curriculum.

In this chapter, I shall argue that the idea of 'the reflective practitioner' has applicability to all students, no matter how theoretical their course or how 'pure' the knowledge fields in which they are working. Despite its having been generated to meet curricular problems in certain fields, 'the reflective practitioner' is an idea which has general validity.

## Being professional

To make the argument, we need first to understand something of the character of professional education. This is worth while in itself, since the growth of professional education is perhaps the most significant feature of the development of higher education in the UK over the past thirty years and generally across the western world. In the UK, there are ninety-plus professional bodies associated with courses offered by universities, colleges and polytechnics. Many higher education courses are designed jointly with professional bodies, or receive accreditation from them such that graduates can either claim exemption from professional qualifications or move – on graduation – directly to a position in the profession (even if under some kind of probation or the tutelage of an experienced practitioner).

It follows that ideas which are claimed to be generally relevant to professional education already have wide applicability. But 'the reflective practitioner' has an even more general validity.

For Schon, the idea of the reflective practitioner is a way of capturing the distinctive character of the professional's use of knowledge. Schon does not discount the possibility that the professional may draw on a wide repertoire of propositional knowledge – knowing that such and such. Schon does, though, insist that in addition to the use of such formal knowledge (textbook knowledge), the professional person is able to use a more dynamic form of knowledge. Many analysts go this far, and accept that professionals also use 'know-how'. Schon, however, argues that professionals are distinctive in their use of 'knowledge-in-use' and, with it, 'reflection-in-action'. The skilled professional has at her command a repertoire of strategies and techniques, the capacity to think creatively in context and the abilities to apply formal knowledge, all of which can be combined at will and called upon in order to produce effective action. It is a kind of real-time reflective thinking; not reflection after the event, but reflection during the event. It is reflection as an integral part of the event.

The skilled professional has, therefore, at her disposal at any one time a range of possible interventions which could be made in the particular situation confronting her. To say this implies two further things. Firstly, the professional is able to create in her imagination different possibilities, without putting them into effect in the real world. Secondly, the professional is able to assess them in her imagination, weighing up alternative courses of action and evaluating them against criteria of different kinds.

It follows from this analysis that the effective professional is a reflective practitioner in the sense of conducting a continuing conversation with herself. The conversation has, too, a critical edge to it, for the professional is always asking the question: what if . . .? Being faced with fresh problems to which there is no single answer, and no one right answer, the professional has a responsibility to appraise the situation and formulate an effective strategy (Birch 1988). This will mean discarding some possible courses of action. The effective professional has, accordingly, to be continually self-critical.

## Spheres of critical ability

I want to press further this idea of being critical in the professional context. This should be of help to us in understanding the character of critical thinking in higher education in general. For professional education is, on the surface at least, a particularly complex form of higher education, having to satisfy a large number of educational objectives; and if we can be clear about critical thinking in that domain, its meaning and development in higher education more generally should be reasonably straightforward. Surprisingly, too, although many in higher education claim to be interested in fostering students' critical abilities, we seem to lack any generally held view as to what the development of students' critical abilities amounts to (McPeck 1981;

*Table 11.1*   Domains of the professional educational curriculum

| | | |
|---|---|---|
| *Cognitive domain:* | (a) Core knowledge | (b) Contextual knowledge |
| *Professional domain:* | (c) Professional action | (d) Professional values |

Siegel 1990). So getting clearer about critical abilities has significance for higher education itself (Weinstein 1991).

Let us then start by attacking the problem in the domain of professional education. In professional education, there are four areas in which students' critical abilities need to be exercised (Table 11.1).

These domains are not entirely separate from each other. On the contrary, interesting interdependencies can be observed between them.

## Core knowledge

By core knowledge, I mean the knowledge that a professional would claim as his own in virtue of which he is a professional. It is for the application and deployment of *that* knowledge that clients and employers (not always the same people) turn to professionals for their services. There are certainly worthwhile questions to be asked about this core knowledge, for it is by no means unproblematic. How are the boundaries of the core knowledge defined? Is all the core knowledge to be acquired in the period of initial professional education? How much of the core knowledge is actually brought into play by professionals in practice? I do not, however, want to dwell on these empirical matters, important as they would be in any serious study of professional education as such. I would just note that, however defined and whatever its uses as a central part of the student's curriculum, the corpus of knowledge that constitutes the core of a programme of professional education should receive the same degree of critical reflection that is normally expected of students in higher education.

To say *that* begs the question: what is meant by critical reflection in higher education? Again, I shall side-step the question for the moment. All I am suggesting here is that, however it is defined and understood in general across higher education, students taking programmes of professional education should be expected to exert the same degree of critical detachment as their counterparts on other 'purer' programmes. This in itself is not without point. There may be motivations on the part of professional bodies to want to define fairly precisely the capacities and 'competencies' that graduates of their approved courses should be in command of. That tight prescriptiveness may unintentionally reduce the openness of the experience which the freedom to develop, and to exert, the student's critical abilities requires.

## Contextual knowledge

What is to count as a contextual discipline? A useful distinction can perhaps be made between *liberal* and *operational* contextual disciplines. For example, in teacher education, philosophy, psychology and sociology are liberal disciplines in so far as they are deployed to illuminate the character of the practice of education. They shed light on it, so that the practice of teaching can be understood in broader ways. The attitudes and abilities of school pupils are brought under intelligible frameworks of interpretation. The wider understanding that these disciplinary frameworks offer the professional bears an internal relationship to the professional practice itself.

We can contrast that with the contribution offered by operational disciplines. Examples, as incorporated into professional education, are the inclusion of management studies in programmes of design education; business studies and languages for engineers; law for social workers and occupational therapists; economics for pharmacists and building science for architects. The role of such operational disciplines is a more instrumental and pragmatic one, compared with that played by the liberal disciplines. Here, the motivation for widening programmes of professional education in such ways springs from a sense of the exigencies of the professional situation at the moment. Their inclusion is a means to the end of producing more effective practitioners: practitioners who can deploy their skills in the ever more complicated patterns of professional life, requiring multidisciplinary competencies whether engaging with other professionals or operating in international settings.

This analysis shows why the liberal disciplines have come under critical scrutiny themselves. It has always been difficult to point to their cash value in terms of enhanced effectiveness for professional practice. The usefulness of the engineer acquiring some business understanding or some linguistic competence has an immediacy which a philosophical perspective in the classroom does not. In an age of demonstrable competencies, the broadening of a professional understanding seems difficult to justify. On the other hand, we are beginning to see the widespread integration of units on ethics in management studies and in medical courses (Bok 1986). So there is some kind of resurgence of a liberal perspective in professional education.

These observations enable us to be clearer about the place of critical thinking in professional education. In relation to the distinction just made, it would appear that critical thinking has more of a role to play in relation to the liberal disciplines than in relation to the operational ones. For example, the desirability of an occupational therapist being taught some law (to enable her to understand her legal liabilities in interacting with her patients or clients) is surely of a lesser priority than her developing a wider insight into attitudes to disability that is offered by the social sciences. It is through the liberal disciplines – the nature of which will vary between programmes of professional education – that students are empowered to critique their professional situations, both the wider social setting in which they are placed and the internal character of the role as defined by their professional bodies.

## Professional action

We can distinguish between proposition-based practice (such as the barrister in the courtroom drawing on his knowledge of case law, and formal court-room procedures including the kinds of question that are legitimate) and non-propositional practice (the actual behaviour, including dress, mannerisms and styles of interaction with other courtroom personnel of the same barrister). But even proposition-based action is itself of different kinds. Compare the surgeon's interactions with his patients with his skills in the operating theatre. In both situations, there will be respect (it is to be hoped) for the patient as an individual; and in the operating theatre, there will be respect towards the inert body. But the immediate demands on the surgeon are of a different order, one depending on inter-communication and the other calling for highly complex motor skills, though both are informed and infused by propositional knowledge. As another example, compare the same surgeon's interactions with other professionals in the hospital (where the ward round team can include a physiotherapist and an occupational therapist) and then again with other kinds of professional (such as the police or social workers).

It is often said that a key characteristic of professional work is the conferring of a service to a client (Downie 1990). But the notion of 'client' is far from straightforward. For example, the client for an architect or engineer may be a large public authority, while for the teacher or doctor it may be a single person (pupil/patient) plus the immediate family members who have to be counselled to assist the pupil's or patient's development or, in the case of death, to cope with their grief.

Professional practice, then, is itself a complex of possibilities. It varies in terms of the client and the other professionals; but it does not require the physical presence of a client (for example, assimilating the contents of a file on a client and her case/problem/illness/proposal, and adding to it in ways which another professional colleague can understand; or working on a commission from a client). It varies in the range and character of the knowledge fields on which the professional has to draw. And it varies in terms of the nature of the client. It follows that, while it is important for the professional to develop a self-critical attitude towards his professional effectiveness, being critical about professional practice is itself a complex of critical abilities. In turn, developing those critical abilities in courses of professional education will call both for a careful analysis of those contrasting forms of critical self-reflection, and for a curriculum designed to form the beginnings of such reflection in all its manifestations.

*En passant*, we can observe that the application of the notion of competence to the activities of the skilled professional is misjudged, for it emphasizes what the professional does. But what he does is unintelligible without an insight into what he knows, perceives, intuits, understands, imagines, assesses, considers and rejects. And those mental acts are not separable from or an adjunct to the action, but are integral to it. Professional action, worth the name, cannot be reduced to mere technique, as the contemporary encouragement (in the UK at least) to embrace the language of competence may seem to imply. Professional activity is an extraordinary amalgam of mind and body, of thought and action, of knowing and doing. Accordingly, professional education – if it is to be worthy of its object – should reflect that complexity and interwovenness.

## Professional values

Values enter inescapably into professional life. The belief that professional actions can be conducted in a value-neutral way is itself a piece of ideological mystification. The question is not whether a set of values is desirable for professional life, but rather which set of values is to inform that life.

We might, pejoratively, call such a set of values an ideology. For a set of values, espoused or followed by the members of a profession, can take on the appearance of a belief system designed to justify the profession's self-interest. Placed under the banner of a proclaimed set of values, actions may be given a spurious legitimacy. Be that as it may, a group of professionals cannot help but act according to some set of values. Whether made explicit or followed tacitly, a value-system there has to be, if those professionals are to be able to act in the world with some kind of predictability and to be recognized as professionals with one particular designation rather than another (as nurses, not doctors; as solicitors, not barristers).

Indeed, however explicit a profession's values, there has to be a tacit element as well. Much of that value structure is acquired over time, as the new entrant is socialized into the profession. But the elements of the value structure will be assimilated in the initial programme of professional education. Unlikely to form a designated part of the undergraduate's curriculum or even a clearly identifiable part of its assessment, the acquisition of the appropriate set of attitudes – towards the client, towards the profession itself and towards the wider world – is an essential element of the programme of initial professional education. Learning the profession's code of ethics, if there is one, is only a small part of the matter. What is demanded is the readiness on the part of the noviciate professional to become the part, to take on the total *Weltanschauung* of the profession.

All this supplies a rich field for the exercise of the student's critical abilities. Various strands of a critique directed at a profession's ideology can be identified. One is the role of the profession in society: how does the profession see itself and what are its dominant motivations? In medicine, for example, is the dominant paradigm of treatment technical and scientistic in character, in which the patient is reduced to a set of biological problems and is largely an adjunct to the techniques available? Is proper attention given to possible interactions between the mind and the body? (Bergendal 1984).

Another level of attack is the interests and assumptions embedded in the role of the profession as such. Why, for example, are barristers (in the UK) and solicitors separated into sub-professions? Whose interests are served by such an arrangement? How are potential clients' interests affected?

A third strand is the role of the professional as such, and the character of the relationships with clients. Is the general stance one of serving the client or of maintaining one's allegiance to the profession? How easy is it for a dissatisfied client to find a member of the profession ready to pursue a claim against another member of the profession? To what extent is the professional providing, in effect, palliatives, securing legitimacy for the state rather than meeting client's interests? In social work, for example, is the professional, in effect, being called upon to ameliorate social problems which deserve a more fundamental attack (such as urban decay)? To what extent are the problems presented consciously by the client or imposed by the social worker? In school teaching, is the pupil seen as having legitimate rights? Does the hidden curriculum encourage a relatively passive role for the pupil, acting as an instrument of social control, or does it encourage independence and autonomy?

Lastly, there are questions about the internal structure of and associated values within the profession itself. To what extent is it one of hierarchy, with communication flows essentially one way, from the established consultants and experts downwards? To what extent is the profession seriously interested in understanding how it works in practice (its values-in-use) as against its espoused values? To what extent is progress within the profession one of time-serving or is open to all regardless of age, sex or social background?

## Critical abilities in professional education

My claim so far in this chapter has been that professional education offers particular problems in taking seriously the notion that essential to any satisfactory programme of higher education is the development of the student's critical abilities. If the schema just outlined is valid, the student's critical abilities should be developed in each of the four domains of professional education. And, as we have seen, each of these domains is a complex in itself. All professions are multidisciplinary in character, but each one is based on a particular mix of knowledge fields. In addition, each profession finds value in particular sets of contextual knowledge; is grounded on particular forms of action; and legitimates its activities through its own ideology and value system.

In the analysis just presented, we have also seen how, in many respects, under the overt or consciously acknowledged character of a profession, there lies a hidden face. In each of the four dimensions – core knowledge, contextual knowledge, action, and values – we should be alert to the possibility of finding that things are not quite the same in reality as the message put across by the practitioners. Again, therefore, the complexity of developing the student's critical abilities becomes even more apparent.

So what might be meant in practice by the exercise of the student's critical abilities? In the context of higher education, the critical abilities in question are the student's capacities critically to reflect on his or her performances or understandings. It is not a dilettante form of self-indulgence, criticizing from an uninformed position what *others* are saying and doing. Certainly, the student is enabled critically to evaluate others' activities, theories and social institutions; but it is on the basis of the student's acquired conceptual apparatus, knowledge and activities.

Critical reflection on the part of the student is fundamentally, therefore, critical *self*-reflection.[1] It has, as a necessary component, an internal dialogue in which the student is able to stand back from his or her offerings and accomplishments, to take a view of them by placing them in the context of a wider framework, to evaluate them and to envisage alternative possibilities. Through this kind of open critique, the student reaches a state of intellectual independence, in which he or she is enabled to see through the apparent givenness of a proposition and its theoretical anchoring and so gain a measure of freedom from entrapment by any conceptual schema.

What is being aimed at is a kind of dialectic in which the student, at or near graduate stage, is self-motivated to test his or her own knowledge, practice and values against those of others and against the professional situations to which he or she is exposed, and through those interactions obtain feedback to reflect on his or her achievements in the different domains. Through that iterative cycle of reflection and action, or metapractice (Barnett *et al.* 1987), new possibilities may be glimpsed which the noviciate practitioner is able to test in practice. The student as an embryonic professional thus becomes a continuous practitioner of action research as part of his or her professional practice (Carr and Kemmis 1986).

These reflections on being critical in the context of professional education have curricular implications. Interdisciplinarity, a real integration of theory and practice, and a partnership between the academic and professional communities in designing and delivering the curriculum, press themselves forward as obvious strategies. Equally, the implied level of student autonomy and independence in thought and action point to a curriculum founded significantly on self-directed learning, at least to the extent that the student is challenged to take full responsibility for his or her claims in thought and in action (Boud and Feletti 1991). Working in groups also suggests itself as an important pedagogical method, for it forces participants to articulate their thoughts, to listen to others, to modify their own suggestions in the light of peer offerings, and creatively to work together; and all of these are typical of contemporary professional activity.

Admittedly, the sheer differences in the role and structure of professions as institutions, and in their knowledge base, values and ideological framework, suggest that no global strategy for developing students' critical abilities is to hand and that specific forms of curricula have to be worked through for each profession. On the other hand, if the schema sketched out here has any validity, it is useful to think in terms of a framework which at least has heuristic value for the development of professional education in general. That a large number of common concerns are arising across the professions, as many of them review the structure, character and purposes of their educational programmes, is testimony to the possibility of meaningful cross-profession dialogue (Goodlad 1984).

## The ubiquity of critical reflection

We have seen that the heart of professional education lies in the student taking on the capacities of the 'reflective practitioner'. That is, the student should begin to acquire the almost subconscious abilities exhibited by the skilled professional of being able to monitor his thoughts and actions as they are being expressed. To recap briefly, Schon demonstrates that the effective professional, while acting in a professional capacity, is all the time envisaging and hypothesizing the implications of different strategies, often in a non-verbalized and non-explicit way. The process of professional action is neither, therefore, one of clinically implementing a theory or set of findings from the world of academic inquiry, nor one of acting as if on automatic pilot (when that happens, something has gone amiss). Professional action is a form of 'knowledge in use' *and* 'reflection in action' (as Schon describes it).

I now want to build on that account by developing my claim that Schon's analysis can help us to understand the kind of learning that we want of students in general. *All* students, I want to argue, whether they have embarked on courses of professional education or on traditional courses based on pure academic disciplines, should come to exhibit signs of being a reflective practitioner.

It is a commonplace assertion across academics that they are trying to develop a critical attitude among their students. And in surveys, students indicate that the acquisition of a critical capacity is one of their main objectives for pursuing a course of higher education (Brennan and McGeevor 1988). Increasingly, too, we are finding that employers and professional bodies use the language of critical abilities to describe the kinds of graduate they are hoping to see come their way. Despite its ubiquity in any expression of views about the purposes of higher education, the nature of critical abilities is surely underdeveloped. It is plausible to think that these various advocates for it would, if pressed, emerge with quite different accounts of what getting a student to be critical means. Even that situation might be too much to hope for; we might equally find that those advocates were unable to give any articulated and substantiated description – still less a justification – of what they had in mind.

At this point, we could easily launch into a detailed examination both of the different senses that being critical has and of the range of justifications that might be adduced for giving it high priority in curricular aims. The conceptions of critical abilities held by the multinational corporation, the civil service, the course leader and the professional bodies could turn out to lead to both contrasting curricular experiences and alternative kinds of ability. Instead of taking that path, I want to press my point that the concept of the reflective practitioner is a vehicle of general utility, likely to command wide support in understanding what the development of the student's critical abilities might mean.

At one level, there is an obvious link between the two ideas in the notion of reflection. Higher education is seen by many as a process in which the student is able to bring powers of high level reflection to bear on his or her experiences. But in another sense, the claim that there is a link between the development of critical abilities in courses of (say) history, mathematics, physics or sociology and the idea of the reflective practitioner is rather surprising. The idea of the reflective practitioner has its home in professional practice, and offers an insight into the way in which skilled professionals are able to carry out informed interventions in the situations which they encounter in professional practice. 'The reflective practitioner' is a shorthand description of informed action: it summarizes the complexities of the situations in which professionals find themselves called upon to act, indicates that they are able to call upon a range of strategies in those situations, implies that they are able to evaluate those strategies, and underlines that they maintain a kind of running (albeit silent) commentary on their own actions as they perform them in interaction with their clients.

Seen in this context, my claim that the idea of the reflective practitioner has application to the whole of higher education, no matter how pure the student's subject matter or how isolated the student in her educational experience, might seem far-fetched. For in what senses are the concepts of (i) action, (ii) interpersonal engagement, (iii) 'reflection-in-action', and (iv) 'knowledge-in-use' (picking up Schon's terminology) applicable to the realms of pure knowledge, and to the student's progress on courses which are not intended to prepare her for any career in particular? Is it not over-stretching matters to claim that *this* idea of the reflective practitioner, with its four components, has applicability across the whole of higher education?

## The student as reflective practitioner

I want to argue to the contrary. To start with the *first* of the four elements I have just identified, that of *action*: we want our students in higher education to be able to evaluate knowledge claims and form their own. Those evaluations and claims should be backed up by the student's use of reasoned argument or empirical evidence. The student has to believe in what she says; her truth claims have to be owned by her. It is not the distinctiveness of the truth claims that counts but their soundness and there being a degree of commitment to them on the part of the student. Sincerity is a necessary part of trying to get at the truth. But, in that case, making statements, forming arguments, putting forward ideas or expressions of understanding – and expecting to be taken seriously – become forms of action. In the cumbersome terminology of Jurgen Habermas, they are forms of 'communicative action'.

It follows, too, from the analysis I have just provided, that being engaged in forms of reasoning (no matter how pure) is a kind of *interpersonal engagement* (to turn to the *second* element). Being serious about getting at the truth involves making claims which, in turn, presupposes a listener. The practice of giving reasons and of substantiating what one is thinking implicitly betokens an audience, and a critical audience at that. The audience may be only one person, where the offering is in a written piece of work or a spoken set of statements made just to the teacher or perhaps to one other student on the course. And the student's knowledge claims may be in the form of a tape or film, or a computer program. Nevertheless, whatever the medium and however many people in practice may encounter what the student has to say, the student has to understand that her views only have substance provided they can withstand some form of critical scrutiny by others.

No psychological processes of persuasion on the student's part are involved here. It is simply the logical fact that truth-telling has a hidden 'this is so, isn't it?'; it is an invitation for a listener to evaluate what has been said or offered. Developing an ability to form ideas by and for oneself and demonstrating capacities to offer them as public claims and to be able to back them up form, therefore, an interpersonal engagement.

So far, we have seen that the first two attributes of the reflective practitioner – action and interpersonal engagement – can be applied to undergraduate courses in pure subjects. What of the *third* attribute, that of *reflection-in-action*? The meaning follows from our discussion of the previous two attributes, which are also components of making truth statements.

A student may make a statement with a claim to objectivity, thereby implying a distance between herself and the statement. If the student has fully taken on the presuppositions of the academic community, the statement will be offered as if it has an independence of its own, to be evaluated in itself. But what appears on the written page is the result of a set of mental operations on the part of the student. The sentences, the paragraphs and the total essay itself do not come into the student's mind fully formed. There has to be some kind of internal dialogue, of which the essay is an outcome. What is presented on paper is simply the current stage of the student's *reflection-in-action*, the reflection occurring during the action of conducting the internal dialogue.

This analysis leaves us just with the *fourth* idea, that of *knowledge-in-use*, to explain as a component of the undergraduate's output, even in the purest of subjects. This phrase is perhaps the key to Schon's idea of the reflective practitioner, and is the most problematic element of the four. In what sense can students taking a course in theoretical physics, philosophy or the history of art be said to be exhibiting the kind of knowledge typical of the skilled professional, able to achieve results in the complex situations with which they are faced?

There *is* an important difference here between the worlds of action and the worlds of thought. Schon's analysis of 'how professionals behave in action' is meant to convey precisely the point that knowledge caught up in the complex of professional action, with its pressures of uniqueness, complexity and time, is not just a matter of applying formal knowledge according to technical rules. The differences between the worlds of thought and action are not to be denied; and that is why courses of professional education should be designed to develop students' abilities to deploy knowledge in professional settings. Knowledge-in-use imposes its own demands. Being able to make sense of the problems presented by a client, to understand what a client is saying, to place it in one's own framework of knowledge and understanding, to imagine alternative solutions, to evaluate them imaginatively (without having the opportunity to put them all into effect), to outline the possibilities to the client, and to put the chosen course of action into effect, steering it through to a definite conclusion: all this calls for capabilities not exactly identical with those ordinarily employed in the academic mode of acquiring knowledge and understanding.

Yet the two forms of knowledge – propositional knowledge and knowledge-in-use – are not entirely distinct. In getting on the inside of propositional knowledge, admittedly there are not the same constraints of time and of interpersonal negotiation as in knowledge-in-use. There are, though, some elements differing only in degree, not kind. Students have to make sense of the different voices around them (whether of the teacher, *other* teachers, or fellow students, as well as those contained in books, journals and other media encountered); they have to identify the problem to hand and to create possible solutions; and they have to work through the solution, ensuring that it leads to a satisfactory conclusion (whether in the laboratory, the studio or the essay). These are all analogous to the elements of knowledge-in-use in the professional situation, even if they do not have the manifold complexities and demands of immediacy experienced by professionals.

## Taking stock

We can fairly judge, therefore, that the idea of the reflective practitioner not just is applicable to the practising professional, but also has considerable value in understanding what we can and should expect of our undergraduates in higher education. To some degree, the four elements of action, interpersonal engagement, reflection-in-action and knowledge-in-use – all of which are contained within the notion of the reflective practitioner – are or should be found in the day-to-day experience of every undergraduate.

To recapitulate the argument of this chapter, and to ward off a challenge, it might be said that the last few sections have focused on a narrow range of curricular experiences and on a restricted set of courses. The argument has been about the application of the idea of the reflective practitioner to the purest of subjects. This is indeed the case, for if the idea of the reflective practitioner is applicable to the student studying pure physics or philosophy then it is applicable elsewhere. The idea of the reflective practitioner springs from the fields of professional practice. So the task before us has been not to show that the idea is relevant to domains of professional education (for that is implied in the notion itself); the challenge has been to show its usefulness for elucidating our expectations of the student in those knowledge fields not oriented towards a particular kind of application in the world.

By showing, therefore, that the idea of the reflective practitioner is applicable to the purest of subjects, I have implicitly tried to demonstrate that it has value in understanding our legitimate expectations of all students.

There is, however, one part of the circle still to be closed. In the first half of this chapter, we saw the complexities of professional education. We identified four separate areas of professional development, such that the student should be developing in each of them in order to become a fully effective professional. The domains that we distinguished were: core knowledge, contextual knowledge, professional action, and professional values. The remaining question is: to what extent is the idea of the reflective practitioner relevant to the student's development in each domain?

My main target in this chapter (and in this book) has not been professional education as such, so a detailed answer is unnecessary. Working it through with any adequacy would deserve a book to itself.

However, it follows from the analysis of this chapter that the development of the student's critical and reflective abilities is, in principle, to be encouraged in every domain. And in this chapter we have seen something of what that might mean. In the activities of students' attempts to think, form defensible propositions, and act effectively and properly, there is much for them to be self-critical and self-evaluative about. But the principle has to be implemented with discretion. The imperative for accountants to be self-reflective about their contextual skills (say, knowing how to use a spreadsheet on a personal computer) does not have the same order of magnitude as being self-critical about their abilities to produce a set of accounts with integrity for a client whose business is in a shaky position.

## Conclusions

What are the implications of this analysis of what it is to develop the student's critical abilities? Again, we can only hint at them here. There are implications for the content of the curriculum and its organization, for the way it is designed and presented, and for the student experience.

For all courses, for instance, the space – intellectual and practical – which self-reflection of the kinds identified calls for, points to significant levels of student autonomy and independence in thought and action. This implies an ethos in which students are expected to exercise responsibility for their own learning. It implies that teachers do not teach that x is the case as such; but offer it as a plausible hypothesis, for students' real assent. This, in turn, suggests that formal didactic teaching should be kept to a minimum, with sessions containing real interaction between teacher and students and between the students themselves (on group exercises). Where lectures (that is, continuous unbroken speech from one person) *have* to be given – perhaps for reasons of resource constraints – they should be carefully thought through so that they do offer students critical overviews to topics, as well as attempting to enthuse the students.

So far as professional courses as such are concerned, the analysis in this chapter points to the use of simulated or actual professional situations, in which students' repertoire of knowledge-in-use can be extended, as well as to opportunities to develop self-critical skills in articulating envisaged possibilities of professional action. But there are also questions to be asked of professional curricula about the extent to which they are genuinely interdisciplinary, interweaving (as the exigencies of professional life demand) different disciplinary perspectives; the degree to which theory and practice are really integrated (does the relevant profession assist both in designing the curriculum and in supporting the students on their placements?); and whether there are opportunities for the very real value questions to be explored (to which the noviciate professional is going shortly to be exposed) or is the professional role simply presented as a technical one, of implementing theories and technologies according to well-defined rules?

Higher learning calls for higher order thinking on the part of the student. Whether engaged in propositional thought or in professional action, students should be enabled to develop the capacity to keep an eye on themselves, and to engage in a critical dialogue with themselves in *all* they think and do. It is a higher order of thinking that is called for here, a metadiscourse; and literally a *higher* education, because it is a reflexive process in which the student interrogates her/his thoughts or actions. The learning outcome to be desired, from *every* student, is that of the reflective practitioner.

# 12

# Beyond Teaching and Learning

## The problem with institutions

On one, admittedly over-simple, reading of our present alternative approaches to quality, we are being presented with two contrasting images. One is the dominant image of an institution of higher education and its performance. That image is supported by an evaluation methodology in which, with performance indicators, institutions' performances are compared in terms of their efficiency and economy, their research ratings and their student output. There is an alternative conception of quality as deriving from the student experience, by the character of students' development and transactions, by the way in which students face up to and surmount the challenges put their way, and in the extent to which students are able to take up well-founded positions of their own.

One set of images and definitions is oriented towards overt institutional performance; the other springs from the attempt, though inevitably flawed, to get inside the mind of the individual student and the character of the experiences put the student's way. In so far as it recognizes students' achievements, the first approach considers that they can be aggregated to form a view of institutional worth. The second is mistrustful of that approach, sensing in it a crude reductionism. But what we appear to end up with are two contrasting approaches, with little in common and no obvious logical way of choosing between them. Is a choice between them possible on any rational grounds, on grounds that are more than subjective opting?

One way out of the dilemma is to dissolve it by claiming that the distinction being drawn here is not a real one, that in practice there is no sharp polarization of positions. It is entirely possible and proper to be concerned with both institutional performance and the character of the individual student's development. They are, though (so the argument might run), different interests and can be met on different levels by appropriate forms of action and evaluation. Institutional managers and national bodies have a legitimate interest in institutional performance as such, while course tutors and staff operating in teaching situations should have a continuing interest in the quality of the students' learning. The two interests, indeed, far from being in conflict, are complementary to each other. Improvement in the institution's performance should help to improve the quality of student learning *and* vice versa.

There is something in that argument. Indeed, this book has been organized around a version of it, with a separate section being given to the way in which institutions can promote the quality of student learning; teaching quality is not just the responsibility of individual teachers. It is, though, a *version* of that argument that this book reflects rather than the argument itself.

There is a fundamental distinction which has to be unravelled here. We have, on the one hand, a claim that institutions as institutions can help to improve the quality of student learning. Call this the secondary conception of quality; it considers that institutions play a secondary, though still important, part in determining the character of student learning.

On the other hand, we have a belief that in assessing the quality of higher education, we can achieve a significant level of understanding by looking at the performance of the institutions themselves. Call this the primary conception of quality; it considers that institutions are in themselves discrete entities, that higher education is an attribute of institutions rather than of minds and that, in viewing higher education, institutions are primary determinants of its character.[1]

Both viewpoints are united in the belief that institutions are real entities in themselves, and are not to be reduced to the collection of programmes that they sponsor. But the primary viewpoint considers that quality is an attribute of the institutions themselves. On the secondary viewpoint, this is a pernicious conception. It is all too easy on the primary conception of institutions to focus our attention on the overt and easily detectable features of institutions, such as their resources, their student flows, their staff and even the characteristics of their students, rather than on the quality of the education that they offer.

This is no accidental error. It derives from the view that higher education can be an attribute of institutions rather than of educational processes and the development of minds. Philosophically speaking, to draw a conceptual connection between higher education and institutions is a 'category mistake' (as Gilbert Ryle might have put it). It is to confuse the location where the desired human practice is to take place with the practice itself.

## The paradigm switch

This way of thinking about quality in higher education is probably so deeply entrenched that it will not be eradicated. Against that conception of quality (in which quality is seen as an attribute of institutions), the argument here can be read in two ways. It can be read as a reminder of an alternative vocabulary, a complementary set of conceptual spectacles, with which to view quality. And, given *this* alternative, the reader is in effect being invited to judge whether there is anything in the alternative vocabulary; whether it

offers useful or interesting insights to place alongside the dominant conception of institutional quality. The invitation amounts to saying that there is no
absolute way of choosing between these vocabularies, no way of arbitrating
finally between their presuppositions, for they are *both* justifiable viewpoints.
In the end, the reader is simply (on this reading) being invited to plump for
one view or the other.

There is nothing amiss with that reading. If the claims about the centrality
of the student experience, the development of the student's mind and the
self-empowerment that higher education should bring amount to a vocabulary in their own right, carrying helpful insights to be placed alongside the
dominant conception of institutions as being central, the task undertaken
here will have been worth while. But the argument can be read in another
way as well.

In this age of postmodernity (in which some claim that 'anything goes'), it
may be felt that there is no way of judging between competing claims in the
sphere of human endeavour, for we have no agreed set of cognitive or moral
foundations on which to fall back (Lawson and Appignanesi 1989; Turner
1990). Given contrasting images, conceptions and aims, all we can do in the
end is to opt for one view or the other on non-rational grounds. It is like one
of those optical illusions which, at one moment, can be viewed in one way (as
a rabbit) and, in the next, can be seen in quite a different way (as a duck).
What we cannot do is to see the picture in both ways at once. At the same
time, there is no way of choosing between the possible perceptions; both are
equally valid. It could be felt that choosing between an institutionally
dominated image of quality and a student-dominated image of quality is
like that: both are equally valid, with their articulation representing rival
vocabularies betweeen which there is no rational way of choosing.

In this book, however, I have been trying to develop a stronger claim. I
have been trying to show that it is possible to choose between those two
viewpoints; and I have also been trying to show that it is necessary to do so.

A rational choice between the two viewpoints is possible if we can show
that one rather than the other is intimately connected with the conceptual
underpinnings of higher education. Just this is what I want to claim for the
student-based conception of quality.

It would be tempting to argue that for 'higher education' to take place, a
student is necessary but an institution is not. In other words, it might seem
plausible to argue that 'higher education' is a description of certain kinds
of development undergone by students; and, seen in this way, institutions
and indeed teachers are neither sufficient nor even necessary for 'higher
education' to occur. Stripped of all its institutional trappings, 'higher
education' in essence can appear to be purely a matter of the attainment by a
student of certain states of mind. That characterization would, of course,
leave open what the required states of mind are to warrant the appellation
'higher education'. Putting that difficulty to one side for the present, the
stance here is that we can judge whether 'higher education' has taken place
simply by seeing what capacities of thought, judgement, insight and so on a

student has to offer. On this conception, therefore, it is entirely legitimate for autodidacts to present themselves to a university claiming that they have given themselves a higher education in subject x, and requesting that they be entitled to present themselves for the relevant examination in order to obtain the appropriate degree.

That is not, though, the claim I have been making in this book. Nor is it a legitimate interpretation of the concept of higher education. In this culture, higher education does have an inescapable institutional connotation.

'Higher education' does imply some kind of more or less structured programme of study, made possible by some kind of institution, with appointed staff having some kind of responsibility for the oversight of the programme. Within those three elements of structured programme, institutional framework and responsible teaching staff, many kinds of programme are possible. 'Institution' does not necessarily mean face-to-face interaction. The Open University requires some kind of face-to-face contact with the student, but it would be difficult to argue that this is a necessary part of the concept of higher education (Weidemeyer 1981). Correspondingly, having some kind of structured programme leaves open all sorts of possible arrangements by which to secure that structure. It could, as with the Independent Study programme offered at the Polytechnic of East London, be a programme mainly determined by and formally negotiated with the student (Robbins 1988). And both examples indicate that the role of 'teacher' within higher education is itself diffuse.

So 'higher education' does have institutional connotations; and it has, obviously, connotations of students (or, less tendentiously in an age of increasing mature students, course participants) and their educational progress. Where, then, does this get us in relation to the distinction I have been arguing between an institutionally focused and a student-focused conception of quality? On the conceptual analysis just made, *both* conceptions seem legitimate. 'Higher education' has both student-developmental and institutional connotations and, therefore, conceptions of quality which favour one or the other appear to be entirely plausible; or which simply combine the two.

Either strategy presents too neat a solution, however; and too easy a get-out. Both assume that the student and the institutional components of 'higher education' are equal in weight and in importance. That is wrong.

In our contemporary understanding of 'higher education', both students and institutions might be (and are) necessary components of the logic of the concept. That does not mean that their 'necessariness' is the same.

## The centrality of the student dimension

'Higher education' is both a descriptive and an evaluative concept. It indicates that certain kinds of process are being conducted, with certain kinds of educational end. The ends are connected with the aims of student autonomy and self-realization. Coming to form a view of the world, even in one disciplinary field, to be able to interpret the offerings of others, to have some deep understanding of what others are saying in a field, and to be able to make some kind of truth claim for oneself, backed up and defended orally or in writing with relevant grounds: these are part of the aims of an educational process which aspires to the title of 'higher education'. So calling a process 'higher education', as well as being descriptive, is evaluative. It indicates that the transactions, the forms of engagement in question, come up to scratch to some degree. The term 'higher education' is a qualitative concept in a double sense. It indicates that the tasks have had some measure of success (are of a particular quality) and have led to the achievement of at least some of the relevant aims, aims that have been the realization of certain human qualities.

But (as we saw in Section 1) it is the student who primarily does the achieving. Teachers, laboratories, computers, resources in general, and the total paraphernalia of institutions are secondary to this end. Students have to give something of themselves if they are to engage authentically with the experiences that confront them. It is to be hoped that the institutional framework will have a positive effect in assisting that process. But there is a gap between institutional provision and personal achievement on the part of the student which can only be leapt by a successful act of commitment by the student. Forming an understanding, making a statement, offering evidence, drawing conclusions, making an inference or producing an insight into or a solution to a problem: it is the student's own personal involvement in these acts (for that is what they are) that is indicative of a genuinely higher education.

So while the institutional dimension of 'higher education' may be a necessary dimension, it is still subsidiary to the student dimension. Putting it simply, the institution is a necessary contributor to the realization of the promise of 'higher education', but the promise of higher education is realized by the student herself. It is no false modesty on the part of the teacher who waves aside the thanks of the proud parents at the degree ceremony, observing that 'the achievement was all hers'.

It would be unrealistic to expect that many could be like John Stuart Mill or Mark Pattison, undertaking the gruelling course of entirely private study at home (which we observed earlier), even if under the close direction of a parent. And the programmes of study associated with higher education are so complex and so highly structured, that they have in those aspects alone become such that they could hardly be undertaken except in an institutional setting of some kind. Our language recognizes this. We cannot seriously employ the vocabulary of 'higher education' in the absence of a presumption of fairly large and complex institutions, providing a number of thought-out programmes of some duration and normally leading to a recognized qualification. But this inescapable institutional component remains subsidiary to the part played by the individual student.

The distinction can perhaps be expressed in this way. Students are a logically necessary part of the concept of higher education. Institutions are an empirical component of the term, but bearing a statistical probability approaching certainty that, wherever higher education of quality is going on, there we will find responsible institutions too.

# Beyond teaching

The discussion in this chapter may so far have seemed purely conceptual, but it has practical bite. If we start from the viewpoint that quality is an attribute of the student experience, then we have to ask of any other surrounding activity, supporting structure or resource whether it is aiding or impeding the student experience. We cannot take it for granted that any other entity is worth while, that is, it is making a positive contribution to this end. This seemingly benign reflection strikes at the heart of the academic enterprise. For instance, the two activities of teaching and research cannot be assumed to be of value in themselves. We are entitled to ask of any teaching or research activity whether it is having a positive contribution or effect on the student experience. There will be, of course, other perfectly acceptable reasons for engaging in research, even if the link is not demonstrable. But it is difficult to justify teaching if it cannot be reasonably argued that the student's development is being enhanced as a result of the teaching he or she experiences.

A stark and unsettling question should be continually in front of every teacher in higher education: would this student have made similar or *even better* progress had I not been teaching her? Of course, the question is not susceptible to any absolute answer. Evidence supporting an answer one way or another is not easy to produce. Students vary as individuals in their reliance on others, and in what they gain from others. And it is impossible to judge the effect of any one teaching session as against the total course unit in which it is set. Nevertheless, the question is worth keeping in the front of the teacher's mind, as he approaches his teaching commitments. It serves as a salutary reminder that it cannot be assumed from the fact that teaching is taking place that learning is also taking place.

Indeed, when we see the differences in teaching patterns across subjects and sectors, the suspicion grows that teaching may often be redundant. Historically, the polytechnic sector has taught more than the university sector; and, across higher education as a whole, substantially more teaching has taken place in the sciences and technologies than in the social sciences and the humanities. Admittedly, much of the former takes place in laboratories; indeed, subjects requiring studio work, such as art and design and architecture, have always required a high commitment of students' time. Nevertheless, the lecture load of students in the sciences and technological subjects is usually relatively still high.

The main problem is not just that so much of the student's time is committed that he has relatively little space to himself for his own explorations in and around the subject (though that is a serious enough matter in itself). The first and most immediate problem is that there is a tendency in some subjects to so overload the curriculum that the student is unable to assimilate with any degree of real understanding what is put in front of him.

The consequence is that teaching, in these circumstances, is actually counterproductive. Real learning, in the sense of a deep understanding and personal insight on the part of the student, becomes impossible as the student struggles simply to cover the material in a superficial way so that it can be reproduced under examination conditions. In other words, an ill-thought-through teaching strategy produces an entirely inadequate quality of learning. It follows that the quality of student learning is not a random variable but is affected by the character of the total learning environment. Teaching may be able to improve the quality of the student's learning; but – the teacher should remind himself – it may also impair the quality of the student's learning. In other words, the student's learning might – in some situations – be better if she were getting on under her own steam.

Support for these observations comes from two directions. Firstly, it comes from reports beginning to be produced by associations of subject teachers, which are starting to be concerned about the quality of students' learning in their disciplinary fields. In the UK, in both physics and engineering, for example, reports have appeared by the relevant professional associations admitting that the undergraduate courses in their fields have been seriously overpacked with factual material, so that the student inevitably struggles simply to assimilate the information on the most superficial level (Sparkes 1989; Institute of Physics 1990). Any kind of deep understanding involving a personal appropriation of the material is rendered impossible.

The second source of evidence for the way in which teaching can be counterproductive comes from international research on student learning over the past twenty years. The empirical work in question has been conducted in different kinds of institution, at different levels of work and in different subjects (Marton *et al.* 1984; Ramsden 1988). It has generated a rich field of insights and concepts, out of which I wish to pick just two.

The first set of findings is that students develop different learning approaches which lead, in turn, to contrasting learning experiences. The learning strategies which students adopt in practice have been distinguished around two polarities: one is a contrast between deep and surface understanding, and the other between a holistic and an atomistic understanding of their learning experiences. The terminology is relatively self-evident, and is indicative of different motivations on the part of the student. Is the student intent just on mastering sufficient material so that it can be reproduced under examination situations? In that case, a surface learning rather than a deep learning strategy will probably be adopted. Is the student trying just to keep his head above water in coping with an overloaded curriculum? Faced with trying to understand this week's material before the topic on the curriculum changes next week, the student is likely to adopt an atomistic approach (learning this item as a discrete unit) rather than stepping back and trying to make connections across his learning, so employing a more holistic approach.

The important point about these findings is that the quality of the student's learning experience neither is given nor occurs randomly, but arises from the learning style and motivation of the student. To that observation, we have to add another and even more significant finding.

Those different learning styles are not just a matter of different personality structures among students, but are much more the outcome of the kind of curriculum experience with which students are faced (Ramsden 1986). Their learning style is a rational attempt to come to terms with the demands placed on them. One student taking a two-subject course may adopt a deep learning approach for one subject and a surface approach for the other. Against findings of this kind, giving students study skills courses can only be a palliative (Entwistle 1989). What is required is a fundamental rethink on the part of those who design the course, for two reasons. Firstly, in *higher* education, the aim should be directly to prompt higher order analytical and critical abilities which necessarily require a deep learning approach. Secondly, there should be a willingness to give students greater insight into their own learning strategies ('metacognition', as it is termed (Baird 1988)). In this way, students can be more in command of their own learning styles and they will be enabled to maximize the effectiveness of their own learning.

To do all these things, we have to find ways of reducing the pressures that produce 'reproducing', 'surface' and 'atomistic' learning responses, so loosening the student's concern merely to assimilate factual material in order to reproduce it in closed examinations.[2] A number of teaching strategies need to be pursued at once. The anxiety that prompts students to adopt 'reproducing' behaviours has to be lightened by ensuring that the sheer workload and assessment demands do not overburden students. Secondly, the learning tasks or experiences should be such as to challenge the students, so as to demand real thought and judgement from them. Factual recall will still be important, particularly in some professional subjects and in the sciences and technologies. But it is the depth to which they comprehend those facts, the connections they make with them, and the ways in which they are used that are important. Thirdly, the students need to feel that they are to some degree in command of their own learning, and are active in its construction. 'Deep learning' is unlikely to take place if students feel uninvolved, having passively to digest what is put before them. Independent learning, whether as individuals or in groups, should be encouraged (Boud and Feletti 1991). Lastly, ways will need to be found of encouraging students to be self-reflective and self-critical. This demand follows from the sense that higher education is, in part, the development of an individual's intellectual autonomy and, for that, some degree of self-referential capacity is required.

It could be said that nothing especially enlightening has been said in the last few paragraphs. They could be caricatured as saying: for learning of a high quality to take place, teaching of a high quality has to be conducted. That, in itself, is worth saying as a continuing reminder that there is a link between the quality of learning and the quality of teaching. But these last paragraphs have implied other things as well.

The first is that high-quality learning can take place without teaching, and that teaching can impair the quality of learning. Secondly, significant implications for teaching and learning derive from our prior conceptions of what counts as higher education.

Thirdly, there are implications for our forms of student assessment, in both their content and their general pattern. If we are serious about promoting higher order thought and judgement in our students, then our assessments have to be designed to prompt exemplifications of such states of mind. Even so-called problem-solving tests can all too easily call for limited and fairly routine skills. Equally, having to sit up to ten closed examinations in the space of two weeks will call forth learning behaviours designed to satisfy those conditions. Indeed, the evidence is that students, in forming their learning strategies for a course of study, will take the examinations as their point of departure and assess what has to be achieved in order to avoid fail-ure (Ramsden 1988; Entwistle 1989). So whatever fine words there may be in the accompanying course booklet about promoting independent and critical thinking, if the students feel that conventional, reproducing behaviours are in practice being required by the examinations, or that – given the curriculum load – that is the way to avoid failure, then those are the learning behaviours that will result.

The pattern, pacing, scope, texture and style of the examinations need to be crafted carefully, therefore, and kept continually under review against the stated and informal aims and objectives of the course, so that they have a beneficial influence on the curriculum. For it follows that if examinations can have a negative effect, calling forth low-level cognitive processes, they can also have a positive effect, encouraging the sought-after states of mind and achievement. The assessment regimen can be part of the hidden curriculum, having a controlling or policing function which ensures that students adopt relatively passive or conservative intellectual behaviours. Or it can be used to encourage precisely those levels of thought – of independence, of evaluation, of critical judgement and of seeing things in a broader perspective – that form the self-understanding of higher education.

## Beyond learning

'Courses' in higher education are a kind of contract. Students attend more or less voluntarily on programmes of study which they have chosen. The new language of students as 'consumers' or 'clients' (Phillips 1989) at least picks out the voluntariness of the student's participation, and the tacit sense of a provider offering services of an acceptable standard. The problem with the new language is that it suggests a product, pre-designed and pre-packaged, that is passed to students in exchange for their attendance and the accompanying fee. It neglects the extent to which a genuine educational encounter is a transaction, is a necessary process of human interaction, between the student and the teacher and between the students themselves. The language is part of the commodification of higher education.

Nevertheless, a 'course' does have a justifiable component of being set in advance of the student's attendance. Given the extraordinary explosion of knowledge over the past 50 years, and the infinite number of ways it can be put together to form a positive educational experience, it makes sense for programmes to be properly designed by competent staff and then offered to the market to see whether there are any takers from prospective students. 'Courses' save the students from having to reinvent the wheel for themselves, or (to put it more formally) they make sense in terms of efficiency, economy and effectiveness. Given a well-designed course, students can expect that their learning efforts are going to be made effective; having a course which is taken by a number of willing participants aids the economical use of the resources of an institution; and with both staff and students engaged on a course in which they have an interest, the energies of all concerned will be made efficient with the non-completion rate of the students presumably being kept low.

A course amounts, then, to a quasi-contract between students and the institution. Students can legitimately expect to encounter a well-organized and well-presented programme so that, with regular attendance and application on their part, both the students and the institution can expect them to be successful at the conclusion of the course. To say this is to put a gloss on the earlier reflection: where we find a high quality curriculum and a high quality of teaching, we are likely also to find a high quality of learning.

I have already made the qualification that high quality learning can take place even if the teaching is poor and even if the curriculum is ill thought out and fails to hang together in any coherent way. So neither 'teaching' nor a 'curriculum' is logically necessary for learning to take place.

The other qualification to be made is to point to the possibility, implied in the general reflection, that high quality teaching can take place even without high quality learning. Philosophers of education, we might note, fall into opposed camps on this matter. Some hold that, conceptually, teaching entails learning; we cannot reasonably say that 't' has taught student 's' unless 's' has learnt something as a result of the interventions of 't'. Others hold that, provided that 't' has taken his professional duties seriously, is on top of his subject and has organized his teaching efforts in a way that can be deemed to offer significant learning opportunities to the student, 't' can be said to have taught irrespective of whether 's' has learnt anything as a result. It hardly makes sense to try to legislate tightly one way or the other. However, there would seem to be little virtue in a lecturer in higher education describing herself as a teacher unless there was some evidence to suggest that she was giving her students positive learning experiences and that at least some of the students were learning to some extent as a result.

There is, though, something profoundly unsatisfactory with this whole way of looking at higher education. I have been saying, in effect, that teachers teach in higher education on sufferance. Students attend voluntarily, and (especially those attending on a part-time basis) will vote with their feet if they are unhappy with the fare put before them. This 'consumer power' may grow in the future, as the student fee becomes an increasing element in institutions' recurrent income. In any case, learning can take place without teaching (even if, on balance, courses of study are an effective means of producing learning). What I now want to argue, though, is that not even learning itself is central to higher education.

'Learning' typically has application where someone can reproduce that which has been taught. Whether a form of propositional knowledge ('knowing-that' such and such is the case) or a form of skill ('knowing-how' to do such and such, which might be verbal, literary or behavioural), we accept that a student has learnt something if the action can be reproduced on request. But this is precisely what a genuine *higher* education is not about.

A higher education is about what a student is able to make of her learning, not about what she has learnt as such. Whether in the field of the performing arts, medicine, engineering, archaeology, law or philosophy: what matters is the extent to which the student has freed herself *from* her learning. This may seem a rather extraordinary claim, but its essence is quite simple. A *higher* education is an educational process in which a student is put in command of her learning. That is, the student is able to do things with her learning. The learning has become a resource which enables the student to conduct herself autonomously in the world and in the company of others. Yes, we want to be sure that the medical student has actually learnt facts about anatomy and physiology, about the central branches of medicine, about drugs, and so forth. But we also want the young doctor to have a sense that every patient is unique, and that all the knowledge and experience acquired through medical training and developed in the professional situation is deployed as the basis of an *infinite* repertoire of possible responses to the presenting cases.

Learning, therefore, can only be a preliminary element in higher education. It cannot constitute higher education. For that to happen, the individual's powers of forming unique responses to her surroundings have to be developed, encouraged and released. Higher education has an essential unpredictability in it. We want the students to wean themselves away from both their teaching *and* their learning.

## Promoting independence

Two courses in UK higher education take the title 'degree in independent learning'; many others are introducing independent learning units. My argument here is that all higher education of any quality has to be, in part, a matter of independent learning, in which students are allowed to form their own responses to their experiences, to offer their own truth claims and to perform their own actions in their own way, provided those offerings are made in a spirit of 'this is so, isn't it'?

On this reading, teaching is a means of enabling students to form well-founded claims of their own, whether in action or in propositional form. (I take a well-founded action to be one that is chosen by a student from a repertoire of possible actions, and where the student can give reasons for her chosen course of action in this instance.) It is tempting to go on to argue that the purpose of teachers is to make themselves redundant. That is a misguided conclusion.

If we regard higher education as a process designed to enable students to be more rational, as well more competent, in specific domains of human activity, higher education takes on the form not simply of introducing students to a conversation but also of enabling them to participate in it. It does not follow that the more students are able to engage in that conversation, the less the teacher can play a useful role. What it does mean is that the relationships in the conversation change, to one approaching equality. The conversation can still go on, albeit at a higher and more discriminatory level.

Most courses in higher education are delivered by more than one member of staff. Justifiably, members of staff will differ in their teaching styles. But if the argument here has validity, certain general principles follow for any curriculum and any teaching activity.

The first point arises from the reflection that both teaching and learning in higher education can easily be redundant, if not actually counterproductive. Teachers should be constantly asking themselves if what they are doing is likely to promote deep understanding and active thought on the part of the students. This is a tough criterion and, if enforced, might lead to much of the work in UK courses of higher education being jettisoned. On this principle, it needs to be asked, for example, if there is any reason to retain the institutionalized lecture, consisting of an uninterrupted monologue for around an hour, often without questions being permitted at its conclusion.

The second point is that there should be a consensus among the teaching staff concerned about the general aims of the course *and* the means of achieving them. This may sound a fairly straightforward point, but the ethos of teaching in higher education remains a relatively solitary one. Where there are regular course team meetings, perhaps they tend to focus on the routine matters of course administration rather than on fundamental matters of teaching aims and styles.

The third point is that students need to be encouraged to attend to their responsibilities for their own learning. In this, students may need educating for they may have a relatively passive learning orientation, especially if their motivation for joining the course is largely instrumental. Getting students to accept responsibility for their own learning does not need to be formalized into learning contracts, though that may help (Knowles *et al.* 1986). It is more a matter of putting into place realistic and attractive open-ended learning tasks, in which the students have to give something of themselves, perhaps in preparation for a session ahead.

Lastly, the cohort of students offers a valuable means of prompting authentic learning. Engaging the students in group tasks provides a non-threatening way of putting the students on the spot, and securing a personal response from them. There is a danger, of which students themselves are often very well aware, of such tasks encouraging anecdotalism and off-the-cuff responses rather than reasoned interventions that draw on appropriate evidence. Learning in groups is no sure route to a learning experience of high quality, but requires careful advance preparation.

## Conclusion

The work on student learning conducted over the past 20 years has been both valuable and misleading. Its value has lain in its showing how far the teaching style, the character of the curriculum and the assessment regime can all profoundly affect the way in which the student tackles her course. The student experience is not simply constructed by the student but is in part presented to her, in the way in which the course is designed and taught. And the rhetoric of the course team may not match the hidden curriculum, the forms of thinking and response which are, in reality, desired of the students.

However, this research programme has been misleading in that it has continued to use the language of learning. 'Deep processing' is not really learning: it is the attempt by the student to impose some personal meaning on to what has been learnt. The drawback in continuing to use the language of learning is that we all too easily slip into using the language of teaching, with connotations of relatively passive and predictable transactions taking place between the teacher and the taught.

Quality in higher education can never be tied to particular kinds of outcome, even particular kinds of learning outcome (cf. Jessup 1991). Yes, it looks to achievements on the part of students, but in large measure, those achievements are unpredictable. If we want students to emerge as autonomous thinking and acting persons (even if only in one or two restricted fields of human endeavour), then the outcomes are necessarily open to some degree. The measure of the quality of our efforts in teaching students lies in their finally being able to participate in a conversation, whether through thought or action. The improvement of the quality of those efforts will come not through any tighter specification of objectives but through increasing openness in the forms of thought and action which we can envisage in our students. Since the educational conceptions and practices in question are always susceptible to further development, the quality of our educational offerings is always open to further improvement.

# Conclusions

In this book, I have been trying to do something quite simple. It is to put students and their learning experience at the centre of our debates on quality in higher education. That may seem uncontroversial. But it runs counter to much of our contemporary language, our developing methods of assessment, our values and our institutional practices, as I have tried to show.

## Technique

If there is a single word that captures the spirit of the age in higher education, it is 'technique'. Technique, as I have indicated, is to be found at the levels of institutional evaluation and curriculum design. Controlling quality or improving quality, at either level, comes to be seen as a matter of technique. On the one hand, we see the imposition of technique as a means of assessing institutional performance through performance indicators. On the other hand, the greater effectiveness of the curriculum is felt to lie in the promotion of specified competencies and outcomes. Here, the curriculum becomes a matter of technology, in which the required outcomes are engineered.

Improving the quality of higher education cannot be accomplished simply as a set of tasks in a technical mode of operation. 'Improving', 'quality', 'higher' and 'education' itself are all value terms; none is merely descriptive. They point to an aiming in a conscious direction and to some end, and are oriented by a set of values. We cannot sensibly employ the term 'quality' in a value-free way. Its use obliges us to take up a value stance, that of declaring in favour of some worthwhile way of doing things. It is that sense, perhaps tacit and unformulated, of there being some kind of approved way of going on, that gives point to this terminology.

If this is the logic of 'quality' in the educational sphere, it follows that the identification, the assessment and the improvement of quality cannot be conducted purely as a technical exercise. Matters of judgement, of taste, and of a sense of rightness inescapably come into play.

The belief that quality should be assessed as a value-free calculation or improved as a value-free operation is a piece of ideological mystification. It is a nice example of bureaucratic reductionism, a pretence that things are simpler than they are (Goodlad 1985). But more perniciously, it contains its own sense of what is desirable and is disinclined to come clean about those values of its own. The dominant values of a performance indicator approach, adopted by agencies of the state, are likely to be well below the surface of debate. The hidden function of such an approach is less to be found, perhaps, in the indicators themselves than in their use for comparative purposes by the state. Performance indicators take great steps to hide their real purpose as being that of control and prediction of the individual institutions that make up the system.

If there is validity in this suggestion that talk of, and the practices surrounding, 'quality' are value-impregnated whether we wish to admit it or not, then we are obliged to be clear about the values that ought to be at the centre of our efforts to maintain and improve quality in higher education. The argument here has been that at whatever level (national, institutional or programme) and whether we have in mind organizational matters or issues of clear academic concern, *if* we are seriously interested in the quality of higher education *then* in the forefront of our considerations should be the improvement of the student experience.

Any attempt to set down a definite position on quality is fraught with difficulty. Talk of 'quality', it has turned out, is an expression of contemporary counter-claims on higher education. There are different voices, not always engaging with each other. In this situation, we can either systematically examine the different voices, their separate claims and their alternative approaches. Or we can attempt to offer a perspective of our own. It is the latter approach that has been attempted here.

Any move to pin down a particular point of view justifiably opens itself to the charge: 'but that is only your value position'. The charge can be directed at the present argument and, at one level, the charge is entirely fair. The view developed here is one view among many possible claims. The 'only' in the charge is pejorative, though, and the key question is whether the view offered here amounts to anything of substance and is worth taking seriously.

# Vocabulary

What I have done is to try to develop a vocabulary alongside the dominant vocabulary of the age, a vocabulary of persons, of intellectual struggle, of student development and maturation, of ends and of connections with the 'life world' (in Habermas's terminology) as well as with the world of work. It is a vocabulary offered in the spirit of: try looking at the world in this way and see if interesting or helpful meanings and insights accrue.

It should be noticed that, in taking up a particular stance, no attempt has been made to offer what might be termed a general theory of quality. That is to say, no attempt has been made to develop an overarching framework which might offer some definitive sense of all the available approaches. It has been implicit in the present argument that *such* an approach would be illegitimate. No super-theory of quality in higher education is available, in the sense of making the subsidiary theories redundant. No ultimate vantage point is attainable through which a unifying normative theory can be glimpsed. This point holds at the levels of definition of quality, of forming systems for assessing and maintaining quality, and of establishing procedures and activities for improving quality. To repeat, such efforts in pursuance of quality reflect contrasting value positions and alternative conceptions of what constitutes a higher education, between which there can be no ultimate resolution.

This does not mean that, in working out our conceptions of quality, anything goes. If our definitions and principles are to have practical feasibility, then we have to have an eye to the rival conceptions on offer, their provenance among different interest groups and the social force that stands behind them. In turn, any approach and conception for which we argue can then be so formed that it is likely to have some chance of attracting wide support. Educational definitions, if they are intended to have some real as against rhetorical effect, have to be developed with some degree of political awareness. One crucial test, therefore, of the argument here is simply the degree of support it gains from the different interest groups concerned (as we noted in our preliminary observations at the outset).

There is one sense in which an overarching theory of quality is possible, however, and that is in the sociological sense. Closing remarks are an unsuitable place to develop the point, but some brief observations may assist in giving a further context to the discussion of this book.

Given the near one thousand years of history behind higher education, the contemporary debate over quality – common across the western world – is sudden and striking. How might we understand it? Some programmatic remarks were offered in the introductory scene-setting but a more fundamental conceptual schema is required if we are to understand the eruption of the debate on quality, with all its associated activity, as a social phenomenon. Talk of 'accountability' and of a movement from 'élite' to 'mass' higher education serves only to draw attention to accompanying features of the social landscape; it does not explain the phenomenon itself. I offer, therefore, as a concluding thought, the following.

## Disenchantment

What we are witnessing in the quality debate is none other than a fundamental shift in the relationship of higher education to society. The arrival of the quality debate is indicative of the host society making new claims on higher education as a social institution. Extraordinary as it might seem, up till the second half of the twentieth century, the preceding 850 years or so of higher education (typified by the university) can be read as a continuous and *uniform* history. Across that period, the university can be seen as essentially the same kind of social institution. As a social institution, it enjoyed and indeed was granted by King and Pope privileges and rights setting it off from other social institutions. Given that position of social independence and implicit societal esteem, its inner relationships took the form (in Durkheimian language) of mechanical solidarity. While there was a gradual evolution of separate epistemic groupings, those groups were able to recognize each other as being in the same enterprise and as having a uniform outlook on the academic function, and on the pedagogic function and its relationship with society. The members of the traditional university cherished common values and were characterized by a degree of replaceability.

One hundred and fifty years late, so to speak, higher education has begun to change from being an institution essentially of an agrarian feudal society, to being an institution of an industrial and bureaucratic society. Correspondingly, the inner life of the institution has begun to move from a mechanical solidarity to an organical solidarity in which the inner social relationships are essentially those of differentiation, lacking any overt uniformity of binding ideas. This form of social order becomes problematic when the wider society begins to exert new claims on the institution. In that situation, rules, relationships and expectations have to be more codified and explicit (Aron 1970; Bernstein 1971).

One explanation for the change in the form of academic life is an internal one, and is to be found in the fragmentation of the single community into a multitude of sub-units with their distinctive loyalties and identities (the disciplines). In that situation, rules have to be articulated and understood as a means of holding the fragmenting segments together and of institutional survival. Integrating cross-institutional ideas like common 'mission', and developing a renewed sense of 'academic leadership', become attractive.

So the urge to codify, to systematize and to make explicit all that was tacit, unsystematic and implicit has come about through both the internal dynamics of the academic community and as a consequence of the incorporation of higher education (no longer just the university) into the institutional apparatus of modern society. No longer is higher education a small affair on the fringes of society, performing the ceremonial functions of an élite clerisy. Now, higher education is a significant player in the mainstream of institutional life, offering key functions in the formation and dissemination of knowledge, on which the post-industrial society rests.

In this sense, the rhetoric of 'quality' is a new-found importance attached to higher education by modern society, and is an expression of the closer relationship between the two now demanded. It is also a reflection of the sense within the host society that higher education has not sufficiently adjusted to the demands of the age.

We can, then, summarize the debate over quality and the underlying social movements in this way. The period from the Middle Ages until comparatively recently was one of *enchantment*. Higher education was somewhat mysterious, an activity in which only very few were engaged, but which somehow carried its own social legitimacy. Its quality was not at issue; the activity saw itself and was seen by the host society as self-justifying.

The modern age is one of *disenchantment*. The host society is no longer prepared to accept that higher education is self-justifying and wishes to expose the activities of the secret garden. With greater expectations being placed on it, higher education is being obliged to examine itself or be examined by others. 'Permeability', 'responsiveness' and 'accountability' are just some of the key words of the age. Against this changing mood and desire for transparency, systems of evaluation are being imported into higher education which may have point in other spheres of modern society but which may fail to do justice to the inner activities of higher education.

## Engagement

In this situation, I have not argued for a retreat to the position *ante bellum*, where the activities are held to have their own inner purpose and be self-justifying. Instead, I have tried to develop the idea of a third stage of quality maintenance, one of *engagement*. This is not a cosy, self-satisfied state of affairs, controlled only by the academic community through its conversations. But neither is it the imposition of inappropriate technical models and systems on a distinctive form of human activity. It is judgemental, open, binding on every participant in the academic community, critical (especially self-critical), collaborative (including the students), eclectic in its approach, and willing to draw on all the evidence available. However, it is driven by two principal considerations: that the central activity of higher education is that of educating individual students; and that it is the continuing improvement in the educational processes that lies at the centre of our concerns over quality. I have called this approach *total quality care*.

In plotting this typification of approaches to quality against a sense of the relationship of higher education to its host society, there is implicit in the third view I am advocating – as there must be – a particular view of that relationship. In this book, I have accepted that society does indeed have legitimate claims on higher education. Sociologically (the actual contemporary position of higher education in society), economically (the community's contribution to and expectations of higher education) and politically (to deny the claims of society is tantamount to wishing a marginal position for higher education in the modern society), the interlocking of higher education and society is a fact of modern life.

Correspondingly, higher education has responsibilities to society, but the fulfilment of those responsibilities – as I have tried to show – cannot be assessed either through specific curricular outcomes or through efficiency indicators. Rather, they will be met by institutions sustaining interactive open processes designed to foster educative transactions. The success of institutions in meeting those responsibilities will be shown principally by illuminating the relevant processes at the levels of the curriculum and of the institution itself.

I have tried to sketch out ways in which our assessments of quality can move forward to this third stage of evolution. There is no reason why our understanding of quality has to be arrested at the disenchantment stage; in theory, our approaches to quality could move on to the third stage of engagement. However, the principal actors – students, academics, the state, employers and professional bodies – all have other agendas, and it is doubtful whether a sufficient constituency exists for the approach being suggested here. I am happy to be proved wrong.

# Appendix: Institutional quality audit: a schema

| Elements of quality assurance | Existence of formal institutional procedures or guidelines | Current practice across the institution | Examples of good practice | Proposed course of action |
|---|---|---|---|---|
| 1. Approval of proposals for new courses | | | | |
| 2. Changes to existing courses | | | | |
| 3. Course monitoring (annual)<br>(a) Intake analysis<br>(b) Cohort analysis and non-completion<br>(c) Results analysis | | | | |
| 4. Periodic course review (involving peer dialogue with course team) | | | | |
| 5. Course committees | | | | |
| 6. Course tutors/course leaders | | | | |
| 7. External examiners<br>(a) Approval of their appointment<br>(b) Action on informal comments<br>(c) Written reports<br>(d) Any wider role (e.g. as course consultant) | | | | |

8. Involvement of students in
   (a) Course committees
   (b) Departmental boards
   (c) Institutional committees

9. Course information for students:
   (a) Course directory/outline
   (b) Prelim. course guides/notes for students
   (c) Study guides/handouts related to individual teaching sessions
   (d) Principles for marking formally assessed coursework

10. Informing students on progress:
   (a) Feedback on work produced during course
   (b) Feedback on formally-assessed work

11. Student feedback:
   (a) On course as a whole
   (b) On teachers and their teaching

| Elements of quality assurance | Existence of formal institutional procedures or guidelines | Current practice across the institution | Examples of good practice | Proposed course of action |
| --- | --- | --- | --- | --- |
| 12. Research students:<br>(a) Upgrading from MPhil to PhD<br>(b) Progress of students<br>(c) Guidelines to students and supervisors | | | | |
| 13. Appeals procedures:<br>(a) For students on taught courses<br>(b) For research students | | | | |
| 14. Staff appraisal | | | | |
| 15. Staff development:<br>(a) Improving teaching effectiveness<br>(b) Improving research competence<br>(c) Improving admin. and managerial skills | | | | |
| 16. Promotion of innovation and good practice in teaching (methods and curricula) | | | | |

# Notes

Chapter 1   *The Quality of Higher Education*
1. cf. Gellner, 1988: 23.
2. cf. Collier, 1982.
3. cf. Barrett, 1979; and the writings of Habermas in general, but especially his earlier writings such as in 1972 and 1978.
4. cf. Boys *et al.* 1988.
5. Admittedly, the evidence is that higher education also brings personal economic added-value.
6. 'Quasi-market' because no developed state would leave higher education entirely to the market. The production of intellectual capital is too important to be left to such uncertain outcomes.
7. cf. Peters, 1975.
8. cf. Hirst, 'Liberal Education . . . ' in 1974.
9. A point Feyerabend makes about the cognitive supremacy, for example, in 1978 and 1982.
10. cf. Astin, 1985; Gellert *et al.* 1990.
11. *Collins English Dictionary*, 1979 ed.
12. cf. Phillips, 1989.
13. cf. Bourdieu and Passeron, 1979.
14. cf. the work of Basil Bernstein on elaborated codes, for example, note (a), chapter 8 in 1975.
15. I develop this point in my book, *The Idea of Higher Education* (Barnett 1990).
16. This formulation of ideology is inevitably over-compressed, the concept of ideology having attracted an extensive literature. The connection of ideology with social interest is explicit in Marx's classic formulation, *The German Ideology*, pp. 65–6 (1974 ed.). For a more modern formulation, McClennan summarizes Habermas as saying that '. . . so societies generate ideologies which are rationalizations of asymmetrical power relations which have been repressed, elided or distorted in language'. Accordingly, here, 'the study of ideology becomes the study of systematically distorted communication' (1986: 77–8).
17. Admittedly, an interest in success rates and retention rates could spring from an educator's interest in assessing his effectiveness. But I am making a point about the social causes behind this new interest establishing a high profile in contemporary system-wide developments.
18. For example, Peters, 1980.
19. Newman, 1976 ed.: 103.

20. For example, Sloman asserted, in setting up the University of Essex, that 'Far from repudiating the accepted idea of a new university we are determined to preserve and perpetuate it'. (The new university) 'must . . . be committed to the pursuit of learning . . . must stand for excellence' (1964). At Sussex, it was intended that the undergraduate 'would become not only an educated person but potentially, at least, a better specialist' (Briggs 1964).
21. A point made by Galbraith, in talking of the way in which higher education has been 'extensively accommodated' to the claims of the major corporations (1969: 372). See also Dickson, 1988, in which he charts the way in which the major industrial and defence interests in the USA have influenced the character of the universities' practices.
22. See Part 2 of my book, *The Idea of Higher Education* (Barnett 1990).
23. cf. Gellner, 1974: 184; Feyerabend, 1987: 157.
24. For example, Schon, 1987; Perry, 1970.

*Chapter 2   Aiming Higher*
1. To express aims in this way is, it might be worth noting, to offer a formulation slightly different from that of R. Peters, for whom aims of education are entirely intrinsic to what we would consider education to be; so 'to ask questions about the aims of education is . . . not to ask for the production of ends extrinsic to education which might explain their activities as educators' (1966: 27–8). To insist on the 'intrinsic' criterion as an attribute of aims seems over-restrictive. Professional education is intended to be educative as well as being oriented to extrinsic ends. Nor does the description 'professional training which is also educational' – as implied by Peters as a possible locution – do justice to the intentions behind professional education.
2. As a recent conference confirmed, autonomy is a problematic concept, but there was little attempt to deny that universities still enjoyed it in significant measure (St Catharine's Report 1990).
3. For example, Whitehead, 1932; White, 1982.
4. On 'ideal speech situation', see Guess, 1981; on the consensus theory of truth, see Rasmussen, 1990. Roderick, 1986 is helpful on both issues.

*Chapter 3   The Idea of Quality*
1. For example, Loder's edited collection (1990). Moodie's introductions to two edited collections (Moodie 1986a; Berdahl *et al.* 1991) make helpful conceptual points, but otherwise both volumes also fall to the charge I am making.
2. Her Majesty's Inspectorate (1989) has identified accommodation and equipment as two of five 'key areas' by which it judges courses and confers its quality ratings. On this basis, it would appear that physical features of courses (matters that lend themselves to inspection) are significant determinants of its overall ratings.

*Chapter 4   Can Quality be Managed?*
1. 'The context of "management" has traditionally been industry and commerce; most theories and models of management have emerged from studies of organizations in these sectors' (Adair and Middlehurst 1988).

*Chapter 6   Inside the Black Box*
1. The University of London, through its Academic Council under the chairmanship of Professor G. Alderman, has established a working party to examine the usefulness of retaining degree classes.
2. The Council for National Academic Awards has been conducting a research

project, investigating the feasibility of establishing a national profiling system as a supplement to awards in higher education.

3. In their book, *Performance Indicators in Higher Education* (1990), Johnes and Taylor point out that correlations between A-level point scores and degree classifications are more meaningful at the level of institutions than at the level of subjects.
4. As Mantz Yorke has reminded me in relation to this latter point.
5. A point expressed by Dr Clark Brundin, Vice-Chancellor, University of Warwick at a seminar and in the columns of the *Times Higher Education Supplement*.
6. See the range of publications produced by CNAA (some in conjunction with CVCP) in connection with the Framework for the Recognition of Access Courses.

*Chapter 7   What's Wrong with Quality Assurance?*
1. Mary Midgley has some interesting things to say around issues such as these (1989).

*Chapter 8   Institutions for Learning*
1. The diagram reflects a suggestion made to me by Mantz Yorke.
2. One institution that has tackled this matter concertedly is Heriot-Watt University which has established an Institute for Computer-Based Learning. An information pack can be obtained from the University, Edinburgh.
3. I understand from Graham Badley that the President of the University of Harvard has recently announced a scheme to encourage all new staff (and eventually all faculty) to prepare their own teaching portfolios.

*Chapter 9   Practice makes Perfect?*
1. In individual disciplines, we see comparable developments; for instance, in management education, the Management Charter Initiative; in legal education (Tribe and Tribe 1992); and in engineering education, an important contemporary review looks to incorporating transferable skills of use in the wider world (Sparkes 1989).
2. See the leaflet on the NCVQ framework, issued by the NCVQ (1991).
3. Manufacturing industry now accounts for only about one quarter of occupations.

*Chapter 10   Communication, Competence and Community*
1. Press release, Polytechnic of Wales, 1989.
2. The ideas in the last sentence are drawn partly from my understanding of Habermas's analysis of rationality. See for example, Roderick, 1986, ch. 4.
3. This latter point, too, is taken from Habermas's 'critical theory'.

*Chapter 11   We're all Reflective Practitioners Now*
1. Tony Giddens in his book, *The Consequences of Modernity*, suggests that being reflective is a general condition of mankind in the postmodern society (1990).

*Chapter 12   Beyond Teaching and Learning*
1. *Performance Indicators in Higher Education*, by Johnes and Taylor (1990) falls into this latter category.
2. Funded by the Council for National Academic Awards, Graham Gibbs is currently completing (1991) a major piece of action research involving a range of courses in different institutions, in which innovative teaching methods are being designed to encourage 'deep learning' strategies from students.

# Bibliography

This bibliography contains a minority of items which, while not referenced in the text, have provided pertinent background to the discussion.

Where the publisher has both a USA and a UK office, I have restricted the reference to the UK location.

Academic Audit Unit (1991a) *Quality Assurance in Universities*. London, CVCP.

Academic Audit Unit (1991b) *Notes for the Guidance of Auditors*. London, CVCP.

Adair, J. and Middlehurst, R. (1988) *Leadership Development in Universities, 1986–1988*. Final report to the Department of Education and Science. Guildford, University of Surrey.

Adelman, C. (ed.) (1984) *The Politics and Ethics of Evaluation*. Beckenham, Croom Helm.

Adelman, C. and Powney, J. (1986) 'Institutional self-validation and course validation'. Paper given to SRHE annual conference.

Allsop, P., Findlay, P., McVicar, M. and Wright, P. (1989) 'Performance indicators within an English polytechnic' *International Journal of Educational Management*, 3 (3), 10–13.

Allsop, P., Findlay, P., McVicar, M. and Wright, P. (1990) *Performance Indicators: the development of common performance indicators, their implementation and critical evaluation*. Final report to CNAA of Performance Indicators Research Group, Portsmouth Polytechnic. London, CNAA.

Alverno College (1987) *Liberal Learning at Alverno College*. Wisconsin, Alverno Productions.

Argyris, C. and Schon, D. (1974) *Theory in Practice*. London, Jossey-Bass.

Aron, R. (1990) *Main Currents in Sociological Thought 2*. Harmondsworth, Penguin.

Astin, A. W. (1985) *Achieving Educational Excellence*. London, Jossey-Bass.

Badley, G. (1989) 'Excellent teaching in the UK' *British Journal of In-Service Education*, Winter, 15 (3), 177–86.

Badley, G. (1992) 'Institutional values and teaching quality' in R. A. Barnett, op. cit.

Baird, J. R. (1988) 'Quality: what should make higher education "higher"?' *Higher Education Research and Development*, 7 (2), 141–52.

Ball, C. (1985) *Fitness for Purpose*. Guildford, SRHE and NFER-Nelson.

Barnett, R. A. (1987) 'The maintenance of quality in the public sector of UK higher education' *Higher Education*, 16, 279–301.

Barnett, R. A. (1989) *Responsiveness and Fulfilment: the values of higher education in the modern world*. Oxford, Higher Education Foundation.

Barnett, R. A. (1990) *The Idea of Higher Education*. Milton Keynes, Open University Press.

Barnett, R. A. (ed.) (1992) *Learning to Effect*. Buckingham, Open University Press.

Barnett, R. A., Becher, R. A. and Cork, M. (1987) 'Models of professional preparation: pharmacy, nursing and teacher education' *Studies in Higher Education*, 12 (1), 51–63.

Barrett, W. (1979) *The Illusion of Technique*. London, William Kimber.

Barrow, R. (1991) 'The educated intelligence'. Paper given to annual conference of Philosophy of Education Society, Roehampton.

Baume, D. (1990) 'Defining quality (and using your definition)' *Bulletin of Teaching and Learning*, 3, Mar, 27–9.

Becher, T. (1989) *Academic Tribes and Territories*. Milton Keynes, Open University Press.

Bee, M. and Dolton, P. (1985) 'Degree class and pass rates: an inter-university comparison' *Higher Education Review*, 17, 45–52.

Berdahl, R. (1988) 'Autonomy and accountability'. Paper given to SRHE annual conference on academic freedom.

Berdahl, R. O., Moodie, G. C. and Spitzberg, I. Jr (eds) (1991) *Quality and Access in Higher Education*. Milton Keynes, Open University Press.

Bergendal, G. (ed.) (1984) *Knowledge Policies and the Traditions of Higher Education*. Stockholm, Almquist and Wiksell.

Bernstein, B. (1971) 'On the classification and framing of educational knowledge' in M. F. D. Young (ed.) *Knowledge and Control*. London, Collier-Macmillan.

Bernstein, B. (1975) *Class, Codes and Control: volume 3, towards a theory of educational transmissions*. London, Routledge.

Bevan, J. (1984) *The Interrelationship and Impact of Performance Criteria for Higher Education*, mimeo. London, National Advisory Body.

Billing, D. (1986) 'Judging institutions' in G. C. Moodie (ed.) op. cit.

Birch, W. (1988) *The Challenge to Higher Education*. Milton Keynes, Open University Press.

Birmingham Polytechnic (1989) *Evaluating Satisfaction with Educational Experience among Part-Time Students*. Birmingham, Birmingham Polytechnic.

Black, H. and Wolf, A. (1990) *Knowledge and Competence: current issues in teaching and education*. Sheffield, COIC/HMSO.

Bligh, D. (1986) *Teach Thinking by Discussion*. Guildford, SRHE and NFER-Nelson.

Bok, D. (1986) *Higher Learning*. London, Harvard University Press.

Boud, D. (1988) *Checklist on Valuing Teaching*. Australia, HERDSA.

Boud, D. and Feletti, G. (eds) (1991) *Open Learning*. London, Kogan Page.

Boud, D. and Prosser, M. (1985) 'Sharing responsibility for learning in a science course' in M. Knowles *et al*. *Learning Contracts*. London, Jossey-Bass.

Bourdieu, P. and Passeron, J-C. (1979) *The Inheritors*. London, University of Chicago.

Bourner, T. *et al*. (1991) *Part-time Students and their Experience of Higher Education*. Milton Keynes, Open University Press.

Boys, C. *et al*. (1988) *Higher Education and the Preparation for Work*. London, Jessica Kingsley.

Bradshaw, D. (1985) 'Transferable intellectual and personal skills' *Oxford Review of Education*, 11 (2), 201–16.

Bradshaw, D. (1989) 'Higher education, personal qualities and employment: team-work' *Oxford Review of Education*, 15 (1), 55–70.

Brennan, J. (1985) 'Preparing students for employment' *Studies in Higher Education*, 10, 151–62.

Brennan, J. and McGeevor, P. (1988) *Graduates at Work*. London, Jessica Kingsley.

Briggs, A. (1964) *Drawing a New Map of Learning*. London, Deutsch.

Brown, G. and Atkins, A. (1990) *Effective Teaching in Higher Education*. London, Routledge.

Burgess, T. (1977) *Education after School*. London, Gollancz.

Burgess, T. (1978) 'Excellence or equality: a dilemma in higher education?' *Higher Education Review*, 10 (2), 41–54.

Burgess, T. (1981) 'Bias is of the essence' in D. Warren-Piper (ed.) *Is Higher Education Fair?* Guildford, SRHE.

Burgess, T. (1982) 'Autonomous and service traditions' in L. Wagner (ed.) *Agenda for Institutional Change in Higher Education*. Leverhulme Seminar 3. Guildford, SRHE.

Burke, J. W. (ed.) (1989) *Competency Based Education and Training*. Lewes, Falmer.

Callaghan, B. (1990) 'British standards and the pursuit of quality' in B. Callaghan *et al.* (eds) *Meeting Needs in the 1990s*. Social Policy Paper No 2. London, Institute for Public Policy Research.

Cameron, J. M. (1978) *On the Idea of a University*. Toronto, University of Toronto Press.

Carr, W. and Kemmis, S. (1986) *Becoming Critical: education, knowledge, and action research*. Lewes, Falmer.

Cave, M., Hanney, S. and Kogan, M. (1991) *The Use of Performance Indicators in Higher Education*, 2nd edn. London, Kogan Page.

Church, C. (1988) 'The qualities of validation' *Studies in Higher Education*, 13 (1), 27–44.

Clark, B. (1983) *The Higher Education System: academic organization in cross-national perspective*. London, University of California Press.

CNAA (1989a) *Quality Assurance Systems: issues for consideration*. Development Services Briefing 16. London, CNAA.

CNAA (1989b) *The Access Effect*. London, CNAA.

CNAA (1989c) *Access Courses to Higher Education: dimensions of quality assurance – models of cooperation between further education and higher education*. London, CNAA.

CNAA (1990a) *Performance Indicators and Quality Assurance*. Information Services discussion paper, no. 4. London, CNAA.

CNAA (1990b) *Quality Assurance and Associated Institutions*. London, CNAA.

CNAA (1990c) *Handbook*. London, CNAA.

CNAA and PCFC (1990) *The Measurement of Value-Added in Higher Education* (joint report). London, CNAA.

Collier, G. (1982) 'Ideological influences in higher education' *Studies in Higher Education*, 7 (1), 13–20.

Collier, G. (1984) 'Higher Education as preparation for the handling of controversial issues' *Studies in Higher Education*, 9 (1), 27–35.

Collier, G. (1990) 'Syndicate methods' in N. Entwistle (ed.) *Handbook of Educational Ideas and Practices*. London, Routledge.

Colling, C. (1990) 'Teaching quality matters' *Bulletin of Teaching and Learning*, 4, July, 10–17.

Colman, A., Garner, A. B. and Jolly, S. (1992) 'Research performance of UK university psychology departments' *Studies in Higher Education*, 17 (1), 97–103.

Cuthbert, R. E. (1988) 'Quality and management in higher education' *Studies in Higher Education*, 13 (1), 59–68.

Cuthbert, R. E. (1991) 'The British binary system and its "missing link"' in R. O. Berdahl *et al.* op. cit.

CVCP (1985) *Report of the Steering Committee on Efficiency Studies in Universities* (Jarratt Report). London, CVCP.

CVCP (1986, 1987, 1988, 1989) *Academic Standards in Universities*, original statement (report of Reynolds Group) plus annual monitoring reports, London, CVCP.

CVCP and UGC (1988) *University Management Statistics and Performance Indicators*. London, CVCP.

Day, B. and Edwards, T. (1990) 'Quality in higher education – the industrial approach' *Bulletin of Teaching and Learning*, 3, March, 6–10.

DES (1985) *The Development of Higher Education into the 1990s*. Cmnd 9524, Green Paper. London, HMSO.

DES (1987) *Higher Education: meeting the challenge*. London, HMSO.

DES (1991) *Higher Education: a new framework*. Cmnd 1541, White Paper. London, HMSO.

Dickson, D. (1988) *The New Politics of Science*. London, University of Chicago.

Downie, R. S. (1990) 'Professions and professionalism' *Journal of Philosophy of Education*, 24 (2), 147–60.

Ellis, R. (1990) *A British Standard for University Teaching*, mimeo. University of Ulster.

Elton, L. (1990) 'Criteria of excellence of teaching and learning and their appraisal' *Bulletin of Teaching and Learning*, 3, March, 2–5.

Elton, L. (1991) 'Teaching excellence and quality assurance' *Zeitschrift für Hochschuldidaktik*, 15, 102–15.

Entwistle, N. (1989) 'Teaching and the quality of learning in higher education' in N. Entwistle (ed.) *Handbook of Educational Ideas and Practices*. London, Routledge.

Eraut, M. (1989a) 'Initial teacher training and the NCVQ model' in J. Burke (ed.) op. cit.

Eraut, M. (1989b) 'Knowledge creation and knowledge use in professional contexts' *Studies in Higher Education*, 10 (2), 117–34.

Eustace, R. (1991) *Gold, Silver, Copper: standards of first degrees* in R. Berdahl *et al.* op. cit.

Evans, N. (1992) *Experiential Learning: assessment and accreditation*. London, Routledge.

Feyerabend, P. (1978) *Against Method*. London, Verso.

Feyerabend, P. (1982) *Science in a Free Society*. London, Verso.

Feyerabend, P. (1987) *Farewell to Reason*. London, Verso.

Frazer, M. (1991) *Assuring Quality*, mimeo. London, CNAA.

Fulton, O. (1981) *Access to Higher Education*. Monograph no. 2, Leverhulme Seminar Series. Guildford, SRHE.

Fulton, O. and Ellwood, S. (1989) *Admissions to Higher Education: policy and practice*. Sheffield, Training Agency.

Galbraith, K. (1969) *The New Industrial State*. Harmondsworth, Penguin.

Gellert, C. *et al.* (eds) (1990) *Research and Teaching at Universities*. Frankfurt, Peter Lang.

Gellner, E. (1964) *Thought and Change*. London, Weidenfeld and Nicolson.

Gellner, E. (1974) *Legitimation of Belief*. London, Cambridge University Press.

Gellner, E. (1988) *Plough, Sword and Book*. London, Paladin.

Geuss, R. (1981) *The Idea of a Critical Theory: Habermas and the Frankfurt School.* Cambridge, Cambridge University Press.

Gibson, R. (1986) *Critical Theory and Education.* Sevenoaks, Hodder and Stoughton.

Giddens, A. (1990) *The Consequences of Modernity.* Cambridge, Polity.

Goedegebuure, L. C. J., Maassen, P. A. M. and Westerheijden, D. F. (eds) (1990) *Peer Review and Performance Indicators: quality assessment in British and Dutch higher education.* Utrecht, Uitgeverij Lemma.

Goodlad, S. (1976) *Conflict and Consensus in Higher Education.* Sevenoaks, Hodder and Stoughton.

Goodlad, S. (1984) *Education for the Professions.* Guildford, SRHE and NFER-Nelson.

Goodlad, S. (1985) 'Bureaucratic reductionism' in A. Peacocke (ed.) *Reductionism in Academic Disciplines.* Guildford, SRHE.

Gorz, A. (1988) *Critique of Economic Reason.* London, Verso.

Gouldner, A. (1979) *Future of Intellectuals and the Rise of the New Class.* London, Macmillan.

Gregory, K. (1991) 'Assessing departmental academic performance: a model' *Higher Education Review*, 23 (2), 48–60.

Gutmann, A. (1987) *Democratic Education.* Guildford, Princeton University Press.

Habermas, J. (1965) *Knowledge and Human Interests: a general perspective.* Reprinted in Habermas, 1978.

Habermas, J. (1972) *Towards a Rational Society.* London, Heinemann.

Habermas, J. (1976) *Legitimation Crisis.* London, Heinemann.

Habermas, J. (1978) *Knowledge and Human Interests.* London, Heinemann.

Habermas, J. (1979) *Communication and the Evolution of Society.* London, Heinemann.

Habermas, J. (1989) *The Theory of Communicative Action*, vol. 2. Cambridge, Polity.

Harris, R. W. (1990) 'The CNAA, accreditation and quality assurance' *Higher Education Review*, 23 (3), 34–54.

Held, D. (1980) *Introduction to Critical Theory: Horkheimer to Habermas.* London, Hutchinson.

Heyck, T. W. (1982) *The Transformation of Intellectual Life in Victorian England.* Beckenham, Croom Helm.

Hirst, P. (1974) *Knowledge and the Curriculum.* London, Routledge.

Hirst, P. and Peters, R. S. (1970) *The Logic of Education.* London, Routledge.

HMI (1989) *Quality in Higher Education.* London, HMI.

HMI (1991a) *Aspects of Education in the USA: quality and its assurance.* London, HMSO.

HMI (1991b) *Performance Indicators in Higher Education: a report by HMI.* Stanmore, DES.

Institute of Physics (1990) *The Future Pattern of Higher Education in Physics.* Final report of a Higher Education Working Party. London, Institute of Physics.

Jansen, J. D. (1990) 'Curriculum policy as compensatory legitimation? A view from the periphery' *Oxford Review of Education*, 16 (1), 29–37.

Jaques, D. (1991) *Learning in Groups.* London, Kogan Page.

Jessup, G. (1991) *Outcomes: NVQs and the emerging model of education and training.* Lewes, Falmer.

Johnes, J. and Taylor, J. (1990) *Performance Indicators in Higher Education.* Milton Keynes, Open University Press.

Kerr, C. (1963) *The Uses of the University.* Massachusetts, Harvard University Press.

Knowles, M. *et al.* (1986) *Using Learning Contracts.* London, Jossey-Bass.

Kuhn, T. (1970) *The Structure of Scientific Revolutions.* London, Chicago University Press.

Lakatos, I. (1977) 'Falsification and the methodology of scientific research pro-grammes' in I. Lakatos and A. Musgrave (eds) *Criticism and the Growth of Scientific Knowledge*. Cambridge, Cambridge University Press.

Lawson, H. and Appignanesi, L. (eds) (1989) *Dismantling Truth, Reality in the Post-modern World*. London, Weidenfeld and Nicolson.

Loder, C. L. (ed.) (1990) *Quality Assurance and Accountability in Higher Education*. London, Kogan Page (Bedford Way series with Institute of Education).

Maassen, P. A. M. (1989) 'Quality assessment in higher education' in M. McVicar (ed.) op. cit.

McClennan, D. (1986) *Ideology*. Milton Keynes, Open University Press.

McIntyre, A. (1971) *Against the Self-Images of the Age*. London, Duckworth.

McIntyre, A. (1985) *After Virtue*. London, Duckworth.

McPeck, J. (1981) *Critical Thinking and Education*. Oxford, Martin Robertson.

McVicar, M. (ed.) (1989) *Performance Indicators and Quality Control*. Portsmouth, Portsmouth Polytechnic.

McVicar, M. (1989) 'Performance indicators in quality assurance: what can we learn from the NHS?' in M. McVicar (ed.) op. cit.

Major, K. (1990) *Quality and Assurance for Teaching and Learning in Universities* (based on BS5750), mimeo. Bath, University of Bath.

Margolis, J. (1986) *Pragmatism without Foundations*. Oxford, Blackwell.

Marton, F. *et al.* (eds) (1984) *The Experience of Learning*. Edinburgh, Scottish Academic Press.

Marx, K. (1974) *The German Ideology*. London, Lawrence and Wishart.

Maxwell, N. (1987) *From Knowledge to Wisdom*. Oxford, Blackwell.

Midgley, M. (1989) *Wisdom, Information and Wonder*. London, Routledge.

Moodie, G. C. (ed.) (1986a) *Standards and Criteria in Higher Education*. Guildford, SRHE and NFER-Nelson.

Moodie, G. C. (1986b) *Fit for What?* in G. C. Moodie (ed.) op. cit.

Moodie, G. C. (1988) 'The debates about higher education quality in Britain and the USA' *Studies in Higher Education*, 13 (1), 5–13.

Moodie, G. C. (1991) *Setting the Scene* in R. O. Berdahl *et al.* op. cit.

Moore, T. (1974) *Educational Theory: an introduction*. London, Routledge.

Muller, D. and Funnell, P. (eds) (1991) *Delivering Quality in Vocational Education*. London, Kogan Page.

Muller, D. and Funnell, P. (1991) 'Delivering quality: a managerial and an industrial perspective' in D. Muller and P. Funnell op. cit.

National Advisory Body for Local Authority Higher Education (1986) *Transferable Skills in Employment*. London, NAB.

National Advisory Body for Local Authority Higher Education (1987) *Management for a Purpose: the Report of the Good Management Practice Group*. London, NAB.

NCVQ (1991) *The NVQ Framework*. London, National Council for Vocational Qualifications.

Neave, M. (1991) *Models of Quality Assurance in Europe*. Discussion Paper 6. London, CNAA.

Newble, D. and Cannon, R. (1991) *A Handbook for Teachers in Universities and Colleges: a guide to improving teaching methods*, 2nd edn. London, Kogan Page.

Newman, J. (1976) *The Idea of a University*. Oxford, Oxford University Press.

Oakeshott, M. (1989) *The Voice of Liberal Learning*. London, Yale University Press.

Partnership Awards (1991) *Partnership Awards*. London, RSA.

Pattison, M. (1969) *Memoirs*. Fontwell, Sussex, Centaur Press.

Perry, P. (1990) 'Is there a need for a higher education inspectorate?' in C. Loder (ed.) op. cit.

Perry, W. G. (1970) *Forms of Intellectual and Ethical Development*. New York, Holt, Rinehart and Winston.

Peters, M. (1992) 'Performance and accountability in post-industrial society: the crisis of British universities' *Studies in Higher Education*, 17 (2) (in press).

Peters, R. (1964) *Education as Initiation*. Inaugural lecture. London, Institute of Education.

Peters, R. (1966) *Ethics and Education*. London, Allen and Unwin.

Peters, R. (1967) 'What is an educational process?' in R. Peters (ed.) *The Concept of Education*. London, Routledge.

Peters, R. (1975) 'Subjectivity and standards' in W. R. Niblett (ed.) *The Sciences, the Humanities and the Technological Threat*. London, Unwin.

Peters, R. (1980) *Education and the Education of Teachers*. London, Routledge.

Pfeffer, N. and Coote, A. (1991) 'Is quality good for you?' Social Policy Paper no. 5. London, Institute for Public Policy Research.

Phillips, D. C. (1987) *Philosophy, Science and Social Inquiry*. Oxford, Pergamon.

Phillips, V. (1989) 'Students: partners, clients or consumers?' in C. Ball and H. Eggins (eds) *Higher Education into the 1990s*. Milton Keynes, Open University Press.

Plato (1971) *The Republic*. Ed. Cornford. Oxford, Oxford University Press.

Polanyi, M. (1966) *The Tacit Dimension*. New York, Doubleday.

Pollitt, C. (1990) 'Measuring university performance: never mind the quality, never mind the width?' *Higher Education Quarterly*, 44 (1), 60–81.

Pollitt, M. (1987) 'The politics of performance assessment: lessons for higher education' *Studies in Higher Education*, 12 (1), 87–98.

Polytechnic and Colleges Funding Council (1990a) *Teaching Quality*. Report of Committee of Enquiry chaired by Baroness Warnock. London, PCFC.

Polytechnic and Colleges Funding Council (1990b) *Performance Indicators*. Report of Committee of Enquiry chaired by Alfred Morris. London, PCFC.

Popper, K. R. (1975) *Objective Knowledge: an evolutionary approach*. Oxford, Oxford University Press.

Prabhu, V. and Lee, P. (1990) 'Implementing total quality management (TQM): Newcastle Business School (NBS) pilot study' *Bulletin of Teaching and Learning*, 3, Mar, 20–24.

Pratt, J. (1983) 'The Council for National Academic Awards' in M. Shattock (ed.) *The Structure and Governance of Higher Education*. Monograph no. 9, Leverhulme seminar series. Guildford, SRHE.

Pratt, J. and Burgess, T. (1974) *Polytechnics: a report*. London, Pitman.

Ramsden, P. (1983) 'Institutional variations in British students' approaches to learning and experiences of teaching' *Higher Education*, 12.

Ramsden, P. (1986) 'Students and quality' in G. C. Moodie (ed.) op. cit.

Ramsden, P. (ed.) (1988) *Improving Student Learning*. London, Kogan Page.

Ramsden, P. (1990) 'A performance indicator of teaching quality in higher education' *Studies in Higher Education*, 16 (2), 129–50.

Rasmussen, D. (1990) *Reading Habermas*. Oxford, Blackwell.

Reeves, M. (1988) *The Crisis in Higher Education*. Milton Keynes, Open University Press.

Robbins, D. (1988) *The Rise of Independent Study*. Milton Keynes, Open University Press.

Robbins, L. (1963) *Higher Education: Report of the Committee.* Cmnd 2154. London, HMSO.

Robinson, E. (1968) *The New Polytechnics.* Harmondsworth, Penguin.

Roderick, R. (1986) *Habermas and the Foundations of Critical Theory.* Basingstoke, Macmillan.

Rorty, R. (1980) *Philosophy and the Mirror of Nature.* Oxford, Oxford University Press.

Rorty, R. (1989) *Contingency, Irony and Solidarity.* Cambridge, Cambridge University Press.

Rutherford, D. (1990) 'A new initiative in departmental reviews: annual meetings in the Faculty of Sciences (University of Birmingham)' *Higher Education*, 19, 195–217.

St. Catharine's (1990) *Autonomy in the Universities.* Conference report, no. 18. Windsor, St. Catharine's, Cumberland Lodge.

Schon, D. (1982) *The Reflective Practitioner: how professionals think in practice.* New York, Basic Books.

Schon, D. (1987) *Educating the Reflective Practitioner.* London, Jossey-Bass.

Schuller, T. (1990a) 'Nearer to the edge' in *Times Higher Educational Supplement.* London, Times Supplements.

Schuller, T. (1990b) 'Performance measurement in higher and continuing education' in C. Bell and D. Harris (eds) *Assessment and Evaluation.* London, Kogan Page.

Scott, P. (1984) *The Crisis of the University.* Beckenham, Croom Helm.

Scott, P. (1990) *Knowledge and Nation.* Edinburgh, Edinburgh University Press.

Shattock, M. L. (1986) 'The UGC and standards' in G. C. Moodie (ed.) op. cit.

Shattock, M. (1991) 'Financial pressures and quality in British universities' in R. O. Berdahl *et al.* op. cit.

Siegel, H. (1990) *Educating Reason: rationality, critical thinking and education.* London, Routledge.

Sizer, J. (1982) 'Assessing institutional performance and progress' in L. Wagner (ed.) *Agenda for Institutional Change in Higher Education.* Guildford, SRHE.

Sizer, J. (1988) 'In search of excellence – performance assessment in the UK' *Higher Education Quarterly*, 46 (2).

Sizer, J. (1989) 'Performance indicators, quality control and the maintenance of standards in higher education' in M. McVicar (ed.) op. cit.

Sizer, J. (1990) 'The role of the funding councils and performance indicators in quality assessment in the UK'. Paper given to CHEPS conference, Utrecht, Netherlands. University of Loughborough, unpublished.

Sloman, A. (1964) *A University in the Making.* London, BBC.

Sparkes, J. (1989) *Quality in Engineering Education.* Report of the Engineering Professors' Conference on Quality in Engineering Education, available from Professor P. B. Morice, Department of Civil Engineering, University of Southampton.

Sparrow, J. (1967) *Pattison and the Idea of a University.* Cambridge, Cambridge University Press.

Sussex, University of (1986) *Teaching and Research in Education at the University of Sussex: two independent appraisals.* Falmer, University of Sussex.

Tan, D. L. (1986) 'The assessment of quality in higher education: a critical review' *Research in Higher Education*, 24 (3), 223–65.

Taylor, W. (1987) *Universities under Scrutiny.* Paris, OECD.

TEED (undated) *Total Quality Management and BS5750: the links explained.* Sheffield, TEED.

Thompson, D. L. (1991) *Moral Values and Higher Education*. USA, Brigham Young University.

Thompson, J. B. (1984) *Studies in the Theory of Ideology*. Cambridge, Polity.

Training Agency (1988) *Enterprise in Higher Education*. Sheffield, Training Agency.

Tribe, D. and Tribe, A. (1992) 'The law teacher's dilemma: skills teaching and assessment' in R. Barnett (ed.) op. cit.

Trow, M. (1974) 'Problems in the transition from elite to mass higher education' *Policies for Higher Education*. Paris, OECD.

Trow, M. (1981) 'Comparative perspectives on access', in O. Fulton (ed.) *Access to Higher Education*. Leverhulme Seminar 3, ch. 3. Guildford, SRHE.

Trow, M. (1987) 'Academic standards and mass higher education' *Higher Education Quarterly*, 41 (3), 268–91.

Turner, B. S. (ed.) (1990) *Theories of Modernity and Postmodernity*. London, Sage.

UDACE (1989a) *Performance Indicators and the Education of Adults*. Leicester, NIACE.

UDACE (1989b) *Understanding Competence*. Leicester, NIACE.

UDACE (1989c) *Understanding Learning Outcomes*. Leicester, NIACE.

UNESCO (1991) *Planning and Management for Excellence and Efficiency of Higher Education*. Caracas, UNESCO/CRESALC.

University Grants Committee/National Advisory Body Joint Statement (1984) *A Strategy for Higher Education in the 1990s*. London, HMSO.

University Grants Committee (1985) *Review of the University Grants Committee* (Croham Report). Circular letter 22/85, quoted in para 6.7, Cmnd 81, 1987. London, HMSO.

Weidemeyer, C. A. (1981) *Learning at the Back Door: reflections on non-traditional learning in the lifespan*. London, University of Wisconsin.

Weiler, H. N. (1990) 'Curriculum Reform and the legitimation of educational objectives: the case of the Federal Germany' *Oxford Review of Education*, 16 (1), 15–27.

Weinstein, M. (1991) 'Critical thinking and educational reform'. Paper given to annual conference of Philosophy of Education Society, Roehampton.

White, J. (1982) *The Aims of Education Restated*. London, Routledge.

Whitehead, A. N. (1932) *The Aims of Education*. London, Williams and Norgate.

Williams, G. (1986) 'The missing bottom line' in G. C. Moodie (ed.) op. cit.

Williams, G. and Loder, C. (1990) *The Importance of Quality and Quality Assurance* in C. Loder (ed.) op. cit.

Wittgenstein, L. (1967) *Philosophical Investigations*. Oxford, Blackwell.

World University Service (1989) *Factors and Conditions Conducive to Academic Freedom*. Report of WUS/UNESCO seminar, Paris, May 1989. Geneva, WUS.

Wright, P. W. G. (1989a) 'Putting learning at the centre of higher education' in O. Fulton (ed.) *Access and Institutional Change*. Milton Keynes, Open University Press.

Wright, P. W. G. (1989b) 'Who defines quality in higher education? Reflections on the role of professional power in determining conceptions of quality in English higher education' *Higher Education*, 18 (2), 149–65.

Wright, P. W. G. (1990a) 'Strategic change in the higher education curriculum: the example of the enterprise in the higher education initiative' in C. Loder (ed.) op. cit.

Wright, P. W. G. (1990b) 'Quality assurance through contractual obligation: the experience of the British Enterprise in Higher Education Initiative'. Paper to 12th EAIR Forum, Lyons, mimeo. Sheffield, TEED.

Yorke, M. (1984) *Effectiveness in Higher Education: a review*. London, CNAA.

Yorke, M. (1988) 'Beyond performance indicators: studying institutional effectiveness in British public sector higher education'. Paper presented to 10th EAIR Forum, Bergen, August, mimeo. Liverpool Polytechnic.

Yorke, M. (1991a) 'Quality in higher education: a conceptualisation and some implications for institutional performance'. Paper given to 31st AIR Forum, San Francisco, 24–29 May, mimeo. Liverpool Polytechnic.

Yorke, M. (1991b) *Quality Control and the Management of Institutions* in D. Muller and P. Funnell (eds) op. cit. (Also in M. McVicar (ed.) (1989) op. cit.)

Yorke, M. (1991c) *Performance Indicators: observations on their use in the assurance of course quality*. CNAA project report, no. 30. London, CNAA.

# Index

# The Society for Research into Higher Education

The Society for Research into Higher Education exists to stimulate and co-ordinate research into all aspects of higher education. It aims to improve the quality of higher education through the encouragement of debate and publication on issues of policy, on the organization and management of higher education institutions, and on the curriculum and teaching methods.

The Society's income is derived from subscriptions, sales of its books and journals, conference fees and grants. It receives no subsidies, and is wholly independent. Its individual members include teachers, researchers, managers and students. Its corporate members are institutions of higher education, research institutes, professional, industrial and governmental bodies. Members are not only from the UK, but from elsewhere in Europe, from America, Canada and Australasia, and it regards its international work as amongst its most important activities.

Under the imprint *SRHE & Open University Press*, the Society is a specialist publisher of research, having some 45 titles in print. The Editorial Board of the Society's Imprint seeks authoritative research or study in the above fields. It offers competitive royalties, a highly recognizable format in both hard- and paperback and the world-wide reputation of the Open University Press.

The Society also publishes *Studies in Higher Education* (three times a year), which is mainly concerned with academic issues, *Higher Education Quarterly* (formerly *Universities Quarterly*), mainly concerned with policy issues, *Research into Higher Education Abstracts* (three times a year), and *SRHE News* (four times a year).

The Society holds a major annual conference in December, jointly with an institution of higher education. In 1990, the topic was 'Industry and Higher Education', at and with the University of Surrey. In 1991, it was 'Research and Higher Education in Europe', with the University of Leicester. Future conferences include, 1992, 'Learning to Effect', with Nottingham Polytechnic, and in 1993, 'Governments and the Higher Education Curriculum' with the University of Sussex. In addition it holds regular seminars and consultations on topics of current interest.

The Society's committees, study groups and branches are run by the members. The groups at present include:

Teacher Education Study Group
Continuing Education Group
Staff Development Group
Excellence in Teaching and Learning
Women in Higher Education Group

# Benefits to members

## *Individual*

Individual members receive:

- *SRHE News*, the Society's publications list, conference details and other material included in mailings.
- Greatly reduced rates for *Studies in Higher Education* and *Higher Education Quarterly*.
- A 35% discount on all Open University Press & SRHE publications.
- Free copies of the Precedings – commissioned papers on the theme of the Annual Conference.
- Free copies of *Research into Higher Education Abstracts*.
- Reduced rates for conferences.
- Extensive contacts and scope for facilitating initiatives.
- Reduced reciprocal memberships.

## *Corporate*

Corporate members receive:

- All benefits of individual members, plus.
- Free copies of *Studies in Higher Education*.
- Unlimited copies of the Society's publications at reduced rates.
- Special rates for its members e.g. to the Annual Conference.

*Membership details:* SRHE, 344–354 Gray's Inn Road, London, WC1X 8BP, UK. Tel: 071 837 7880
*Catalogue: SRHE & Open University Press*, Celtic Court, 22 Ballmoor, Buckingham MK18 1XW. Tel: (0280) 823388